INTERNATIONAL CASH MANAGEMENT

GW00763544

International Cash Management

A Practical Guide to Managing
Cash Flows, Liquidity, Working Capital
and Short-term Financial Risks

Lex van der Wielen

in cooperation with
Willem van Alphen
Joost Bergen
Phillip Lindow

CIP-GEGEVENS KONINKLIJKE BIBLIOTHEEK, DEN HAAG

International Cash Management
International Cash Management – A Practical Guide to Managing Cash Flows, Liquidity, Working Capital and Short-term Financial Risks/Wielen, Lex van der (in cooperation with Alphen, Willem van, Bergen, Joost and Lindow, Phillip).

NUR 782
treasury, (international) cash management, working capital (management), liquidity management, foreign exchange risk, interest rate risk, cash flow management, financial risk management, short-term investments, payment processing, clearing, settlement.

ISBN-10: 90-802323-8-6
ISBN-13: 978-90-802323-8-9
Includes index

Published by Riskmatrix
P.O. Box 176
3970 AD Driebergen
The Netherlands
www.riskmatrix.eu
www.riskmatrix.nl

Produced in cooperation with the Netherlands Institute for Banking, Insurance and Investment (NIBE-SVV)
P.O. Box 2285
1000 CG Amsterdam
The Netherlands
uitgeverij@nibesvv.nl
www.nibesvv.nl

Although the utmost care has been taken in preparing this publication, the author or the publisher cannot be held liable for information that may be incorrect or out of date.

Typography and cover design by Magenta Ontwerpers, Bussum
Printed by Printforce, Alphen a/d Rijn

Preface

Welcome to the second edition of the practical guide to International Cash Management. We decided to write this second edition in part due to the success of the first – it is now sold out and the publishers have received requests for more copies. However, this is also a very welcome occasion for an update. Many developments in cash management, including increased regulations by public authorities as well as newly available solutions allowing for improved operating efficiency, present both significant opportunities and a few challenges.

The modern cash manager should keep up to date with the latest changes. After all, the globalisation of large, and increasingly medium sized, companies and their treasuries, as well as ongoing developments in market infrastructure and bank software systems, continues to change dramatically the duties of the cash manager. The treasurer and cash manager can make significant financial contributions to the company, and as such, need to be aware of emerging opportunities and best practices. The cash manager plays an active role in achieving optimal liquidity management and often has a major advisory role in various aspects of working capital management.

In a complex organisation, operating in a multinational environment, a modern internal cash management structure is indispensable for the achievement of optimal cash management. Times have moved on since it was sufficient to search for appropriate means of effecting international payments and conducting feasibility studies for multilateral netting operations. Advancing technology and evolving market infrastructures are even now leading to dramatic developments. For example, in the area of cash pooling, advancements are such that we are beginning to see automated multi-bank sweeping and multi-currency cash pools being managed on a global basis. Bank technology is also allowing corporations to outsource many of the more routine cash management tasks. In the field of market infrastructure, the introduction of a Single Euro Payments Area (SEPA) from 2008 will be a major catalyst for further change and consolidations.

Meanwhile, corporations continue to search for ways to improve their financial management even further. They are looking to maximise investment returns from surplus funds and have a constantly evolving range of modern financial and investment instruments to help them. These same companies are constantly seeking ways of improving risk management, especially related to currency and interest rate risk, and are employing a growing range of derivatives to manage these exposures.

This book gives those officials responsible for cash management in a corporate treasury a clear overview of the techniques and instruments available to ensure optimal cash management. This is a wide-ranging overview of the entire field of operation designed to be used by a professional in a corporate treasury of a non-financial company. Additionally, this handbook may also be successfully employed by those who are active in this sector, for example, in an advisory capacity at a bank. All key aspects of cash management are dealt with, from the beginning when cash flow is established, to the actual management of liquidity.

But although this book was originally written for financial professionals, the previous edition was also used by students in finance and treasury university programs. It is particularly useful for students wishing to acquire practical knowledge with a view to a later career in the financial industry, in addition to the more academic topics and research activities of traditional university programs.

I would like to express our thanks to all those who have helped us produce this enhanced second edition. It is my pleasure to welcome Phillip Lindow as co-author. Phillip has worked for different banks in North America and brings a vast amount of experience in financial markets and global liquidity management. His contribution has enabled us to broaden the scope of the book even further to include more of the US aspects of cash management. We thank Christopher Gonzalez who helped us update the chapter about delivery channels and we acknowledge the invaluable contribution by our editors Rupert Bruce and Jim Kosters.

Prof. Dr Mattheus van der Nat

Director of the postgraduate treasury program of the VUA University (Vrije Universiteit) in Amsterdam

About the authors

LEX VAN DER WIELEN

Lex van der Wielen is currently working as financial risk manager at the Dutch State Treasury Agency. He is on a free-lance basis associated as a trainer, text writer and consultant with NIBE-SVV, the Dutch educational organisation for financial institutions, and RISKMATRIX, a company that offers support in treasury management and financial management to corporations and non-profit organisations. Also he gives lectures on interest rate risk management for the post-graduate Treasury course at the Vrije Universiteit in Amsterdam.

For NIBE-SVV he has written a number of study books on a wide range of topics, such as banking risks, private investments and interest rate derivatives. Recently he finished a handbook on the Financial Markets (Dutch written). He started his career at the Asset & Liability department of the former AMRO Bank. Next, he spent many years working in the financial markets department of ABN AMRO Bank and ING Bank. In this capacity he advised numerous corporations on interest rate risk management and currency risk management.

WILLEM VAN ALPHEN

Willem van Alphen is currently Senior Vice President and Head of Global Cash Pooling within Transaction Banking of ABN AMRO Bank N.V. He is responsible for product management, strategy and advising corporate clients on cross-border liquidity solutions. Mr. van Alphen started his career with the Dutch Central Bank working on international monetary matters and joined AMRO Bank in 1978. He led the bank's corporate treasury management consulting group, which role he continued after the merger between ABN and AMRO in 1991. Mr. van Alphen contributed to the successful development and marketing of ABN AMRO's euro cash management solutions and was responsible for Global Cash Management Advisory and Training within the bank's transaction banking unit.

JOOST BERGEN

Joost Bergen is currently a Vice President responsible for Short Term Liquidity Investments in Europe of ABN AMRO Bank N.V. In this role Bergen advises corporate clients on their liquidity investment strategy across all investment products of the bank including asset management and global market services.

Bergen started his career as a treasury consultant and joined ABN AMRO Bank in 2000. He holds a Masters in Financial Economics and a training teacher's degree. Next to this he is frequent speaker for internal and external clients and industry forums, he is a writer on treasury and cash management topics and he regularly provides treasury related trainings for Risk Matrix.

PHILLIP LINDOW

Phillip Lindow serves as Executive Director and Head of Global Treasury and Investment Management in the Transaction Banking Business Unit Division of ABN AMRO BANK N.V. Lindow directs product management, strategy and solutions development in liquidity management, transactional FX/netting, and investment services for the bank's clients.

Mr. Lindow developed most of his 19-year career with two of the most well known names in the financial services industry: At JPMorgan and its predecessor Chase Manhattan Bank and Deutsche Bank and its predecessor Bankers Trust.

Table of contents

B

Transaction Banking

Chapter 4

Chapter 5

Chapter 10
Investment management

Chapter 11
Cash flow management

D

Working Capital Management and Financial Risk Management   **235**

Chapter 12

xvi

E

Related Topics   **337**

Chapter 15

Cryptography   **339**

Chapter 16

Overview of clearing and settlement systems   **347**

Introduction

As globalisation has conquered the corporate world, so one aspect of this has been the centralisation and increased efficiency of cash management. Treasury and cash management have attracted growing attention in the past decades, with the 1999 introduction of the euro increasing the potential benefits of professional management in this area for companies operating in Europe. While this was un-doubtedly a catalyst for more professional cash management services, the march of progress has continued and there are many new ways in which a treasurer or cash manager can further improve efficiency.

Since the first edition of this book was published in 2002, there have been notable advances in bank technology and market infrastructure. Banks increasingly re-gard cash management as a core service. They are constantly investing in cash management technology, and this is now leading to such innovations as global cash pooling, multi-bank sweeping and cross-currency pooling. This enables banks to automate much of the treasury function, allowing corporates to cost-effectively outsource many of their more routine tasks to the banks.

On the infrastructure side, the introduction of a Single Euro Payments Area (SEPA) from 2008 will obviously have major advantages for companies operating in Eu-rope. It will change how these companies process transactions dramatically, while also affecting how they structure liquidity management. There is also progress with the SWIFT payments network, with companies being offered greater access to the SWIFTNET system, allowing them to communicate with mltiple banks.

What this adds up to is simpler and far more effective international cash manage-ment. A practice that used to be very complex and difficult is becoming far sim-pler. The developments we are discussing have transformed what was once an ac-tivity conducted on a country by country basis to one conducted on a regional basis. Cash management is now becoming even more centralised, with small trea-sury teams potentially organising payments globally and managing global liquidi-ty pools.

This book describes the evolving cash management function within a multinational corporation (MNC). In dealing with the role of the cash manager within the MNC, we will describe the internal environment within which the cash manager operates (i.e. the company where the cash manager works), the cash manager's various tasks, the instruments at the cash manager's disposal, his or her day-to-day activities and objectives. Finally, we portray the financial world that the cash manager must deal with.

The book is strongly oriented towards actual practice within MNCs. It contains a large number of examples to give a clear and accurate picture of the working environment and daily operations of the cash manager.

2

The book consists of five parts. The content of each is briefly described below:

A. The Multinational Corporation (chapters 1 - 3)
B. Transaction Banking (chapters 4 - 7)
C. Core Cash Management Activities (chapters 8 - 11)
D. Working Capital Management and Financial Risk Management (chapters 12 - 14)
E. Related Topics (chapters 15 - 19)

A. THE MULTINATIONAL CORPORATION
In this first part, we describe the multinational corporation (MNC), focusing on the methods used to organise procurement, sales and distribution. These methods largely determine the financial function, the international money flows of the company and, consequently, the cash management function. Next, we describe the treasury's place within the MNC's finance department and the role of the cash management function within treasury. In chapter three we zoom in on the treasury itself, taking a closer look at its three principal tasks, i.e. cash management, financial risk management and corporate finance. We also look at its three subsidiary tasks – working capital management, investor relations and other tasks. We then move on to the treasury policy of the company, the organisation of the treasury department and the risks associated with treasury activities. We end with a brief description of the treasury systems available to support the treasurer.

B. TRANSACTION BANKING
Our first subject in this part is the current account. Among other things, we deal with the documentation required for opening accounts, as well as with the costs and revenues of current accounts. In chapter five, we describe payment products for outgoing and incoming payments. First, we describe the outgoing payment products. We start with the electronic credit transfer. Then we focus on two other alternatives for outgoing transfers, the cheque payment and letter of credit. In the second part of the chapter, we deal with all the incoming products available to the

cash manager for dealing with the various types of collections. We describe the incoming credit transfer, the incoming cheque payment, direct debits, documentary collections, card payments and, finally, cash payments. Chapter six focuses on the different ways a company may deliver its payment instructions. We describe the features of desktop systems, direct link systems, web-based systems and also a new alternative: SWIFTNet. At the end of the chapter we give a short overview of the safety aspects of these systems. We then broadly discuss the routing of payments, explaining the difference between gross and net settlement, as well as the differences between local and international payments. We also deal with the evolving role of SWIFT.

C. CORE CASH MANAGEMENT ACTIVITIES $\quad$
In chapters eight, nine and ten we deal with liquidity management. This breaks down into cash balances management and investment management. Cash balances management concerns the management of the company's current account balances. It is aimed at controlling balance positions and optimising the total interest income from the company's accounts. We continue by discussing cash pooling, an important tool for cash balances management, and an area of significant innovation with the development of global and multi-bank sweeping as well as multi-currency cash pools. Next, we deal with investment management, i.e. the management of the company's liquidity positions. Investment management involves determining the future liquidity positions, so that the funding of future shortages or investment of future surpluses can take place in the money market at the best possible rates.

We then move on to another key task of the cash manager, cash flow management, which is aimed at minimising the costs of the company's internal and external payment flows. We describe three possible ways in which the cash manager can reach this goal. First he or she may try to reduce the costs of the payment flows, leaving the cash flow structure and the internal organisation structure of the company unchanged. In this respect, he may negotiate on tariffs and banking float. Another possibility is to change to more efficient payment products. Also, the cash manager might try to fine tune the company's payments and collections. He or she may investigate the possibilities of substituting cross-border cash flows for (remote) local cash flows and / or the possibilities of changing the routing of inter-company cash flows. A second option for the cash manager could involve setting up a netting system to offset inter-company cash flows. Thirdly, the cash manager may set up a payment and collection factory in order to achieve economies of scale in executing the payables and collections of the company.

Chapter twelve focuses on working capital management. Although this is not a core task for the treasurer, he or she is closely involved in all aspects of working capital management. After all, the size and composition of the working capital largely determine the company's liquidity position. We describe the actions the cash manager can take to keep the cash cycle as short as possible. We look at accounts receivable management and accounts payable management and at stock management, as distinguishable parts of the cash conversion cycle. Here, we also describe the possibilities of electronic commerce and outline the role of so-called shared service centres (SSCs). We end this part by calculating the duration of the cash conversion cycle, using days receivable, days sales outstanding and days inventories.

Then, we deal with currency risk and interest rate risk. First, we give a definition of currency risk and formulate the goals of currency risk management. After a short description of the currency market, we describe the most important currency products. We deal with spot transactions, forward transactions, currency futures, options and currency swaps. Chapter fourteen focuses on interest rate risk. Again, we start with a definition of interest rate risk. We then describe the goals of interest rate risk management and the most commonly used interest rate products. We explain forward rate agreements, money market futures, interest rate swaps and interest options such as caps, floors and collars.

E. RELATED TOPICS
This part contains of a number of chapters most of which can be seen as elaborate appendices to previous chapters. First, as an addition to the chapter about delivery channels, chapter fifteen deals with cryptography. This is an important safety tool used to secure payment messages. Chapter sixteen is a supplement to the chapter dealing with clearing and settlement. It provides an extensive overview of the clearing and settlement institutions and systems in the United States, the euro zone, the United Kingdom and Japan. In this chapter, we also describe the Continuous Linked Settlement system. Chapters seventeen and eightteen can be seen as a supplement to the chapter about investment management. First, we deal with credit ratings as a means of indicating a debtor's creditworthyness. Then, we sketch a picture of the financial market in which the cash manager operates while fullfilling his investment management duties: the money market. We describe the US and European money markets. Finally we present a list of the most commonly used ISO currency codes.

A
The Multinational Corporation

Chapter 1
MNC's organisation

Introduction

Multinational corporations (MNCs) enjoy several advantages over companies operating in only one country or on a limited regional scale. In addition to benefiting from greater economies of scale that help to spread out the costs of production and research, MNCs are also better positioned to take advantage of commercial opportunities that cut across national borders. They also have stronger negotiating positions with local suppliers and government agencies. The major drawbacks of a multinational structure, however, are that it is more difficult to manage and often such companies are less flexible in responding to commercial opportunities.

MNCs vary greatly in the degree to which they are centralised, and this affects how the cash management function is structured. For example, corporations with independently operating subsidiaries will usually have a largely decentralised cash management function, in which the various operating units carry out their own treasury and cash management tasks.

The role of the treasurer and cash manager depends to a significant degree on the geographical arrangement of the MNC's procurement, production and sales operations. Their relative locations determine the cash flow volumes and patterns that the cash manager must control. These locations, in turn, are often driven by tax and other considerations.

1
The structure of multinational corporations (MNCs)

The degree of centralisation in the decision-making structures of MNCs varies widely, with some comprised of largely autonomous operating companies while others take most decisions at the head-office level. In decentralised MNCs, individual operating companies carry out their own treasury activities, and only consolidated financial statements are prepared at group level. Decentralised organisations often set up a holding company, a separate legal entity that is responsible for carrying out certain activities on behalf of the entire company. These can include:

- tax affairs
- legal affairs
- treasury functions
- other support functions

With this structure, the company strategy, and sometimes the central marketing strategy, are also determined at holding company level. An MNC may also use the holding company model as a way of managing ownership relations and corporate governance issues.

2
Location of procurement, production and sales

We can gain an insight into the MNC's cash flows by examining where its procurement, production and sales take place.

Our first case concerns an international company that has its production and procurement units in the same country where it sells its goods and services. In this case all creditor and debtor payments are local. As a result, the operating companies are not exposed to foreign exchange risk, as all payments take place in the local currency. This situation represents something of an ideal for a financial director because the cost of payments is low and the risks are limited. However, it is difficult to achieve in practice and can diminish the key benefits of cross-regional sourcing for the MNC.

A more common case is an international company with production units located near its sales market, which imports unfinished inputs from a third country. The treasurer and cash manager, then, are confronted with international payments and associated foreign exchange risks.

With many other MNCs the situation is even more complicated where the operating companies sell their products in various country markets and buy their raw materials and semi-finished products in still other countries. In addition, the various operating units within the MNC may conduct transactions with one another, resulting in a multitude of international intra-company cash flows in several currencies. The cash manager is tasked with ensuring that all cash flows are pro-

cessed and settled as efficiently as possible, while minimising any adverse consequences arising from foreign exchange risks.

The examples below show the different ways that MNCs can organise their procurement, production and sales.

Local production for local sales
Samas, a European manufacturer of office furniture, has its own local factory in every country of sale, so
production is thus aimed exclusively at local needs. As a result, Samas has virtually no international cash
flows.

Local production for local sales, international procurement
An international supermarket chain sources most products and sells them to customers locally, so the
resulting cash flows are also local. Many supermarket chains, however, must also import products from
abroad, either from external suppliers or from their own foreign-based business units, resulting in
outgoing international payments.

Many multinationals seek to locate their factories as close as possible to their customers. Unilever, for
instance, operates food and detergent factories in a very large number of sales areas.

Centralised production, international procurement and sales
Car manufacturers typically have a limited number of production locations, but a widespread international customer network. The car parts are often imported from various countries. So car companies are
confronted with a huge number of relatively low-value incoming and outgoing cross-border payments.

Centralised production for international sales
Shell has a number of oil and gas fields in production in fixed locations with refining operations in both
those same countries and a small number of other countries. The end users of petrol, however, are
spread throughout the world. Shell's inward cash flows come from all over the world, but its outgoing
cash flows are concentrated in a handful of countries.

International procurement, production and sales

General Electric (GE) comprises many operating companies around the world, across numerous industry sectors. Each of these operating companies produces for markets in several countries and procures goods from other countries. GE's central cash manager is confronted with a huge number of payments, including inter-company transactions, to and from foreign countries in many different currencies.

Chapter 2
MNC's financial organisation

Introduction

Within each multinational corporation (MNC), a broad range of financial management functions must be fulfilled. These tasks are often split between the control and treasury departments. The control department's primary responsibility is to provide financial information on the company's affairs. Meanwhile, the treasury focuses on the company's short- and long-term cash positions, and on risk management issues. Within these broad areas of responsibility the treasury carries out financial risk management, cash management and corporate finance. In some companies, the treasurer is also responsible for working capital management, investor relations and 'other' activities such as taxes.

Each company has to report its financial progress, most importantly through its annual report, which consists of a balance sheet, and a profit and loss account (plus notes). These two analyses offer quantitative insight into a company's financial position. While the balance sheet details total assets and liabilities, the profit and loss account reveals information such as the income from and costs of the operations.

Most MNCs use enterprise resource planning systems, which integrate all information used by large companies, including financial information.

1
The organisation and tasks of financial management

The treasury and control departments both have important financial management responsibilities. Control has a retrospective brief, reporting on what has happened in the previous period. Meanwhile, treasury 'looks to the future' as it manages financial risks, cash and corporate finance.

Within stockmarket-listed companies, there is often a financial director (corporate financial officer (CFO)) who is senior to the treasurer and controller. The CFO is responsible for all the company's financial functions. He is either a member of the board of directors or reports directly to it. In companies with a separate board of directors, the Chief Executive Officer (CEO) is the chairman of this board. However, in other companies, only one board of executive and non-executive directors exists. In this case, the role of chairman is more and more fulfilled by one of the non-executive directors.

The financial management functions within a large company are illustrated in figure 1.

Figure 1   *Organisation of the financial management in the company*

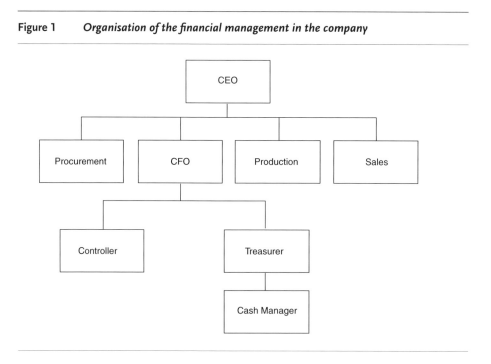

The figure shows that the controller and the treasurer operate at the same level.

1.1 The Controller

One of the controller's tasks is to collect and arrange the information required for financial decision making at all levels within the company. He has a central position in the supply of financial information. In this connection, a distinction is made between internal reporting (management accounting) and external reporting (financial accounting). In some cases, however, departments other than control may be responsible for making budgets or other calculations.

The most important internal reporting tasks are:

- drawing up forecasts and budgets
- recording the financial data
- reporting (e.g. in the balance sheet and the profit and loss account)
- the analysis and assessment of the financial results
- treasury control

External reporting (financial accounting) comprises preparation of the annual accounts, where the controller reports the composition and size of the company's capital and assets, as well as its profit or loss.

1.2 Treasurer

The treasurer has overall responsibility for all treasury tasks. A principal objective is to ensure that sufficient cash is available at all times to carry out primary business processes. Another important objective is to ensure that all interest rate and foreign exchange risks conform with the risk management policy. A derived objective is to ensure that the costs of cash flows and cash inventory are minimised and/or the revenues are maximised.

The treasurer's principal activities can be sub-divided as follows:

- cash management
- financial risk management
- corporate finance
- other topics

CASH MANAGEMENT
Cash management is defined as the management of account balances and cash flows. The cash manager aims to manage the cash position, keeping the costs of cash flows as low as possible, while minimising interest expenditure and maximising interest income.

This includes working capital management, where working capital refers to the difference between current assets (cash and those assets that can quickly be converted to cash, including investments) and current liabilities (debts repayable within one year). Within working capital management, we distinguish between accounts receivable management, accounts payable management and inventory management.

FINANCIAL RISK MANAGEMENT

The financial risk management of the company involves the management of the interest rate risks and the foreign exchange risks.

CORPORATE FINANCE

Corporate finance is the optimisation of the size and composition of the company's assets.

OTHER TOPICS

In addition to the tasks mentioned above, many treasury departments carry out activities in areas such as tax, insurance and pensions. Treasurers may also play an advising role in investor relations, which is the function charged with communicating with shareholders, analysts, portfolio managers and the financial press.

In small companies the managing director fulfills the roles of both controller and treasurer, co-ordinating all financial activities. But as the company grows, these tasks become more specialised. Small and medium-sized companies often appoint a financial director to perform both the control and treasury tasks. In large companies the treasury task is split from the control function. In even larger companies, the treasury function itself is split into separate departments for cash management and other functions such as accounts receivable management.

2
Financial reporting

Companies have to include various financial reports in their annual report. The most important of these reports are the balance sheet and the profit and loss account and the management board's explanatory notes. In some cases, the annual accounts must be accompanied by an auditor's report, which can consist of the following opinions:

- an unqualified opinion
- a qualified opinion
- a disclaimer of opinion
- an adverse opinion

A note of caution is in order here. An unqualified opinion is no guarantee that a company cannot go bankrupt. It merely means that the annual accounts have been prepared in accordance with the applicable standards.

2.1 The balance sheet

The balance sheet is an administrative snapshot of the financial position of a company at a given moment, e.g. at the end of the financial year. It has an "assets" or debit side and a "liabilities" or credit side.

The assets side is a summary of the available assets (the totality of possessions and receivables). The liabilities side indicates how the totality of the assets is financed. Sources of finance are:

–   own funds, shareholders' equity
–   funds borrowed: the borrowed capital

Total assets and total liabilities are by definition equal. The total on either side is also referred to as the balance sheet total. Balance sheets' principal headings can be itemised further. A typical company balance sheet is shown below.

(x EUR 1,000.–)

fixed assets			equity		
intangible fixed assets:			shares	200	
goodwill		50	share premium account	100	
				–––––	
real fixed assets			total		300
buildings	150				
machinery	150		provisions		
	–––––		pensions	50	
total		300	taxes	50	
				–––––	
financial fixed assets			total		100
participations		50			
		–––––	long term liabilities		
total fixed assets		400	bank loans	200	
			bonds	200	
floating assets				–––––	
inventory:			total		400
raw materials	100				
goods	200		short term liabilities		
			bank	70	
receivables			accounts payable	130	
accounts receivable	250			–––––	
			total		200
cash	50				
total floating assets		600			
		–––––			–––––
total assets		1.000	total liabilities		1.000

16

2.2 Assets

The assets side of the balance sheet indicates the assets in which a company has invested. As we see, the capital is partly invested in fixed assets (the tied-up funds)
and partly in current assets.

2.2.1 Fixed assets

Fixed assets are means of production with a long, useful life. An investment in
fixed assets is a long-term investment. The capital invested is earned back during
or even after an extended period of time.

Fixed assets include:

- buildings
- machinery
- land
- intangible assets

Intangible assets are resources other than physical assets. Patents, permits, computer programs or goodwill are examples of intangible assets. Goodwill is typically the result of a buyout of a company that does not have many assets. For example, suppose a company has a book value (assets minus liabilities) of USD 10 million, but is purchased for USD 100 million. The difference between the two – USD 90 million – is considered goodwill and is booked accordingly on the asset side of the balance sheet.

2.2.2 Current assets

Current assets are means of production that generate cash in the short-term. Cash is also recognised as a current asset. Current assets include:

- accounts receivable
- inventory
- cash

The fact that investments in fixed assets are earned back over a longer period than investments in current assets has consequences for funding methods, i.e. for the liabilities side of the balance sheet. Fixed assets must, in principle, be financed with shareholders' equity and long-term loans. Current assets can be financed with short-term borrowings (short-term bank loans or supplier credit).

The following types of current assets are especially important for the company's cash management:

- accounts receivable
- inventory

ACCOUNTS RECEIVABLE
Most transactions between companies rely on credit. In other words, a seller receives payment from his customer some time after the goods have been received. This outstanding payment is called a receivable and is posted to accounts receivable. The balance sheet shows the receivables that are still outstanding on balance sheet date.

If the debtors are creditworthy, receivables may be stated at face value in the balance sheet. However, the company may know from experience that a certain percentage of its sales are never paid for. This can be taken into account when valuing the accounts receivable item.

Under normal circumstances, there is a more or less fixed relationship between accounts receivable and turnover. A disproportionate rise in accounts receivable relative to turnover indicates that the credit term is becoming longer. This entails an increased risk of non-payment and means that a higher proportion of the financial resources is tied up.

INVENTORY
As a rule, there are fairly fixed relationships between inventory on the one hand, and production and sales on the other. If a substantial increase in inventory is not attributable to an increase in production and sales, another explanation must be found. The reason may be that unmarketable inventory remains stated at its full value in the balance sheet. If so, the value should be adjusted downwards. Obviously there may be another clear reason. If a winter is exceptionally mild, for instance, the inventory of an ice-skate factory will naturally remain unsold.

2.3 Liabilities

The liabilities side of the balance sheet indicates how the assets are financed. The various sources can be sub-divided into four:

- shareholders' equity
- provisions (long-term)
- long-term liabilities (long-term loans)
- current liabilities (short-term loans)

2.3.1 Shareholders' equity

When a company is started up, the founders contribute capital and/or goods. This constitutes the shareholders' equity of the company. The shareholders' equity can be enlarged by means of fresh contributions, but the lion's share of any increases will be realised through profit appropriation. Conversely, losses are charged to shareholders' equity.

The shareholders' equity of a company includes, among others, the following elements:

- share capital
- share premium account
- reserves

The face value of the issued shares is stated as share capital. The capital raised by issuing shares remains permanently in the company, and need never be paid back to the shareholders. A shareholder who wants his money back must sell his shares in the stock exchange, provided that they are listed.

Shares can be assigned four different types of value:

- face value
- issue price
- intrinsic value
- market value

The face value is the 'official' value of a share, for instance EUR 100 or EUR 250. This value is comparable with the face value, or nominal value, of a bond. One difference between shares and bonds is that shares are generally not issued at face value. When a company issues new shares, we speak of an issue or offering. A share with a face value of EUR 100 can have an issue price of EUR 150. In other words, if the company issues shares worth a nominal amount of EUR 100,000,000, it receives EUR 150,000,000. The issue proceeds are posted to two different items: EUR 100,000,000 to the issued share capital and the remaining EUR 50,000,000 to the share premium account. The number of shares outstanding can be calculated by dividing the share capital by the face value of the share.

The intrinsic value of a share is determined by the real net worth of the company. It is calculated by subtracting the market value of the liabilities from the market value of the assets and dividing the outcome by the number of shares outstanding.

Finally, every share also has a market value, which reflects the stockmarket's valuation of the company. The market value of a share may differ strongly from the intrinsic value. This is typically the case when investors overestimate or underestimate the company.

A company does not benefit directly from an increase in its share price. Issued shares continue to be recognised in the balance sheet at the issue price (face value

+ share premium account). The company only reaps the rewards of a higher share price when it issues new shares. The new shares can then be offered at a higher price. It is only now that the share capital and the share premium account change.

2.3.2 Provisions

Apart from reserves, most companies also make provisions, which are sums set aside to cover foreseeable future costs or expected losses. A company can make provisions to protect itself against a wide range of contingencies. These all have one common factor: uncertainty. It is, for instance, not completely certain whether, when and for what amount the company might be confronted with obligations arising from existing contracts or foreseeable future developments. As most of these risks and obligations relate to periods longer than one year, the associated provisions are generally stated as long-term liabilities. Where provisions are required for periods shorter than one year, they are often included in accounts payable. The best-known provisions are for pension commitments, tax liabilities and for matters such as customer claims.

2.3.3 Long-term liabilities

Debts to third parties that are not payable within one year are classified as long-term liabilities or long-term borrowing. The best-known examples are:

- medium/long-term bank loans
- bonds and debentures

MEDIUM/LONG-TERM BANK LOANS
Banks often extend long-term corporate loans. Before doing so, they thoroughly check the company's creditworthiness. In addition, they request all sorts of security to cover themselves against the risk of non-performance. They often ask for collateral such as a building or machinery. Moreover, a clause frequently stipulates that the company must maintain a specific ratio between shareholders' equity and borrowed capital during the term of the loan. Long-term loans involve a higher level of risk for the bank than short-term loans. After all, more can go wrong in a longer period than in a short period. For this reason, the bank charges a higher margin on top of the market rate for longer-term loans than for short-term loans.

Long-term bank loans are often extended at a fixed rate, which in most cases means that the interest of the loan is fixed during the term of the loan. But sometimes long-term bank loans have floating rates of interest, which are reviewed at regular intervals (e.g. once every three or six months).

Apart from long-term bank loans, many MNCs also issue bonds to meet their funding requirements. Bonds are debentures ('I owe you' notes) from the company, which are issued and traded on an exchange. Both domestic and foreign investors buy these bonds. When the bonds are issued, the investors buy the bonds from the company – virtually always at face value. The company recognises the issue proceeds in the bonds item on its balance sheet. In contrast with the capital received from a share issue, the company is obliged to repay the bonds. Bonds, therefore, have a certain term. The company must repay an amount exactly equal to the face value at the end of the term. Bonds have a market price, which varies according to the market interest rate. In the balance sheet, however, bonds are always stated at their face value, irrespective of the market price.

An alternative to bonds are medium term notes. These debentures are generally not listed on an exchange, and are issued under a program, organised to issue notes up to a specified maximum total outstanding amount. The main advantage of medium term notes over bonds is their flexibility.

2.3.4 Current liabilities

Current liabilities are a company's financial commitments due in less than one year. They include:

- trade accounts payable
- short-term bank credit (including overdrafts)
- commercial paper
- tax
- social security contributions
- bonds with a term to maturity of less than one year
- profit distribution

The trade accounts payable item, or "accounts payable" for short, comprises the amounts payable to the suppliers of goods or services to the company. This item is the most important in relation to cash management.

2.4 Balance sheet ratios

In order to assess the financial strength of a company, the management and external analysts use balance sheet ratios. These balance sheet ratios indicate the illiquidity risk faced by a company; this is the risk of being unable to raise cash to meet its obligations. Illiquidity manifests itself as an excess of current payments due, over cash currently available. Illiquidity may occur in the short-run, or in the long-run. In the latter case it is commonly referred to as insolvency. We will now describe two different types of ratios which indicate the company's liquidity and solvency:

– liquidity ratios
– solvency ratios

LIQUIDITY RATIOS

Liquidity ratios calculate the risk of (short-term) illiquidity by comparing the short-term claims against the assets already in the form of cash or that will be converted to cash shortly. We will show two broadly used ratios to indicate a company's liquidity position.

The *current ratio* compares all current assets to the current liabilities of the company. This includes inventory, although one must remember that it may not be be possible to convert inventory into cash at short notice, especially in times of emergency. Therefore, companies also use a more stringent test of liquidity by calculating the so called *quick ratio* or acid test. The quick ratio considers only cash and current assets that can be most quickly converted into cash, i.e. marketable securities and receivables. The formulas of the liquidity ratios are:

$$\text{current ratio} = \frac{\text{current assets}}{\text{current liabilities}}$$

and

$$\text{quick ratio} = \frac{\text{quick assets}}{\text{current liabilities}}$$

The higher the current and the quick ratio, the less risk a company will run that it will face illiquidity.

SOLVENCY RATIOS

Leverage or solvency ratios calculate the extent to which a company relies on debt. In doing so, these ratios indicate the solvency of the company, or the extent to which it is able to comply with its financial obligations in the long-run. The most important measures of leverage is the debt-to-asset ratio (D/A ratio), which focuses on the structure of a company's long-term financing structure. The D/A ratio shows what portion of its assets a company finances with debt. The formula is as follows:

$$\text{Debt to asset} = \frac{\text{total debt}}{\text{total assets}}$$

The higher the D/A ratio, the more the company relies on external debt. Companies with a low D/A ratio have relatively small equity and are considered to be more vulnerable to adverse commercial and financial circumstances. As a rule of thumb, the debt-to-asset ratio should be at least between 25% and 50%. Of course, the target figure varies with the type of industry.

In practice, these ratios do not always give adequate information about the company's financial strength. Watching how these ratios develop over time gives greater insight.

2.5 The profit and loss account

The profit and loss account of a public or private limited company must be formatted according to one of the legally prescribed models. Broadly speaking, these models are structured in such a way that income from, and costs of, ordinary activities are clearly distinguished from extraordinary income and expenditure. Every country has its own rules for drawing up the profit and loss account; notably the rules governing recognition of treasury positions have evolved significantly in the past years. In most countries, treasury positions must be revalued periodically, while any profits or losses arising from these positions must be recognised at the report dates.

2.5.1 Operating income, EBIT

The first item on the profit and loss account is turnover. This is the most important element of the operating income. If operating expenses are deducted from turnover, you get operating income or EBIT (earnings before interest and tax). Operating expenses include all sorts of cost items, such as raw materials and wages. For Elditor, EBIT can be calculated as follows:

(x EUR 1,000,–)	
turnover	10,000
operating costs	9,000
	–
EBIT (operating profit)	1,000

Turnover and EBIT are of major importance to every company. All of the company's efforts are aimed at realising the highest possible sales at the lowest possible costs. The profit and loss account reveals whether the company has succeeded in this aim.

By comparing these figures with competitors in the same sector, a company's position in the market can be determined.

2.5.2 Interest

Most profit and loss (P&L) accounts show interest paid and received as a separate item. For the treasurer and cash manager this is one of the most important P&L items. They are, after all, responsible for optimising the company's interest performance.

In certain periods companies can have extremely large cash reserves. This can occur, for instance, immediately after an economic recession. Profits are starting to pick up, but businesses are putting off their investments until there is more certainty regarding the strength of the revival. In this period interest received exceeds interest paid. The company may also have a 'war chest', i.e. a large amount of ready cash to permit rapid takeovers.

2.5.3 Extraordinary income and expenditure

One difficulty in assessing the results of a company is that the extraordinary income or expenditure often obscure the true picture. This income and expenditure does not belong to the ordinary activities. In some cases the distinction is straightforward. If, for instance, a coffee trading firm sells part of its real estate, then the realised book profit must be treated as extraordinary income. A natural disaster, by contrast, will result in an extraordinary expenditure.

2.5.4 Profit before and after tax

To calculate the profit or loss from ordinary activities before tax, the balance of financial income and expenditure (e.g. the interest payable and receivable) must be deducted from the operating result. By subsequently deducting the taxation on the profit or loss from ordinary activities, we get the profit or loss from ordinary activities after tax.

Similarly, by deducting tax on the balance of extraordinary income and expenditure from this item, we get the extraordinary income or expenditure after tax.

These two results jointly make up the net profit (or net loss). Let's now complete the profit and loss account for Elditor.

24

Profit and loss account Elditor Inc.

(x EUR 1.000,–)		
turnover		10,000
operating costs		−9,000
EBIT (operating income)		1,000
net interest income		100
gross profit		1.100
taxes		−440
net profit before extraordinary results		660
extraordinary profit	50	
taxes on extra ordinary profit	−20	
extraordinary profit after taxes		30
net profit		690

2.5.5 *Profit margins*

The results can be expressed as a percentage of turnover. This allows us to make rapid comparisons with other companies or with preceding years. The formula read:

$$\text{gross profit margin} = \frac{\text{gross profit}}{\text{turnover}} \text{ x } 100\%$$

For Elditor, this is : $\frac{1.100.000}{10.000.000}$ x 100% = 11%

and

$$\text{net profit margin} = \frac{\text{net profit}}{\text{trunover}} \text{ x } 100\%$$

For Elditor, this is : $\frac{690.000}{10.000.000}$ x 100% = 6,9%.

Another ratio in this respect is the *times interest earned ratio*. This indicates the company's ability to service its interest and redemption obligations of its external debt. Times interest earned is calculated using the company's earnings before interest and taxes, because these are earnings available to pay the interest. In formula:

$$\text{Times interest earned} = \frac{\text{earnings before interest and taxes}}{\text{interest expenses}}$$

Normally, the times interest earned ratio is supposes to be between three and five. If the ratio were lower, suppliers of external funds might become reluctant to grant new loans to the company, and might tighten the terms of new loans.

3
Enterprise resource planning systems

In the past, the financial information of a company was administered in a separate book-keeping system. Nowadays, large companies use integrated systems which cover the whole range of functions for all departments of the company, including the financial information. Those systems are called enterprise resource planning (ERP) systems. Examples of suppliers of ERP systems are SAP, Oracle, JD Edwards, People Soft, GDE and PS.

Prior to the introduction of ERP systems, each department within a company maintained separate departmental databases to manage information, such as employee records, customer data, purchasing orders and inventory.

Also, departments often used different systems to manage information. The different systems could be standard software packages, but often departments used self-built spreadsheet applications. In many cases, the separate systems used could not communicate with one another, resulting in manual re-entering of data from one system to another, which was both time-consuming and prone to errors. Sometimes, the separate systems were integrated by self-built interfaces. Interface are computer programs which are specifically designed to connect different computer systems. However, the effectiveness of such self-built interfaces was very much dependant on the employee of the IT department that developed them. If this employee left the company, the interfaces might not be maintained anymore.

With ERP systems, all company employees can now use one and the same information, stored in one and the same database.

A customer of a company calls to inquire about the progress of an important order. Prior to ERP-systems, the sales department would be forced to track down the order by making multiple calls to the company's manufacturing, shipping or the accounts receivable department.

If the company uses an ERP system, the question can easily be answered with one glance at the shared database.

Apart from integrating all information within the company, another advantage of ERP systems is that they can easily be connected to computer systems outside the company, such as bank systems or the computer systems of business partners. As a result, ERP systems not only improve the internal flow of information but they also contribute to efficient external communications.

Chapter 3
Treasury organisation

Introduction

When setting up a treasury department, a company must first draw up rules and guidelines. Treasury tasks must be defined clearly, and the company must decide whether treasury activities should be profit-making, or confined to minimising costs and optimising revenues arising from cash management activities.

Also, the company must determine how the treasury will be organised, including where treasury activities will be carried out and how responsibilities and lines authority will be allocated. The treasurer must identify the nature and level of the financial risks to which the company is exposed, as well as how they are to be managed.

1
The increased interest in treasury activities

More and more companies are now realising the importance of treasury activities. The reasons for this increased emphasis on treasury management include:

- an increase in international trading opportunities
- growing complexity of financial markets
- greater emphasis on shareholder value (profit)
- greater emphasis on optimal balance sheet ratios
- increasing awareness of the importance of financial risk management and oversight
- advances in information technology
- introduction of the euro
- decreasing monetary restrictions

AN INCREASE IN INTERNATIONAL TRADING OPPORTUNITIES

Increased participation in global trade bodies like the World Trade Organisation and the expansion of regional trade zones like the European Union, has encouraged many companies to look abroad for new markets and new locations for procurement and production. In the process they have set up new foreign operating companies, and acquired control of existing companies in their countries of interest. This globalisation has created more complicated trade flows, including intercompany transactions across borders. Other consequences are a greater exposure to foreign exchange risks, and contact with different tax and regulatory regimes.

THE GROWING COMPLEXITY OF THE FINANCIAL MARKETS

The deregulation of the capital markets has sparked a tremendous increase in the use of both existing and new investment and financing instruments. Companies must keep abreast of new funding alternatives, and carefully assess their advantages and disadvantages, making sure they meet their financing requirements at the lowest cost.

GREATER EMPHASIS ON SHAREHOLDER VALUE (PROFIT)

In recent years companies have been under increased pressure to create value for shareholders. This has led to ambitious profit targets and a growing need to limit any losses on financial positions. Most treasury departments are now expected to neutralise the effects of adverse interest rate and foreign exchange movements, while at the same time limiting the costs of treasury activities and optimising income earned on cash surpluses. The goal of outperforming 'the market' is now the rule rather than the exception.

GREATER EMPHASIS ON OPTIMAL BALANCE SHEET RATIOS

Banks and investors are also looking ever more critically at the composition of the company's balance sheet. Treasurers are expected to create and maintain optimal balance sheet ratios, which they impact by adjusting key drivers of the debt / equity ratio and the long-term debt / short-term debt ratio, and by pursuing active working capital management.

INCREASING AWARENESS OF THE IMPORTANCE OF FINANCIAL RISK MANAGEMENT

Companies are increasingly aware of the financial risks they face, resulting from new regulatory pressures and new emphases in corporate governance. Increasing risk awareness is the main reason that most companies, despite their aim of creating shareholder value, do not go so far as to organise treasury departments as a profit centres. Treasurers who operate their departments as profit centres risk taking unwise gambles with the corporate balance sheet in an effort to drive treasury revenues.

The rapid advance of information technology has given companies unprecedented opportunities to automate all aspects of business, including treasury operations. New technology has made it easier to collect, analyse and act upon financial information, whether produced internally or externally. Financial information providers offer companies with timely information on cash balances and account movements, as well as foreign exchange and money market rates. Meanwhile, companies' own internal systems provide statements of positions and liquidity forecasts. Taken together, these sources of information provide companies with valuable tools for managing their liquidity and cash flows, as well as accounts receivables and payables.

INTRODUCTION OF THE EURO
The introduction of the euro on 1 January 1999 presented multinational corporations (MNCs) with tremendous cash management opportunities. The single currency meant that balances of accounts in different European countries could now be combined without foreign exchange conversions and associated risks. Many European companies have spent the past few years redesigning their cash management structures, and in the process have frequently switched over to banks or groups of banks better able to meet their evolving requirements. Ongoing enlargement of the euro zone is creating further treasury consolidation opportunities.

The introduction of the euro has also affected capital market structures and the corporate finance function. This can be seen in the increasing importance of euro dominated medium-term note programmes.

THE DISAPPEARANCE OF MONETARY RESTRICTIONS
Many Central European countries abolished their monetary restrictions after the fall of the Berlin Wall in 1989. As a result, the currencies of many of these countries are now freely convertible and any profits made in these countries can be transferred elsewhere without restriction. While many countries globally still have restrictions, there is a general trend towards greater liberating flows.

2
Treasury tasks

The first step in mapping out the treasury policy is to distinguish the treasury tasks from those of the other financial functions. The treasury function spans several different fields. These are briefly summarised below:

Figure 1   *The fields of the treasury function*

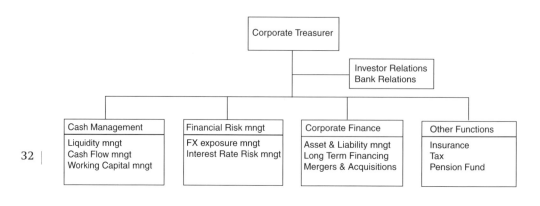

A company must make sure that the scope of these tasks is properly defined. This is particularly the case in the fields of corporate finance and insurance. In order to create an unambiguous segregation of tasks and responsibilities, the company must clearly identify the tasks that do and do not fit within the treasurer's remit.

2.1 Cash management

Cash management is defined here as the management of cash balances and funds flows. In this context, the cash manager aims to manage the cash position, keeping the costs arising from cash flows as low as possible, while minimising interest costs and maximising interest income. The following sub-tasks are distinguished in this context:

- liquidity management: cash balances management and funds management
- cash flow management
- working capital management

LIQUIDITY MANAGEMENT
Liquidity management can be divided into cash balances management and funds management. Cash balances management refers to the day-to-day management of the company's current accounts. Every day the cash manager seeks to control the company's cash balances in such a manner that the interest result on these balances is optimised.

Funds management refers to the management of the company's cash positions. In contrast with cash balances management, this involves cash positions that exist for a longer period of time (for instance longer than a week).

CASH FLOW MANAGEMENT

Organisation of commercial payments is another important cash management task. Cash flow management aims to reduce the number of payments, cutting the transfer costs per payment and effectively managing the outgoing payments while accelerating the incoming payments. Another task for the cash manager is to support accounts payable and accounts receivable administration.

WORKING CAPITAL MANAGEMENT

In some companies, working capital management is also one of the cash manager's tasks. Working capital is the difference between current assets (cash and quickly realisable assets, including investments) and current liabilities (liabilities that are repayable within one year). The size and composition of working capital largely determines the company's liquidity. Working capital management breaks down into:

- accounts receivable management
- accounts payable management
- stock management

Important considerations for the cash manager are: How quickly do customers pay their bills? How long do stocks remain on the balance sheet? How long can the company wait before paying its suppliers? Some of these activities can be delegated to other specialists or departments. A separate department can, for instance, be set up under the direction of a credit manager to manage accounts payable. Stock management is usually entrusted to the production department. However, the cash manager will always keep close track of all the variables that influence cash flows. This is natural considering the company's cash position depends largely on the quality of its working capital management.

2.2 Financial risk management

Financial risk management is the activity dedicated to controlling the interest rate and foreign exchange risks of a company.

2.2.1 Foreign exchange risk management

Foreign exchange risk is the risk that fluctuating foreign exchange rates will have a negative impact on the company's results or value.

We distinguish three types of foreign exchange risk:

- transaction risk
- translation risk
- economic risk

TRANSACTION RISK

Transaction risk is the risk that the company's profit is eroded by exchange rate movements that negatively affect purchasing costs or selling prices. This risk arises when imports or exports are settled in foreign currency. Virtually all international companies are exposed to transaction risk.

TRANSLATION RISK

Translation risk is the risk that foreign exchange fluctuations have a direct impact on the company's asset value. A company is exposed to translation risk when it has assets denominated in one currency, without offsetting liabilities in that same currency.

ECONOMIC RISK

Economic risk is the risk that a country where production takes place becomes expensive compared to others, so causing a deterioration in the company's competitiveness. Possible causes are higher labour costs or a structurally strong currency in the country of production.

The following tasks can be distinguished in relation to foreign exchange risks:

- determining the foreign exchange strategy
- monitoring the foreign exchange positions
- deploying various instruments to reduce and/or hedge the positions

2.2.2 Interest rate risk management

At its highest level, interest rate risk is the risk that interest rate movements will have a negative impact on operating results. This risk arises when future interest flows from cash positions are not fixed. Interest rate risk may also arise from a change in interest rates that impacts the value of assets or liabilities, or the value of a company's financial contracts.

Most companies are sensitive to fluctuations in interest rates. The treasurer's task is to reduce the negative impact of these fluctuations. Money market and capital market rates change may change every moment and these fluctuations must be expertly handled to achieve effective interest rate risk management. In this respect the treasurer is expected to:

- develop an interest rate vision
- monitor the company's interest rate positions
- conclude transactions in the money and derivatives markets

2.3 Corporate finance

The corporate finance function has the following roles:

- financing policy
- optimising the balance sheet structure (asset & liability management)
- producing a financing plan

The treasurer first determines the period during which financing is needed as well as the required currency. Next, he explores the available financing methods, such as bank credits or alternative instruments like bonds or commercial paper. He will generally try to match the term and currency of the finance with the company's assets. In other words, he will seek to finance fixed assets with long-term loans, and current assets with short-term loans. Matching the company's liabilities with its assets is called asset and liability management.

2.4 Investor relations, bank relations, and other activities

Bank relations involve the exchange of information with banks as well as the direct negotiations on terms and conditions. Bank relations are commonly carried out by the treasury department.

Investor relations has a broader scope than bank relations and involves the supply of information to all (potential) suppliers of funds. Investor relations, therefore, are of great strategic importance. These activities are often carried out by a board level director, but the corporate treasurer may have an advisory role. The most important aim of investor relations is to obtain and retain access to the financial markets. From a financing point of view, the company must have strong contacts in the financial world. A well-known example of an investor relations activity is the organisation of roadshows for share or bond issues.

Apart from the tasks already mentioned, many treasury departments also perform tax insurance and pensions activities. Where the treasurer combines financing expertise with an in-depth knowledge of tax affairs, he can devise a highly tax-efficient financing structure for the MNC.

3
The mission of the treasury department

The company must give the treasury department a mission. In general terms the mission statement can be described as follows: to make a contribution to the financial position of the company, so that sufficient cash is always available, and the interest rate and foreign exchange risks are always effectively managed.

One vital question is the strategy for handling interest rate and foreign exchange risks. These risks can be controlled in various ways:

– defensive: the complete coverage (or hedging) of interest rate and foreign exchange positions
– offensive: the selective coverage (or hedging) of interest rate and foreign exchange positions
– aggressive: the deliberate creation of interest rate and foreign exchange positions

When the company chooses the third strategy, one of the treasury's objectives is to make a profit on the positions taken. These positions can be unrelated to the operating activities. Most companies, however, limit the scope of their treasury activities to the (partial) hedging of positions.

When the company opts for an offensive or an aggressive treasury strategy, it must formulate interest rate and currency views as a framework for decision-making. These are often devised by a treasury steering committee, where the financial director, treasurer and usually the cash manager play key roles. These views guide the company's transactions in the foreign exchange and money markets.

4

The organisation of the treasury department

A third important decision-making area concerns the organisation of the treasury department. The following aspects play a role here:

- the degree of centralisation of the treasury activities
- the geographical organisation of the treasury function
- allocation or costs and revenue activities
- the segregation of tasks
- the determination of limits
- the management of the risks

4.1 The degree of centralisation of the treasury activities

The first question is: Where is the most beneficial location for treasury activities to be carried out? Should all operating companies be responsible for their own treasury activities or are these treasury activities to be carried out centrally? To varying degrees, most international companies have centralised their treasury and cash management activities. MNCs generally strive to centralise cash management as far as possible.

When companies first venture into international markets, they often initially opt for a decentralised structure with foreign business units enjoying considerable autonomy. In this phase the cash management activities are usually also decentralised. Local cash managers carry full responsibility for managing their own liquidity and currency positions. All transactions are settled with local banks.

Over time, MNCs realise significant efficiencies and financial benefits can be achieved by centralising treasury activities. The following phases in this process can be distinguished:

- central interest rate, currency risk management, and central management of large liquidity positions
- central interest rate, currency risk management, and cash balance and liquidity management
- fully centralised treasury

The figure below indicates which activities are centralised in each phase, and which activities are still carried out at the individual business units.

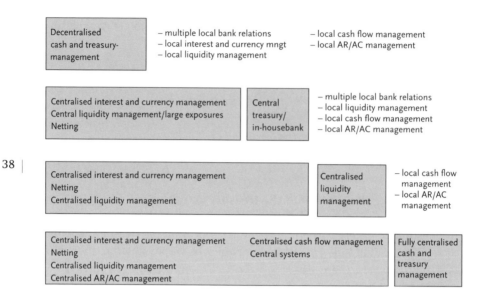

38

4.1.1 Step 1: centralisation of interest rate and currency risk management

The first step towards the centralisation of treasury activities involves the creation of a central treasury department, which carries out a number of tasks for the group. In the first stage, treasury activities will be confined to the following tasks:

- interest rate risk management
- currency risk management
- management of large liquidity positions

The central treasury department can take various shapes. Two of the most common are discussed below. These are: multi currency centres and in-house banks.

MULTI CURRENCY CENTRES
Over the past decades many US companies with European activities have set up 'multi currency centres' in Europe. Multi currency centres are treasury units that open central accounts in all relevant European currencies. These accounts are then used for the central collection of all balances from the European business units. Transfers from the business units to the central treasury must be sufficient-

ly frequent to avoid the occurrence of large decentralised balances (and related currency risks). The great advantage of multi-currency centres is that all currency transactions are executed centrally for all European business units. Credit and debit balances can thus be set off against each other. In addition, multi currency centres can generally obtain more favourable rates from banks than individual business units could acting independently.

The arrival of the euro reduced the tasks of multi currency centres, but they can still add value. After all, many currencies continue to exist alongside the euro in Europe. In addition, the euro has opened up more opportunities for cash balances management. Multi-currency centres are, therefore, increasingly focusing on the creation of euro cash pools.

In this phase, each operating company conducts most of its own cash management tasks. The local cash managers manage their own accounts, and conclude some of the required money market and currency transactions. Debtor and creditor management, as well as the related payments, also take place at the operating companies.

A central treasury can let the business units participate in arrangements made with the banks concerning e.g.:

- payment services
- credit facilities
- credit insurance
- electronic banking

THE IN-HOUSE BANK

Some central treasury departments process transactions in the name of, and for, the accounts of the business units. In this case, they act as an agent for the business units. Central treasury departments first consolidate all the business units' positions and then cover the group positions. Here, the central treasury department acts as the counterparty of the bank, and concludes internal transactions with the individual business units. Because the central treasury deals with the bank on behalf of the business units, and provides the business units with services that were formerly supplied by a bank, it is referred to as the in-house bank.

To fulfil its intermediary function, the in-house bank needs an internal system of current accounts and a central settlement administration.

The scope of operations undertaken by an in-house bank differs from company to company. Some companies with a central treasury or in-house bank allow their operating companies to use the services of an external bank. In this case, however, they are still generally required to ask the central treasury for a price quotation. At other companies, however, the operating companies are obliged to use the services of the in-house bank. All transactions above a certain size must then be concluded at the central treasury.

4.1.2 Step 2: centralisation of liquidity management

The second step towards fully centralised cash management is the centralisation of liquidity management. In the first phase, the various business units maintained accounts at local banks. These accounts did not usually form part of a cash pool. The local cash managers were responsible for managing these local accounts as well as for depositing liquidity surpluses and replenishing liquidity deficits in the money market. As we saw, in this phase the local cash managers are usually already required to transfer very large positions to the central treasury.

The centralisation of liquidity management often takes place in steps. Three successive steps that the central treasurer can make to arrive at central liquidity management are.

- creation of local cash pools
- creation of an international cash pool
- replacement of accounts at local banks with accounts at the principal bank

4.1.3 Step 3: centralisation of transaction processing

The final step towards fully centralised cash management involves the centralisation of all incoming and outgoing payments. In some cases, documentary payments are also centralised. Centralising the transaction processing system can be time-consuming, but offers many advantages such as: more accurate cash flow forecasts and lower transaction costs.

Before the company centralises the processing of debtor and creditor payments, all business units manage their own payments and the local cash managers are responsible for the resulting cash flows. The characteristics of decentralised processing of debtor and creditor payments are:

- use of many different banks
- use of different debtor and creditor systems
- use of several electronic banking systems
- local management of payments

The centralisation of the transaction processing system can take place in the following phases:

- centralisation of payments; payment and collection factory
- centralisation of the entire debtor and creditor management; shared service centres
- outsourcing of the entire debtor and creditor management

PAYMENT AND COLLECTION FACTORIES

The first step towards the centralisation of debtor and creditor management concerns the centralisation of all incoming and outgoing payments relating to these debtors and creditors. To this end, the company sets up a new central business unit: the payment and collection factory. The local business units continue to conduct their own debtor and creditor administration, but all transfers are carried out by the payment and collection factory.

SHARED SERVICE CENTRES

Some companies take the centralisation of services a step further. They opt to centralise their entire debtor and creditor management. The business units are relieved of this administrative burden and can concentrate completely on their core activities. The unit where the central debtor and creditor management takes place is called a shared service centre (SSC). Such an SSC can also carry out other non-core tasks, such as salary administration and back-office activities.

The degree to which the financial functions are transferred to an SSC differs from company to company. Sometimes the operating companies themselves prefer to continue carrying out certain parts of the transaction processing. They may, for instance, want to receive invoices directly from suppliers and then forward these to the payments and collection factory. Sometimes the collection of outstanding debtor payments can be more conveniently arranged at local level.

OUTSOURCING

Companies can realise substantial cost savings by centralising certain cash management activities. At a certain point, however, the opportunities for cost savings through internal centralisation will be exhausted. Then, further cost reductions can only be achieved by outsourcing a number of activities. Various market parties currently offer transaction processing services. These include treasury consultancy agencies, accountancy firms and banks.

A growing number of medium-sized companies are tending to outsource parts of their cash management activities in order to concentrate on their core activities. Though outsourcing in specific situations may significantly reduce overhead costs, many companies are reluctant to embrace this option. This is understandable, particularly if they have gone to great expense and effort to set up their own shared service centre. Also, many companies feel that direct management of cash flowing through the company provides a means to keeping a finger on the pulse of the company. A change in cash flows can be an early indicator of future problems.

4.1.4 Advantages and disadvantages of centralisation

The advantages of centralisation are:

-   concentration of knowledge and experience, leading to improved results with fewer people and reduced risk of error
-   matching of financial positions and cash flows (where applicable), leading to a better margin and lower costs
-   central purchasing of financial services, leading to larger volumes and more competitive rates
-   tighter control to ensure implementation is in line with treasury policy

The disadvantages of centralisation are:

-   reduction of local know how
-   local opposition to the relinquishment of powers
-   reduced attention at operating companies for centralised cash management tasks
-   complex management information system (MIS) flows and demands on enterprise resource planning (ERP) systems

On balance, the advantages of centralisation often outweigh the disadvantages.

4.2 Geographical organisation of the treasury function

MNCs with worldwide activities often open regional treasury centres in three key time zones:

-   Asian time zone
-   European time zone
-   American time zone

These regional treasury centres perform the treasury operations of all subsidiaries in the relevant time zone. Though the regional treasury centres are frequently located in a different country from the holding company, they form a critical functional part of this holding company.

Wherever possible, the regional treasury centres are located in a country with a friendly monetary and investment climate. In Europe, this includes cities such as Brussels, Amsterdam, Dublin, Zurich and London. These locations are called 'financial centres'. The diagram below illustrates the organisational structure of a European MNC with a regional treasury centre.

Figure 3   *A holding structure with a European treasury centre*

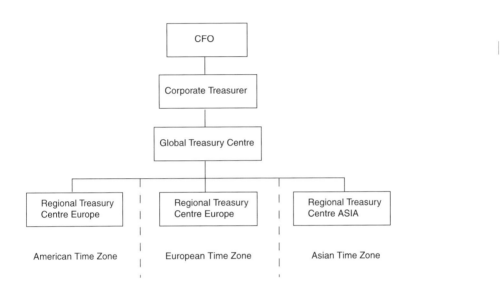

4.3 Allocation of costs and revenues of treasury activities

Where all or some of the treasury tasks are centralised, it is necessary to determine who bears the risks of the treasury activities, and how the resulting costs and revenues are distributed across the central treasury and the operating companies. There are two possibilities, depending on whether the central treasury is a profit centre or a cost centre.

PROFIT CENTRE
If the treasury is a profit centre, it has its own profit target. To comply with this target, the treasury is allowed to take financial positions that are not related to the positions of the company's operating businesses. Transfer pricing policies will

help determine where treasury mark-ups/mark-downs can be taken. This, of course, must be done with clear advice form tax departments.

COST CENTRE

If the treasury department has no profit target of its own, it is called a cost centre. In some cases, the treasury is obliged to hedge immediately all positions arising from a company's business (defensive strategy). In other cases, the treasury department is allowed to postpone the necessary hedge transaction, or to leave a part of the position open (offensive strategy). In the latter case, the treasury department is sometimes referred to as service centre.

4.4 Segregation of tasks

Once the tasks of the treasury department have been clearly established, the various functions must be accurately defined within the treasury department. The day-to-day work of the treasury department consists of managing the cash balances, determining the positions, concluding financial contracts. The following functions are undertaken in the performance of these activities:

- front-office functions: responsible for concluding treasury transactions
- back-office functions
    - deal check
    - deal authorisation
    - deal settlement
    - confirmation
    - contract administration
    - provision of position information
    - monitoring of the maturity calendar (items falling due)
- financial accounting functions: responsible for processing the transactions in the group accounts

For control purposes, tasks belonging to these functions must be separated as far as possible. One of the greatest organisational risk factors is the failure to segregate clearly responsibilities, powers, and tasks. Unambiguous answers must, therefore, be given to the questions: Who is, and who is not, allowed to do what?; Who must do what?; and, finally, Who controls, approves, and reviews?

The most important segregation of duties is between front and back office activities. The officer concluding a deal must never actually control resulting payment flows. The diagram below illustrates the segregation of functions within the treasury department.

Figure 4 *Workflow of a treasury deal*

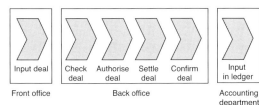

| Input deal | Check deal | Authorise deal | Settle deal | Confirm deal | Input in ledger |

Front office | Back office | Accounting department

Sometimes, companies set up a specific department between the front-office and the back-office, called the mid-office. The mid-office assumes some of the other departments' tasks, with the drawing up of position reports, performance reports and risk reports usually its main responsibility.

4.5 Treasury control

The treasury faces two main types of risk: operational risk and position risk. Operational risks arise from shortcomings within the organisation itself. Examples are procedural weaknesses, system errors, human error and fraudulent actions. Position risks are attributable to the existence of 'open positions' that expose the company to foreign exchange risk. The company can take several steps to minimise these risks.

4.5.1 Limits

A limits system must be set up to facilitate risk management. The system indicates exactly what transactions are permitted, with which counterparties and up to what amount. Exceptional approval must be obtained for transactions out side these limits. A limits system defines the following aspects:

- (types of) instrument
- (types of) counterparty
- countries and currencies
- officers, groups and/or departments

INSTRUMENTS
Most companies set restrictions on the number of products that the treasurer may use to cover positions. The use of financial derivatives, for instance, is forbidden at

many companies. Derivatives are financial products whose value is derived from other financial products.

COUNTERPARTIES

The company must also determine the parties with which the treasury is allowed to do business. A total limit is frequently set per counterparty. This means that the total amount of all transactions with a particular counterparty must remain within the set limit.

COUNTRIES AND CURRENCIES

Very often the trading activities of the treasury department are subject to strict limits in terms of currencies and countries. Apart from the home country's currency, trading will usually be restricted to the currencies of the OECD countries (i.e. the most industrialised countries) and those of the main trading partners outside the OECD area.

OFFICERS AND DEPARTMENTS

The organisation must define the type of transactions that each officer is allowed to conclude, as well as the maximum transaction sizes. These are called the 'transaction limits'. The company must also establish for each staff member (including the treasurer), whether and to what amount he is authorised to make or approve external transactions, such as outgoing payment transfers, foreign exchange transactions, money market transactions or derivative transactions. All transactions should require a separate initiator and approver.

4.5.2 Internal and position control

Treasury activities give rise to two types of risks. Correspondingly, a company has to set up to two types of controls: internal control and position control.

INTERNAL CONTROL

Internal control is the control over the operational risks of the treasury, and is carried out by the internal auditor or the controller. Internal control includes retrospective checks to ensure that contracts have been concluded and settled in compliance with the adopted procedures, guidelines and limits. The internal auditor checks the following points in this context:

- power of attorney (who is allowed to sign and up to what amount)
- authorisation (who must approve what in advance)
- adherence to limits
- compliance with procedures

Position control is aimed at monitoring the value of outstanding contracts. The treasurer is responsible for this. In this connection, the treasurer will calculate the short- and long-term effects of all open positions, both individually and in conjunction with each other. To this end, the treasurer will need frequent – at minimum daily - reports on all open positions to permit timely corrective action if positions become unbalanced. In emergencies, multiple 'intra-day' updates will be necessary.

5
Treasury systems | 47

An accurate information system is an absolute must for the modern treasurer. Apart from an electronic banking system provided by the bank, the treasurer should have a treasury information system which captures all the treasury flows. The most important functionalities of such a system are:

- deal capture
- reporting
- decision support

In order to present the right information, a treasury system needs to import information from other systems, such as an electronic banking system and Accounts Payable/Accounts Receivable systems, EXP and payroll, as well as information from data vendors, such as Reuters and Bloomberg. Most systems are also directly linked with the ledger. The reporting format of the treasury system should, therefore, be compatible with the general accounting standards of the company.

The diagram below shows the most important input, functionalities and output of a treasury system.

Figure 5   *Input, functionalities and output of a treasury system*

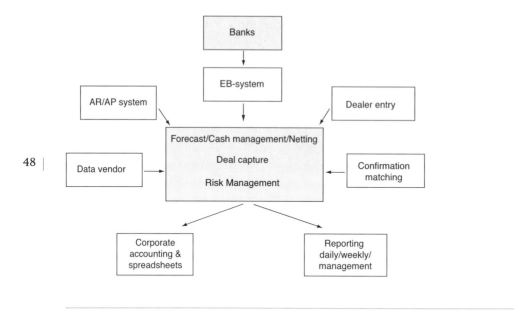

48

5.1 Deal capture

In the modern trading environment, most deals are entered directly into a treasury system by the traders – the actual execution remains subject to back-office authorisation. All the limits and the selected counterparties are captured in this module to avoid unnecessary risk such as fraud.

5.2 Reporting

A treasury system may be used to measure the result of all treasury management activities. Periodically, the system should provide information on interest income and foreign exchange results. Also, the revenues of deposits and other financial investments and the costs of funding, may be evaluated and compared with market average to determine whether the treasurer has performed at market level. This routine may also be applied to assess the effectiveness of foreign exchange transactions.

The output of treasury systems also includes key management information reports on current and future liquidity positions, and interest and currency positions.

5.3 Decision support: risk management

In most MNCs, treasurers play key roles in the corporate risk management process. Treasurers' experience with the management of counterparty, currency and interest risk, as well as their expertise of valuation and risk measurement techniques, make them well-equipped for this job. As risk management becomes more and more important for the treasurer, a treasury system needs to assist in valuing open interest rate and currency positions.

The most important risks measurement concepts are:

- duration
- Value-at-Risk
- stress testing

DURATION

The duration allows us to express the interest rate sensitivity of, for instance, a loan portfolio. The duration is defined as the percentage change in market value as a result of a small change in interest rates. With duration analysis we can calculate the fall in a portfolio's value given a 1% rise in interest rates. For completeness sake, it must be remarked that the duration is approximately equal to a kind of a weighted tenure of the portfolio.

In professional trading, interest rate movements are expressed in basis points (1 basis point = 0.01%). The fall in a portfolio's value due to an interest rate increase of 1 basis point is called the 'Basis Point Value' (BPV).

VALUE-AT-RISK (VAR)

A method that can be used to measure the risks of all kinds of portfolios is Value-at-Risk analysis. With this method, the risk of a position or portfolio is shown in one single figure. The VaR technique is based on the calculation of probability and indicates a loss value that, with a certain degree of probability, will not be exceeded. This loss value is called the Value-at-Risk of the portfolio. The VaR method assumes a model where, notably, the volatilities of the market variables, i.e. the risk parameters, are the main determinants. The volatilities of the risk parameters are used to calculate the extent to which the market value of a portfolio will change relative to the current market value. The VaR model thus gives possible results of changes in the value of the current portfolio. To calculate the Value at Risk of a loan portfolio, the assumed change of the market interest rate is multiplied by the duration.

But which of these possible results is the Value at Risk, 'the possible loss?' To answer this question, all possible results of the model are ordered, starting with the largest possible losses and progressing via declining losses and growing profits to the largest profits. As will be clear, because the VaR is a risk analysis tool, the VaR method focuses exclusively on the possible losses. This, after all, is where the risk lies. Next, a line is drawn at, say, 95% of the observations. We can thus identify the loss value which is exceeded in only 5% of the cases.

EXAMPLE

A company has a loan portfolio of USD 3 billion with a duration of 4,8. With 95% probability the maximum change in interest rate is 20 basis points.

The Value at Risk of the loan portfolio is: USD 3 bn x 4.8 x 0.20% = USD 28.8 mio.

The VaR technique cannot only be used to calculate the negative change in market value. It can also be used to calculate a negative change in interest income or in credit loss. The concept, however, is the same.

VaR gives a good indication of the possible losses under regular market conditions; that is VaR gives the loss figure that will not be exceeded in 95% of the cases. However no indication is given what happens in one of the 5% of the cases left. How much loss may occur then?

STRESS TESTING

In normal circumstances, the VaR is a good instrument for measuring the risk of a portfolio. As we saw, however, the method fails in extreme situations. For this reason, an additional method that provides more information on risks run in extreme market conditions is necessary. This additional method is called 'stress testing.'

Stress testing is a generic title for a range of techniques. The basic concept of stress testing is the analysis of the risks a portfolio runs under conditions of extreme price or rate movements. Stress testing examines whether the company could survive under conditions of a market breakdown. Most commonly, stress tests are carried out as scenario analyses. The treasurer has to set up certain assumptions on possible extreme market conditions. The assumed changes in market conditions should, however, not be too small. If this were the case, stress tests would not distinguish themselves sufficiently from regular VaR analyses. Conversely, the test parameters should not be too large, making the chosen scenario improbable and unbelievable. In other words, the treasurer has to set up credible worst case scenarios that the board of directors will take seriously.

B
Transaction Banking

Chapter 4
Bank accounts

Introduction

The current account is the most elementary cash management product offered by banks. All companies need current accounts to initiate and receive payments. In this chapter we will discuss the various types of accounts, the documentation required to open an account, as well as the costs and benefits of operating a current account. We'll also look at non-resident accounts in foreign countries, also called 'offshore accounts'.

1
Types of bank account

There are various types of bank accounts. The most familiar types are the current account, the deposit account, the money market deposit accounts and the loan account.

1.1 Current account

The current account is the traditional bank account, or 'operating account', used for almost all types of transactions. In the United States they are commonly known as 'checking accounts' or Demand Deposit Accounts (DDAs), and account holders are normally issued with a cheque book when opening an account. With a current account, the holder has immediate access to the available funds, and in most countries current accounts are interest bearing. In other countries, however, banks do not pay credit interest because either they are forbidden by law from doing so or it is not customary practice.

In many countries a credit, or 'overdraft', facility can be attached to the current account, which offers the account holder the opportunity to overdraw the account within a certain limit. Alternatively, a credit limit can be attached to a group of accounts, which is called 'balance compensation'. The bank sets the maximum amount to which the account can be overdrawn and the debit interest rate that will be charged on the debit balance. The overdraft facility allows the company to accommodate unexpected shortfalls without incurring high overdraft penalties.

1.2 Deposit account

In order to obtain a higher yield on cash balances, companies may open a separate account, known as 'deposit account' or 'investment account', which generally does not allow payments to or from third parties, does not have a cheque book, and offers only limited access to the deposited funds. Usually, the greater the restrictions placed on the account, the higher the interest paid.

Some banks in Europe offer companies an investment account, which has a competitive interest rate that applies only when the balance exceeds a certain amount. When the balance drops below this amount, the bank pays a lower rate of interest. The company can freely move funds from the current account into the investment account or transfer funds from it into the current account, which may result in a lower interest rate being applied.

1.3 Money market deposit account

In the United States banks are not allowed to pay credit interest on current accounts (DDAs), but companies can obtain credit interest by opening a Money Market Deposit Account (MMDA), which is a high-yield checking account with monthly disbursement restrictions defined by the Federal Reserve (the US central bank). These regulations limit the number of payments to three cheques and three electronic disbursements per month. MMDAs are viewed as low risk and very liquid investments compared with other money market investment instruments.

1.4 Loan account

As mentioned above, companies can obtain an overdraft facility attached to their current account, but if they have regular borrowing requirements, a separate loan facility can be arranged. A bank can open a 'corporate loan account' for the company, in which borrowed money is simply debited to the loan account and credited to a current account. The company can then use the money as it wishes. By agreeing in advance to make regular repayments, the company can negotiate competitive terms for the credit facility.

2
Documentation

Under anti money-laundering legislation, the account-opening process has become subject to increasingly stringent procedures in recent years. Banks are now required to obtain more information from potential customers as a deterrent against money laundering and fraud, making the opening of an account a time-consuming activity.

A company opening an account must normally submit to the bank specific account-opening forms and one or more of the following corporate documents:

– certificate of incorporation
– articles of association
– powers of attorney and/or board resolutions
– extracts from the commercial register
– legally acceptable identification of the account's authorised signatories

Banks need the company's act of incorporation and proof of registration in public registers to verify the company's identity in the event of money laundering activities. To make sure that the persons representing the company are actually authorised to legally bind the company, the bank requires two or more of the following:

– signed powers of attorney
– minutes of board resolutions
– the company's signature book

Articles of association can be used to ascertain the company's authority structure and to establish whether the company is a legal entity in its home country and subject to local law.

Opening a non-resident account generally involves even more administrative work. One reason for this is that the banks are generally less familiar with non-residents than with residents, but legal factors also play a role, such as deciding which legislation is binding in the event of disputes. Many countries, therefore, apply stricter rules when opening accounts for non-residents. These can include:

– requiring that passports and other documents be verified by a recognised bank or a public notary in the company's home country
– employing the services of independent firms, such as Dun & Bradstreet, to gather information about companies, the cost of which is normally charged back to the customer

- in some countries, such as Germany and France, requiring that documents be
translated into the local language.

3
Current account operating costs

Opening and maintaining accounts will incur costs in most countries, and these
include an account-opening fee and administrative expenses.

3.1 Account opening charge

Many banks charge a fee for opening an account. This fee will generally be higher
for a non-resident account because opening it requires more administration time.

3.2 Administrative expenses

Banks usually charge customers for maintaining accounts, and costs can include:

- a monthly or quarterly maintenance fee
- a required minimum balance at no or very low interest
- fees for meeting central bank reporting requirements

Charges like these are used by banks to cover the costs of sending daily statements
and providing client support.

Today, many multinational corporations (MNCs) use internal accounts for making
inter-company payments to settle internal deliveries or concentrate cash in a centralised account for the group. As with an ordinary bank account, internal accounts generate operating costs, and research shows that the costs of internal accounts can run up to EUR 3,000 per year per account. They stem from setting up
the account in the central administration, executing internal transactions and
providing balance and transaction information.

4
Current account interest income and expenditure

In Western Europe, most banks pay credit interest, but practices vary from country to country. It's common practice to pay interest in Britain and the Netherlands, but in France banks were not allowed to do so until the prohibition was successfully challenged in court in 2005. As a result, companies in France may now

receive interest on their current accounts. In Eastern Europe and Asia, it is less common to pay interest on current account balances, and only larger companies are able to negotiate current-account terms that include credit interest, and usually it is at levels well below money market rates. In certain countries, like the United States and Hong Kong, it is illegal to pay interest, while in other countries, such as China, interest is paid at a rate prescribed by law.

The treasurer must consider four factors when evaluating a bank's offered terms of interest:

- value dating
- level of interest
- interest calculation method
- withholding tax on interest

4.1 Value dating

Bank statements and electronic banking reports show two different types of balances: the book balance and the value balance. The book balance represents the legal relationship between a bank and its customers, and the amount shown as the book balance legally belongs to the customer and is at their free disposal. The value balance is the sum on which the bank pays or charges interest.

How do they differ in practice? Many banks apply 'value dating' when calculating interest accrued on an account, which means that during a certain period the bank pays no interest on funds received on the account. An amount transferred to an account will, for example, only start earning interest one or more days after it has been posted to the account. In this case, the incoming amount is immediately added to the book balance, but is not yet included in the value balance. With outgoing payments, the bank stops paying credit interest or, in the case of a debit balance, starts charging (extra) debit interest one or more days before the amount is debited from the account. Banks generally apply value dating only in relation to transactions below a certain amount, and it has traditionally been used by banks to compensate for having kept transaction fees low. Larger companies in Western Europe are increasingly rejecting value dating, preferring instead transparent fee structures for payment services.

Value dating is different from float, which occurs when a payment is on the way to the beneficiary, but the money is sitting on a bank's internal account (with the payer's bank, the intermediary bank or the beneficiary's bank). With value dating the money is actually on the customer's account, but is not yet earning interest.

The date on which the bank processes a transfer is called the 'book' or 'entry' date, and the date on which the bank starts including the transfer in the interest calculation is called the 'value date'.

In the case of transfers arising from transactions between a company and its bank, the book date and value date are always the same. This applies to, for example, loan repayments, interest payments and foreign currency settlements.

With the implementation of the Single Euro Payments Area in Europe (SEPA), a common legal framework will go into effect from 2008, prohibiting value dating on all euro payments. Transaction fees will then be the only compensation for transaction services.

4.2 Level of interest

With credit interest rates a distinction can be made between a fixed rate or a floating rate and between a universal rate or a tiered rate.

4.2.1 Fixed rate or floating rate

Smaller companies often receive a fixed rate of interest on their credit balances, which do not reflect market rates. In order for them to benefit from raising interest rates, they would have to actively invest surplus funds in money market instruments, such as term deposits.

In Europe and Asia large companies often receive a floating rate on credit balances, which is linked to a reference rate in the money market. The reference rate for euro credit balances is the Euro Over Night Index Average (EONIA), the official one-day interest rate in the euro money market. Credit interest could, for example, be calculated as EONIA - 100 basis points (= EONIA - 1%) and debit interest could be EONIA + 150 basis points.

Here are the most commonly used daily money-market reference rates, by currency, used for pricing interest on current accounts:

euro	Euro Overnight Index Average (EONIA)
US dollar	Fed Funds Effective (FFE)
British Pound	Sterling Overnight Index Average (SONIA)

4.2.2 Universal or tiered rate

With a universal rate, the traditional way in which interest rates are set in most countries, interest is calculated on the entire balance.

With a tiered rate, two or more different interest rates may be applied to different parts of the balance. Banks use this pricing method to attract higher balances (normal tiering) or to avoid clients dumping large amounts of cash into attractively priced accounts (reverse tiering).

Normal tiering is sometimes used by banks in Western Europe to attract investment cash that would otherwise be invested in the money market. The bank is prepared to pay a higher rate for the investment cash, but wants to protect its margin on the normal operating balances.

EXAMPLE

Normal Tiering

A large company has a euro account with a credit interest rate of EONIA – 100 bps, and the current account shows an operating balance of EUR 5 million. In addition, the company has EUR 50 million invested in very short term deposits. The company is investing the funds every day and is looking for ways to simplify its treasury operations.

Responding to this need the bank offers the following tiered interest rates:
Tier 1 = EUR 5 million : EONIA – 100bps
Tier 2 > EUR 5 million: EONIA – 50 bps

The company can now leave all excess cash on the current account and still make a good return, while saving time in its day-to-day treasury operations.

Reversed Tiering

A large pension fund has a euro account with the following tiered interest rates:
Tier 1 = EUR 10 million : EONIA – 50 bps
Tier 2 > EUR 10 million : EONIA – 100 bps

These rates have been set because the pension fund sometimes sells bonds and shares, in which case the bank may receive huge amounts of cash on the current account by the end of the day. In order to avoid situations whereby the bank's treasury position is frustrated, the bank has agreed reversed tiering with the client.

4.3 Interest calculation method and payment frequency

Credit and debit interest can be calculated in different ways, with the most common conventions being: actual / 360, 30 / 360 and actual/actual. The term 'actual' above the line stands for the actual number of days that a balance has been on the account and '30' means that a month is set at 30 days. Below the line 'actual' stands for the actual number of days in a year, whereas '360' means that the year is set at 360 days. A slightly different system is used in Britain and most Commonwealth countries: actual / 365, which ignores leap years. Depending on the absolute level of the interest, the various conventions can lead to differences in compound return from approximately 4 basis points (0.04%) on an interest rate of 3% to about 14 basis points (0.14%) on an interest rate of 10%.

Maturity calculation method

Actual /360	Exact number of days and 360-day years
30/360	30-day months and 360-day years
Actual/365	Exact number of days and 365-day years
Actual/Actual	Exact number of days and exact number of days in the year (365 or 366)

The following examples show the differences in income according to the various conventions.

EXAMPLE

Fortex GMBH has EUR 2 million on current accounts at two different banks from 5 July to 7 September. On 7 September the cash manager of Fortex withdraws the money from both accounts. Both banks apply an interest rate of 2.50% and pay out interest when the account balance is reduced to zero.

Bank A calculates the payable interest on the basis of actual / 360.
Bank B calculates the payable interest on the basis of 30 / 360.

What amount of interest would the cash manager of Fortex receive on 7 September from each of the two banks?

Bank A calculates interest on the following number of days: 17 days in July, 31 days in August and 6 days in September, for a total of 54 days. (Note: the first day is always included in the interest calculation, but the last day is excluded.)
Interest payment: (EUR 2m x 54 x 0.025) / 360 = EUR 7,500.

Bank B calculates interest on the following number of days: 16 days in July, 30 days in August and 6 days in September, for a total of 52 days.

Interest payment: (EUR 2m x 52 x 0.025) / 360 = EUR 7,222.22.

In this example, the cash manager of Fortex would most likely place its surplus cash with bank A or renegotiate interest terms with bank B.

The frequency of the interest payments is also important for the compound interest result, and this can vary from once per month to once per year. If the bank pays out interest every month, the company can immediately place this interest on deposit and generate extra interest revenue. If the bank pays interest annually (and in arrears, as is customary) the company does not have this option.

When calculating the debit and credit interest, the cash manager must also check whether different methods are used to calculate debit interest and credit interest. In some cases debit interest may be set according to actual / 360, while credit interest is calculated according to 30/360.

4.4 Earnings credit and compensating balances

Instead of investing short-term cash in money market instruments, companies may consider leaving the balances on the current account in order to off-set banking fees with earnings credit. In the United States many companies maximise their use of excess cash this way. The 'Earnings Credit Rate' (ECR) or 'Compensating Balances' represents a soft dollar return on balances left on current account at a predetermined ECR rate. This is an interest rate, usually very competitive and close to the going money market rate, used for calculation purposes. The 'virtual' interest income calculated on the balances is used to reduce banking fees for transaction services.

EXAMPLE

A company in the United States has significant excess balances and monthly payment fees of USD 50,000. The bank has offered an ECR of 4% (while the Fed Funds rate is 4.5%). The balances required for full off-set of fees are:

$$\text{Required balances} = \frac{\text{Annual fees USD 600,000}}{\text{ECR 4\%}} = \text{USD 15,000,000}$$

When the company manages to keep an average balance of USD 15 m on the account, it will actually avoid paying any fees for transaction services that month.

The bank will provide an account analysis statement calculating the required balances for full off-set of fees. If the actual balance is lower than the required balance, the company receives a residual invoice. If the actual balance exceeds the 100% off-set level, then the exceeding amount does not earn a return.

The company normally tries to manage its account balances close to the required balance, and by doing so it realises a high yield on its cash balances. Companies may also choose this solution for tax reasons because the ECR can help to reduce taxable income.

4.5 Withholding tax

In some countries withholding tax (levied on income at the source) is levied on interest earned on current account balances. For example, if a German company keeps cash on an account with a bank in Germany, the cash balance is the source generating the interest income that attracts withholding tax.

Withholding tax is charged to the recipient of the interest payment by withholding a portion of the proceeds being sent to the recipient. In this case, the German company is the recipient of the interest, and the bank, as the payer of interest, generally acts as the withholding agent. As such, it is responsible for deducting and remitting the withholding tax to the German tax authorities.

Suppose the bank pays a gross interest amount of EUR 7,500, and we assume a withholding tax in Germany of 30% on bank interest. The bank is obliged to withhold EUR 2,250 and pay it to the German tax authorities, leaving the company with just EUR 5,250 in interest.

Figure 1 *Withholding tax, German company in Germany*

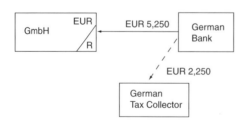

Withholding tax may be levied on domestic interest payments or on cross-border interest payments. Different tax rates may apply to these two situations.

In domestic situations, both the recipient and payer are tax residents of the same country. In cross-border situations the recipient and payer of the tax are residents of different countries or tax jurisdictions. Note that even though the tax recipient and the source account (i.e. the company's bank account) are physically located in the same country, the receiving and paying parties can still be treated as tax residents of two different countries.

Take the example of a German company that keeps an account in Portugal. Even though the company is a German resident for tax purposes, the Portuguese bank acts as the withholding agent of the Portuguese taxing authority. Suppose there's a withholding tax of 20% on an interest amount of EUR 7,500, the Portuguese bank pays EUR 6,000 to its client and transfers EUR 1,500 to the local tax authorities.

Figure 2   *Withholding cross-border situation, German company in Portugal*

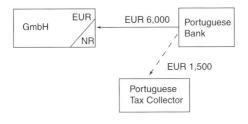

Residency for tax purposes is determined by the residency of the interest payer and recipient, not by the physical location of the account. Take, for example, a German company making a payment from its non-resident bank account with a Dutch bank in Amsterdam to a non-resident account in the same bank held by a French company. For tax purposes this is considered a payment from Germany to France, not a domestic payment within the Netherlands.

Not every country levies withholding tax. The applied percentages differ from country to country and may also differ according to whether the client is a resident or a non-resident. Usually there is a tax treaty between the country where withholding tax has been deducted and the customer's resident country. The company can then reclaim (part of) the tax paid from the tax authority in its own country, in which case it only suffers loss of interest on the withheld tax.

Some countries, like the Netherlands, Ireland, the UK, Singapore and Hong Kong, do not charge withholding tax on interest revenue and are therefore popular locations for maintaining surplus liquidity.

So far we have focused on withholding tax levied on interest paid by banks, but it may also be levied on interest paid to one company from another within the same MNC. This may occur in a physical sweeping cash pool, when the parent company receives excess cash from its operating companies. In such instances, sweeps create inter-company loans between companies, and they are obliged to pay interest to each other at the going market rate.

In the European Union (EU), there has been a trend towards reducing or even abolishing withholding taxes on inter-company interest because they are considered to create barriers to the free movement of capital between member states. Since 2004, withholding taxes on interest between subsidiaries of 'associated' companies within the EU (a few countries excepted) have been abolished.

5
Non-resident accounts

Non-resident accounts, also called 'offshore accounts', are those held with a bank outside the home country of the account holder, and they are opened by companies to facilitate transactions with suppliers or customers in the foreign country. There are a number of factors to consider when opening non-resident accounts, and these are discussed below.

5.1 Reasons for opening non-resident accounts

There are many different reasons to operate a non-resident account in a foreign country, but the most important one is to get access to local clearing.

Payments can be processed most efficiently in the country (or region) where the currency is cleared; for example, clearing US dollars in the United States, British pounds in Britain, and euros in Western Europe. Local clearing enables companies to enjoy the lowest possible costs and benefit from the extensive local service window of the local bank. Using a non-resident account for collecting money from foreign customers is also beneficial, because companies receive the funds a few days earlier than with a foreign currency account in their home country, thereby improving their liquidity position.

By contrast, making cross-border payments from a foreign currency account in the home country of the company incurs the higher costs of cross-border transfers, plus the company has to work around the often inconvenient cut-off time of the foreign currency when making payments.

An Italian company that frequently imports products from the United States and pays for these imports in US dollars can decide to open a dollar account in the United States. The company is then able to make payments locally and benefit from the lower clearing and transaction costs. The corporate treasury will have to fund the account in the United States from time to time to ensure that there is enough balance in order to avoid debit balances, which are not permitted in the United States unless an overdraft facility has been agreed with the bank.

A company wants to open an account in a foreign country where it is selling products to local customers, so to spare its customers the trouble and expense of foreign money transfers, the company can open a local 'collection account'. This is a non-resident account in the name of the company that it can use to settle their invoices by means of local payments into this account. The company can periodically transfer the balance of this collection account to an account in its home country.

Figure 3   *Collecting cross-border or through a collection account*

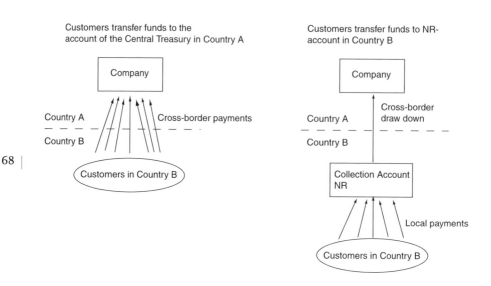

Customers transfer funds to the account of the Central Treasury in Country A

Customers transfer funds to NR-account in Country B

There are other reasons why companies consider opening non-resident accounts. They may have a need for local banking services, such as collecting cheques or depositing cash, or they may require advice and support from a local bank. The account manager of the local bank can assist the company with information or by arranging introductions to new business partners. In addition, local accounts can give the company a local presence, which may make a positive impression on customers.

What type of bank should companies choose for opening an offshore account? This will depend on the type of services required. When specific local services are needed, such as extensive cheque collections or cash deposits, the company may prefer to use a local bank. Alternatively, the company can use a branch of an international network bank or a partner bank of its main bank, with the advantage that the company can more easily manage its cash balances using cross-border pooling services.

5.2 Disadvantages of offshore accounts

The costs of opening and maintaining an offshore account are higher than those of a domestic account; it also requires more time and effort than opening a domestic account. Furthermore, local banking services may be of a different quality than the company is used to in its home country because the quality of banking service differs from country to country and bank to bank.

Another consideration is how the central treasury can manage the balances on the non-resident account. When deficits occur, due to outgoing payments and/or delayed incoming payments, the company needs an overdraft facility attached to the non-resident account. Alternatively, the company can make urgent transfers from the home country or borrow funds in the foreign market. When access cash is generated, it has to be invested in the local market or transferred to the home country, so it is critical that the central treasury receives up-to-date electronic balance and transaction reports from the non-resident account.

In order to assess whether the advantages outweigh the disadvantages, companies should consider the following points when opening non-resident accounts:

- the number of outgoing and incoming payments
- local transaction fees versus cross-border transaction fees
- specific local banking and transaction services needed
- account opening and maintenance fees
- the value of the expected inflows and outflows on the account
- expected balance positions
- interest conditions on the local account versus accounts in the home country
- local investment and funding options

5.3 Consequences of SEPA

In Europe, the Single Euro Payments Area (SEPA) will be implemented during 2008–2010. SEPA will effectively create a technical and legal infrastructure for making domestic payments at domestic conditions across all euro countries. Costs of cross-border transfers will be equal to those of domestic transfers. The question is whether companies in this situation still need local accounts or will they concentrate all transaction accounts in their home country. SEPA will create new dynamics and will stimulate companies to review their account structures. Smaller companies may centralise their accounts in one country, but it is possible that large companies will keep their decentralised accounts and cash pooling structures. The main reasons for keeping local accounts could be that companies may want to ensure that they receive incoming funds as soon as possible, to use local transaction instruments (which are not supported by SEPA) and to enable local customers to pay to local bank accounts.

Chapter 5
Transaction types

Introduction

When a company is making a payment or collecting a receivable, funds will be transferred from one current account to another. To initiate an outgoing payment, a company will issue a payment instruction. Banks have developed a wide range of instruments for this purpose.

Incoming receipts are even more important to a company then outgoing payments. While they affect a company's liquidity position, they are outside its control. As the number of receipts may be very large, it may be difficult for the accounts receivable department to process them efficiently.

Also for incoming transfers, there is a variety of instruments which a company can use. Depending on a company's relationship with its customers, it may be able to determine how they make payments. With some products, such as direct debits, the transaction can be initiated by the receiver. These types of product give the receiver greater control over the transaction and its timing.

1
Scope of the payment process

When two parties enter into a business transaction in which one party buys goods or services from another, there are usually three successive steps:

1. The buyer places an order with the seller
2. The seller delivers the goods or services and sends an invoice
3. The buyer pays for the goods or services.

In rare cases, the buyer is allowed to settle his payment obligation by in turn delivering goods or services to the seller. We call this barter trade. In most cases, however, the buyer has to transfer an amount of money to the seller. This is usually done through a credit transfer. At least three parties are involved in a credit transfer:

- the payer(the buyer of the goods or services) who requests the transfer of a certain amount from his account
- the beneficiary (the seller of the goods or services), whose account is credited with the transferred amount
- the bank (and other institutions) acting as intermediary

The payer can use several payment instruments, including credit transfers, cheques, debit cards, credit cards and new payment instruments such as electronic money. The payment can also be initiated by the receiver, as is the case with direct debits.

Companies can choose beteen the following payment products to execute a payment transaction:

- credit transfers:
    - high value payments (also called wire transfers);
    - low value payments.
- cheque payments.
- documentary credits.

The following collection products are generally available to a company:

- incoming credit transfers
- cheque collections
- direct debits
- documentary collections
- incoming card payments
- cash receipts.

Payment orders have to be delivered to the banks before a certain time for immediate processing. This is called the cut-off time. Every bank and clearing institution has its own specific cut-off time. Banks set their cut-off times earlier than the cut-off times of the clearing institutions. This is because the bank will need time for internal processing and sending the instructions on to the clearing institutions.

2
The credit transfer

Credit transfers involve funds moving from one account to another without meeting any specific conditions agreed between the trading partners. These unconditional transfers are sometimes referred to as clean payments as opposed to documentary payments, where documents need to be presented and validated before the transaction can be executed. A credit transfer is regarded as an outgoing transfer because the paying party takes the initiative.

Credit transfers can be used for both, low value payments and high value payments. Low value payments are transfers of relatively small amounts where immediate (real-time) execution is not necessary. This will usually apply to normal vendor payments as well as payroll payments. These payments, where time is not critical, are also referred to as retail or bulk payments.

High value payments often need to be executed and settled urgently. They are used for all kinds of time-critical transactions, such as treasury payments (i.e. money market and foreign exchange transactions), real estate transactions and tax payments. High value payments are also commonly used in the transport sector to secure the rapid release of goods at seaports.

With a credit transfer, the customer delivers a transfer instruction to the bank, specifying:

- the currency and the amount to be transferred
- the account to be charged
- the account of the beneficiary
- beneficiary bank details
- a value date (optional)
- additional information for the beneficiary (optional)
- instructions for the routing of the payment (optional)

2.1 Costs of outgoing credit transfers

Banks charge fees or commissions for outgoing payments. Obviously, it is important for the payer and the beneficiary to know who is liable to pay the transaction charges. With international payments it is quite common for both the payer and the beneficiary to be charged by their banks. If the payer wants the commissions to be fully charged to itself, or to the beneficiary, this must be stated explicitly in the payment instruction. The following codes are used for international credit transfers:

- if the total costs are borne by the payer, the transfer instruction carries the code OUR
- if the total costs are borne by the beneficiary, the transfer instruction carries the code BEN ('beneficiary')
- if the payer and the beneficiary share the costs, the transfer instruction carries the code SHA ('shared')

2.2 Advantages and disadvantages of outgoing credit transfers

The most important advantage of ordinary credit transfers is that they are relatively cheap. This is because the bank does not have to carry out any additional operations (which it does with documentary payments), and because the processing of credit transfers is largely standardised.

This applies specifically to in-country low-value transfers in many developed economies. These transfers are processed efficiently by the local clearing institutions. By comparison, cross-border transfers are generally still processed through correspondent banks. As a result companies try to avoid the high costs of cross-border transactions by routing them through in-country collection or disbursement accounts.

A supplier may ask the customer to pay in advance. If the customer does so and pays by means of a credit transfer, there is no certainty that the goods will be delivered. This lack of certainty is the biggest disadvantage of credit transfers. In most cases, however, payments take place after delivery and the supplier bears the risk.

3
Outgoing cheque payments

Many companies in Anglo-Saxon countries use cheques instead of credit transfers. When they have to pay a supplier, they pull out their cheque book, write a cheque and send it to the beneficiary. As with the credit transfers discussed above, with cheque payments the debtor takes the initiative.

3.1 The parties involved in cheque payments

The following individuals and institutions are involved in cheque payments:

- the payer
- the payer's bank

- the beneficiary
- the beneficiary's bank

THE PAYER

The payer is the person who writes the cheque and sends it to the beneficiary. He or she is the person who buys the goods or services. The payer is also the one whose account is ultimately charged. Other names used for the payer are: 'issuer', 'remitter' or 'drawer'.

THE PAYER'S BANK

This bank pays the cheque out to the beneficiary's bank to the debit of the drawer's account. The payer's bank is often referred to as the 'issuing bank' or 'drawee bank'. | 75

THE BENEFICIARY

The beneficiary or 'payee' is the person who receives the cheque in payment. He is the supplier of the goods or services delivered to the payer.

THE BENEFICIARY'S BANK

In most cases, the beneficiary's bank receives the cheque from the beneficiary and sends it to the payer's bank for collection. At a later point in time, the beneficiary's bank will receive the cheque amount from the payer's bank and will credit the account of the beneficiary.

Two types of cheques are used in the world of international commerce and payments: company cheques and bank cheques.

3.2 Company cheques

A company cheque or personal cheque is an 'ordinary' cheque. It is a cheque that a payer or issuer draws on his bank (the issuer's bank) and, subsequently, delivers or sends to the beneficiary and supplier of the goods.

In Figure 1, we can see how a company cheque is routed though the banking industry.

Figure 1   *Cheque processing*

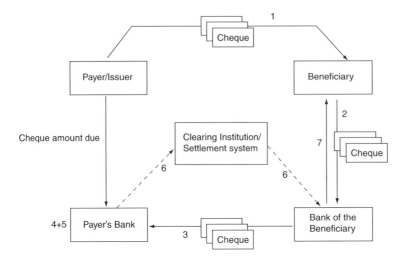

1. The payer / issuer issues a cheque and sends the cheque to the beneficiary
2. The beneficiary receives the cheque and forwards the cheque to his bank or an institute that processes the cheques for the banks
3. The beneficiary's bank forwards the cheque to the payer's bank
4. The payer's bank checks the payer's balance
5. The payer's bank debits the payer's account
6. The payer's bank transfers the money to the account of the supplier's bank through a clearing and settlement system
7. The beneficiary's bank credits the beneficiary's account

3.3 Bank cheques (bank drafts)

Because company cheques do not offer the beneficiary any payment security, trading parties often agree that the payer will use a different kind of cheque, the bank cheque. A bank cheque, or bank draft, is a cheque which is drawn by a bank on behalf of the payer. The bank does this on the instruction of the payer, but in this case the bank enters into an obligation to pay.

When a payer instructs the bank to issue a bank check, the bank will immediately debit the payer's account for the transaction amount. This is different from a company cheque where the payer's account is debited later in the process.

3.4 Advantages and disadvantages of cheque payments

Generally speaking, a company cheque is advantageous to the payer and disadvantageous to the beneficiary. When a company pays a supplier in a foreign country, it can take one or two weeks before the cheque is delivered to the payer's bank. This is advantageous to the paying company, as its account will be charged later. In this way, a company cheque basically provides the payer with a form of credit.

With a bank cheque, the drawing bank debits the payer's account immediately upon issuing the cheque. So the bank cheque has already been settled on the payer's account before it reaches the beneficiary. As with a company cheque, some time will pass before the cheque arrives back at the drawing bank. The interest benefit is now for the drawing bank. After all, the bank only credits the account of the beneficiary's bank after receiving the cheque.

The commercial relationship between the payer and the beneficiary usually determines whether a bank cheque or a company cheque is used.

4
Documentary credits

One risk faced by exporters is that the payer, or the payer's bank, is unable to meet its obligations. This is called credit risk. Such risk exists with domestic payments, but is greater in the case of cross-border payments, especially when companies are trading in less developed economies. It is more difficult to assess the credit quality of a foreign debtor, or its bank, than that of domestic parties. Additionally, when problems occur they are more difficult to resolve. Companies in other countries are often subject to a different legal system, making it more difficult to take legal action. Therefore, exporters are keen to use payment methods that offer a high degree of security.

A way in which exporters can do so is by getting the importer to issue a documentary credit. A documentary credit is applied for by the importer, i.e. the payer. It is, therefore, an outgoing payment product.

A documentary credit works as follows: the 'issuing bank' issues a documentary credit on behalf of the importer (or 'applicant'). This means that the bank enters into an obligation to pay the exporter (or 'beneficiary') during a certain period of time (the period of validity) when certain documents have been submitted.

4.1 The documents with a documentary credit

In order to be eligible for the payment, the exporter must meet certain conditions (the credit conditions). To this end, he must present a number of documents to the bank.

The documents that the importer wants to receive before the bank is permitted to make the payment are specified in a letter of credit (LC). The letter of credit is drawn up by the importer's bank in cooperation with the importer. The importer stipulates which documents must be handed over before the bank pays the exporter. As a rule, this involves the following documents:

- proof of ownership
- transport document, proving that the goods have been dispatched
- certificate of insurance
- quality certificate

The payment of the documentary credit depends on whether the exporter supplies the required documents. However, the delivery of the correct documents does not, in itself, prove that the actual goods will be delivered as agreed. The documents merely provide assurance that the goods have been dispatched, are insured and were in a good condition at the time of inspection. But the documents provide no guarantee as to the quality of the goods upon arrival at the importer's premises, or even whether they will ever arrive at all. The documents can be perfect, but the goods may be worthless! Disputes over the quality of the goods must be settled on the basis of the contract of sale between buyer and seller, and not on the basis of the documentary credit.

4.2 The parties involved in a documentary credit

The following parties are involved in a documentary credit:

- the payer or issuer (this is the importer)
- the payer's bank or issuing bank
- the beneficiary (this is the exporter)
- the beneficiary's bank or nominated bank

THE PAYER'S BANK
This is the importer's bank, also called the 'issuing bank'. The issuing bank makes the credit available and draws up the letter of credit together with the importer.

The issuing bank sends the letter of credit to the beneficiary's bank, also called the 'nominated bank'. The nominated bank passes the letter of credit on to the exporter and pays the outstanding amount if the exporter presents the stipulated documents.

If the nominated bank does not undertake to pay the outstanding amount, it is referred to as the 'advising bank'. In this case, the nominated bank sends the documents to the issuing bank and waits for it to pay. Once the advising bank has received payment, it will pay the amount in question to the exporter. In this case, the documentary credit is called 'advised'.

Sometimes the exporter will negotiate additional assurances, e.g. because it does not know the issuing bank. In this case, it can ask the nominated bank to 'confirm' the documentary credit. This means that the nominated bank enters into an obligation to pay immediately upon receipt of the stipulated documents. It is then referred to as the 'confirming bank'. The documentary credit is now described as 'confirmed'.

4.3 The routing of a documentary credit

We will now describe the entire process that a documentary credit goes through from application to final payment. Our example assumes that a consignment of Danish textile products is to be delivered to Nigeria under a confirmed documentary credit.

EXAMPLE

The Copenhagen-based company, Nielsen Casuals A/S (the exporter), concludes a contract in January 2005 with Lagostyle Ltd., based at Lagos, Nigeria (the importer), for the delivery of textiles to the value of GBP 20,000.

Delivery will be at Lagos, shipment by African Lines, with the latest date of shipment 30 May 2005. Payment under a letter of credit is to be issued by the First Nigerian in Lagos (the bank of Lagostyle) and confirmed by the Den Danske Bank in Copenhagen (the bank of Nielsen Casuals). Both parties pay the costs of their own banks. In Figure 2, we show the different steps in the routing process of this documentary credit.

Figure 2   *Routing of a documentary credit*

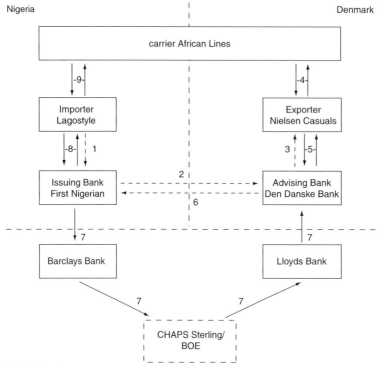

Nigeria | Denmark

carrier African Lines

-9-

Importer
Lagostyle

-8-   1

2

Issuing Bank
First Nigerian

6

Barclays Bank

7

7

-4-

Exporter
Nielsen Casuals

3   -5-

Advising Bank
Den Danske Bank

7

Lloyds Bank

7

CHAPS Sterling/
BOE

United Kingdom

1. Lagostyle requests its bank – the First Nigerian Ltd. – to issue a documentary credit to be confirmed by the Den Danske Bank.
2. The First Nigerian assesses the application from Lagostyle, issues the letter of credit and requests the Den Danske Bank to confirm this letter of credit.
3. The Den Danske Bank responds positively to the request for confirmation. After adding its confirmation, it sends an advice note, together with the letter of credit, to Nielsen Casuals.
4. Nielsen Casuals ships the goods by African Lines, from which it receives the bill of loading, and makes/receives the other required documents.
6. Nielsen Casuals presents the documents to the Den Danske Bank, which examines them and, on approval, pays Nielsen Casuals GBP 20,000 less costs.
6. The Den Danske Bank sends the documents to the First Nigerian, which also examines them.
7. On approval, First Nigerian transfers GBP 20,000 to Den Danske Bank. Since this the payment is nominated in GBP, the payment will be executed in the United Kingdom. The routing of the payment is as follows: First Nigerian sends a payment instruction to Barclays, its correspondent bank, in favour of Lloyds Bank, the correspondent bank of Den Danske Bank, in favour of Den Danske Bank. The payment will be processed via CHAPS and ultimately will be settled through the Bank of England (BOE).

8. The First Nigerian puts the documents at the disposal of Lagostyle while simultaneously charging the account of Lagostyle for GBP 20,000 or the equivalent in another currency plus its commission and costs.

9. On arrival of the goods, Lagostyle takes the bill of loading to African Lines, clears the goods with the aid of the documents and takes delivery of the goods.

When the issuing bank receives the correct documents, it will charge the importer's account. Its next step is to transfer the money to the exporter's bank. This payment made under the documentary credit is a straightforward cross-border transfer.

If the credit has not been confirmed, the advising bank will credit the beneficiary's account on receipt of payment, while applying the usual value-dating rules. With a confirmed credit, the confirming bank credits the beneficiary's account at the moment when the beneficiary presents the documents. In determining the value date of this credit entry, the confirming bank will take into account that it too will only receive the amount after a certain delay. After all, it must first send the documents to the issuing bank, which will then examine the documents. It is only after examining and approving the documents that the issuing bank will transfer the credit amount to the confirming bank.

4.4 Advantages and disadvantages of a documentary credit

The most important advantage of a documentary credit for the importer is that it receives both:

– the proof of title to the goods, and
– the documents proving that the goods have been dispatched, insured (optional) and inspected.

Though this provides no guarantee that the goods will actually arrive in good condition, it still gives the importer a certain degree of security.

The documentary credit gives the exporter a high level of payment security. This is particularly true with a confirmed credit. For in this case, the exporter's own bank guarantees the payment. If the credit has not been confirmed, the exporter still has a claim on the importer's bank. And a claim on the bank naturally provides greater payment security than a claim on the importer company.

One disadvantage of the documentary credit is cost. A documentary credit is fairly labour-intensive as it requires much paperwork over and above the actual transfer:

- the issuing bank must issue the documentary credit and draft the letter of credit
- the issuing bank must inform the advising bank
- the advising bank must take receipt of the documents and forward them to the issuing bank
- the issuing bank must examine the documents

5
Incoming credit transfers / collections

82 | Most collections are credit transfers. After execution of the credit transfers, a company will receive information on the collections from the bank, either through electronic banking, the Internet or a mainframe connection. This will enable the accounts receivable department to process the collections in the accounts receivable records. This process is called reconciliation.

Payment by credit transfer has the commercial advantage that customers are not bothered by all sorts of difficult payment methods. It is also easy from an accounting point of view: the accounting department only needs to check that the payment has been received, and does not have to examine letters of credit or deal with any other kind of paperwork.

The disadvantages of collections by means of clean payments have already been mentioned: there is no certainty when, or even if, the payer will actually pay. But there is a commercial relationship, which the client (payer) probably does not want to jeopardise.

6
Incoming cheque payments

Apart from credit transfers, customers in many countries still pay by cheque. As we said, this is particularly common in the Anglo-Saxon countries.

6.1 The collection of cheques

When a company has received a payment by company cheque, it will present the cheque to its own bank in order to cash the cheque. The beneficiary's bank may accept the cheque under usual reserve or for collection.

6.1.1 Acceptance under usual reserve

If the beneficiary's bank knows the beneficiary well enough, and believes the beneficiary to be creditworthy, it may accept the cheque 'under usual reserve'. This means that the accepting bank immediately credits the beneficiary's bank account for the cheque amount, or pays the cheque amount out in cash. However, the beneficiary's bank will recover the money from the beneficiary if it turns out that the cheque cannot be cashed from the issuing bank.

When the beneficiary's bank forwards the cheque to the issuing bank, there are two possibilities:

– the issuing bank pays the amount of the cheque to the beneficiary's bank and the matter is closed.
– the issuing bank does not pay the amount of the cheque. The beneficiary's bank will receive this message. It will then cancel the initial credit entry and debit the amount paid from the beneficiary's account. Reasons for the issuing bank's refusal to pay the cheque may be either that the issuer does not have the necessary funds or credit line, or that the cheque is fraudulent.

6.1.2 Acceptance for collection

The beneficiary's bank may accept a presented cheque 'for collection'. This means that it does not pay out immediately, but sends the cheque to the issuing bank and waits for the issuing bank to pay the cheque amount. The beneficiary's bank may have the following reasons for this:

– there are doubts about the beneficiary's creditworthiness
– there are doubts about the payer (issuer) or the issuing bank
– the cheque is presented to the bank by someone who is not a regular customer

Again, there are two possibilities here:

– the issuing bank transfers the cheque amount without any problem. After receiving the amount, the beneficiary's bank will credit the beneficiary's account (after deduction of charges).
– the issuing bank sends the cheque back with the message 'no advice to effect payment'. This is a discreet way of saying that the payer does not have sufficient funds in his account, or that the issuing bank was unable or unwilling to pay.

In the latter case, the beneficiary will then have to find some other way of securing payment or try to repatriate the goods.

6.2 The processing of cheques via a lockbox

Generally, it takes a long time before the beneficiary receives the funds via the cheque collection procedure. The payer sends the cheque usually via mail, which will cause delays for the beneficiary in collecting the cheque. This is called 'mail float'. After receiving the cheque, the beneficiary will present it to its bank. This also takes some time. In order to shorten this period, banks and other service providers provide 'lockbox' services.

A lockbox service is a cheque collection and processing service, where the beneficiary of cheques outsources to a third party the physical collection of the paper and accompanying documentation. This means that the actual cheque no longer passes through the beneficiary's hands. The lockbox service receives the cheques on behalf of the client, deposits the funds into the local clearing system, and sends the information relating to each cheque to its client for reconciliation.

There are three types of lockbox services offered today. While the basic purpose and functionality appear to be the same, they serve different customers:

- retail lockbox services, processing low value and more uniform cheque receivables with few accompanying documents
- wholesale lockbox services, processing high value and less uniform cheque receivables with more accompanying documents
- wholetail lockbox services, processing both types of cheque receivables

Figure 3

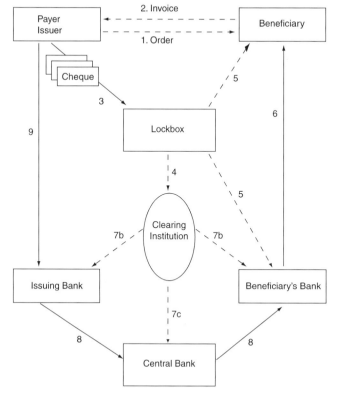

1. The buyer places an order with the seller.
2. The seller sends an invoice to the buyer.
3. The buyer (now called payer) issues a cheque and sends it to the lockbox which is assigned by the beneficiary's bank.
4. The lockbox company will clear the lockbox every day and pass the local cheques into the local cheque clearing system that day.
5. The lockbox company sends the information relating to the cheque electronically to the beneficiary and to the beneficiary's bank.
6. The beneficiary's bank credits the beneficiary's account on the same day that the cheque is received. This goes under usual reserve.
7. Clearing:
   a. Sorting of cheque payment instructions and calculation of settlement claims
   b. Sending detailed payment information to the issuing bank and to the beneficiary's bank
   c. Sending settlement instructions to the central bank
8. Settlement at the central bank.
9. The issuing bank debits the payer's account.

A lockbox service allows companies to outsource all the activities associated with receiving, handling and processing their cheque receivables. This, in turn, reduces the time taken by companies to clear cheque receivables, simplifies their reconciliation process and reduces the overall costs associated with collecting cheque receivables across a number of countries. Furthermore, it eases the hassle associated with handling and clearing different types of cheques and currencies.

In summary, the advantages of a lockbox service are:

- reduced mail float
- reduced information float, i.e. earlier reception of remittance information
- increased efficiency: by outsourcing the cheque collection activities the company can concentrate on its core business
- reduced hassle factor

6.3 The value-dating of incoming cheques

When the bank pays out the amount of the cheque under usual reserve, the beneficiary's account is immediately credited. But the beneficiary's bank has not yet received the money. So the beneficiary's account has, basically, been credited with a cash amount that must still be collected by the beneficiary's bank.

The beneficiary's bank, therefore, posts the amount with a later value date than the book date, i.e. the 'presumed date of receipt'. The difference is based on the number of days that the collection procedure normally takes to complete. The beneficiary's bank and the payer's bank can make bilateral arrangements, so that the date of receipt is usually known beforehand.

The value date can consequently differ, depending on the payer's or issuing bank's country of origin.

6.4 Advantages and disadvantages of incoming cheque payments

Company cheques offer the beneficiary virtually no advantages. Cheques are labour-intensive and their collection is time-consuming. What's more, company cheques provide no payment security. Practice shows, however, that payers still frequently prefer to pay by cheque. In many cases, the beneficiary company has no choice but to accept this payment method. Otherwise the company will lose business.

Compared to a company cheque, a bank cheque is more favourable for the beneficiary. The bank cheque provides greater payment security as the drawing bank will pay immediately once the cheque is presented. Also, the beneficiary's bank will be more inclined to collect a bank cheque under usual reserve rather than a company cheque. This means that the beneficiary's account will be credited earlier compared to a company cheque.

7
Direct debits

Where a company's debtors pay their bills by credit transfer or cheque, the company can only wait to see whether, and when, the money is received. To address this, collection products have been developed where the receiving party plays an active role. These are called 'direct debits' (DDs).

With direct debits, the receiving company can transfer amounts from the payer's account to the company account. To this end, the payer provides the beneficiary with prior written authorisation in the form of a mandate.

On the basis of this mandate, the beneficiary sends a direct debiting instruction to the bank or to a clearing centre, which, in turn, contacts the payer's bank. The payer's bank checks whether the mandate is legally valid and whether the collectible amount is within the agreed limits. Next, the payer's bank debits the payer's account and transfers the amount to the beneficiary's bank. The payer's bank is allowed to reject the direct debit, e.g. because the payer has insufficient funds. A rejected direct debit is reported to the beneficiary.

Mandates can be given for one-off or regularly recurring (periodic) payments.

7.1 Cross-border direct debits in the euro-area

In January 2006, 59 major payment banks in Europe agreed to underwrite the project of the European Banking Association to develop an infrastructure for processing pan-European Direct Debits (PEDDs). The system is planned to be operational in mid-2007 and will enable the banks to offer their customers direct debit services.

The PEDD-service will be based on the EBA STEP2 platform. Apart from international direct debits, the service supports domestic direct debits and electronic bill presentment and payments. Hence the system is called "Multi-purpose Pan-European Direct Debit service", or M-PEDD.

7.2 Advantages and disadvantages of direct debts

The direct debit is a fast and cheap collection method because the entire processing is automated. The greatest advantage for the beneficiary is that it can initiate the payment. But the direct debit does not usually provide a payment guarantee, as the payer is often entitled to reverse the payment and sometimes even to cancel the mandate. Also, there may be insufficient funds in the account, in which case the transfer will not be carried out.

However, the fact that the payer has signed a direct debit mandate is encouraging. It at least suggests the payer intends to pay promptly at the agreed moment in time.

8
Documentary collection

Documentary collections also provide the possibility for the beneficiary to act as the initiator of the payment. As with documentary credits, documentary collections are normally used for international transactions. With a documentary collection, the beneficiary does not charge the payer's account directly. Instead, the beneficiary only hands over the required documents (including the proof of ownership) to the payer in exchange for payment or a promise to pay. Handing over documents and collecting payment is entrusted to a bank located in the payer's country. The same documents are used for documentary collection as for documentary credits.

8.1 The parties involved in documentary collections

The following parties are involved in a documentary collection:

- the beneficiary or seller, i.e. the exporter who gives the instruction to his bank
- the payer, i.e. the buyer or importer
- the 'remitting bank', i.e. the bank that receives a collection instruction from the beneficiary
- the 'presenting bank', i.e. the bank that actually presents the documents to the payer

The presenting bank is usually the same as the collecting bank. This is the bank that is assigned by the remitting bank for the collection of the documents. This is a correspondent bank of the remitting bank, or a foreign local branch in case of an international network bank. However, the payer is free to ask if its regular bank can act as presenting bank.

With documentary collections, banks are merely intermediaries acting on behalf of their customers.

8.2 The routing of a documentary collection

The diagram below illustrates a documentary collection issued by Unilever Ltd. in the United Kingdom at its bank, Royal Bank of Scotland. The importer is the Taiwanese company Fu-san, which banks at the Huang Bank in Taiwan. The Huang Bank holds a GBP-account with NatWest.

Figure 4 *The routing of a documentary collection*

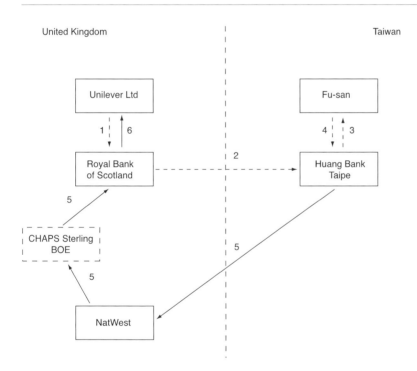

1. Unilever Ltd. sends the documents with a collection instruction to the remitting bank, Royal Bank of Scotland in London;
2. Royal Bank of Scotland sends the documents with instructions to the presenting bank, the Huang Bank in Taipe;
3. The Huang Bank offers the documents to the importer, the Fu-san company.

4. Fu-san sends a valid payment instruction to the Huang Bank in favour of the account of Unilever Ltd. at the Royal Bank of Scotland in London;

5. After the Fu-san company has paid, the Huang bank in Taipe sends a payment instruction in favour of the Royal Bank of Scotland through SWIFT. In this example, the Huang Bank holds an GBP-account with NatWest in London. Therefore, Huang Bank sends a SWIFT message to NatWest instructing NatWest to transfer money in favour of Royal Bank of Scotland in favour of Unilver Ltd by debiting her own GBP-account with NatWest. The payment is processed by CHAPS sterling and settled by the Bank of England.

6. Finally, Royal Bank of Scotland credits the account of Unilever Ltd.

Note that the actual transportation of the goods is not shown in this picture.

8.3 Advantages and disadvantages of documentary collections

For the exporter a documentary collection has the advantage that payment is guaranteed provided it hands over the correct documents. The importer has slightly less certainty. It will receive the correct documents against payment, but still has to wait and see whether the goods are in decent condition. As with documentary credits, the great disadvantages are the labour involved and, consequently, the high cost of this payment method.

9
Incoming card payments

These days many customers use a whole range of plastic cards equipped with a magnetic strip or chip to pay in shops, hotels, restaurants, etc. In addition, such cards are increasingly being used for distance payments, particularly via the Internet. We successively discuss the debit card and the credit card.

9.1 The debit card

A debit card is a bank card that gives the cardholder electronic access to his current account. The cardholder can use it to draw cash from cash machines (automated teller machines or ATMs) and to make electronic payments at a terminal, both at home and abroad. The cash machines and terminals can only be used if they display one of the logos (e.g. Cirrus or Maestro) that is also shown on the card itself.

To provide this electronic payment service, a company must have both a terminal and a telecommunication line. A terminal consists in principle of a card reader with a keypad for the retailer, a transaction slip printer and a keypad on which the customer keys in the PIN (personal identification number).

9.2 The credit card

In contrast with debit cards, credit cards are not linked directly to a current account. A credit card, therefore, does not state an account number but only the card number. With certain credit cards, it is not the bank but the credit card organisation which guarantees the payment. Another important difference with the debit card is that both the crediting and debiting take place at a later time.

Parties involved with international credit card payments are:

-   card holder, this is the customer who buys goods from the merchant
-   beneficiary, this is the merchant who accepts card payments
-   acquiring bank, the bank of the merchant
-   issuing bank, the bank that issues the credit card to the card holder

Credit card processing within one and the same country is well-established, but using credit cards to collect receivables in other countries is less straightforward. Firstly, if the invoice is in a company's home currency, the cardholder will not know in advance how much will be debited from his account. If the invoice is in the buyer's currency, a company will have to make arrangements with an acquirer in each country where it has buyers specifying the exchange rates used. An acquirer acts as a collector. It collects the funds from the bank of the card user, and then pays the beneficiary company the amount of the card transaction less charges. The beneficiary company is, therefore, subject to different service levels and pricing levels in each country.

Figure 5   *Credit card collections through an acquire*

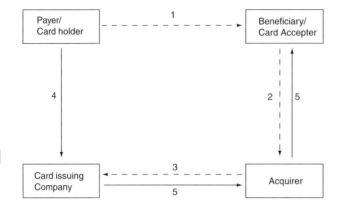

1. The payer pays the beneficiary using a credit card; i.e. he gives an electronic payment instruction to the card issuer to transfer funds to the beneficiary's account at the expense of the payer's current account;

2. If applicable, the merchant performs an authorisation and accepts the transaction if authorised. The payment instruction is then sent to the local acquirer;

3. In turn, the local acquirer sends the payment instruction to the card issuing company;

4. The card company pays the acquirer;

5. The acquirer pays the amount less charges to the beneficiary;

6. If the card company is a bank, it debits the account of the payer with itself. If not, the card company uses a direct debit to debit the card holder's account with his bank.

Many credit cards are not really credit instruments. The 'credit' is limited to a few weeks' postponement of payment. These cards are also called 'charge cards' to distinguish them from real credit cards. The typical characteristic of a charge card is that the cardholder is usually charged once a month for the total amount of his purchases. This means that all his outstanding bills are settled in one go by means of a credit transfer. Unless specific credit arrangements have been made, the cardholder must ensure that there are sufficient funds in his account at the month end.

The characteristic of a real credit card is the standard credit facility. This means that the cardholder can spread out payment of the total amount over a longer period. Interest is naturally payable on the outstanding amount.

9.3 Advantages and disadvantages of card collections

Card payments are an easily accessible payment method for private clients. They serve as an alternative for cash payments. Holding a card is much safer than holding cash money. Another advantage is that credit card payments may be executed through the Internet.

With both debit and credit card payments, the beneficiary faces extra costs. The receiving company needs a specific infrastructure, a terminal and telecommunication line. In addition, the beneficiary has to pay the card issuer for each transaction. Especially with credit card payment, the costs involved can be very high.

10
Cash receipts

Some businesses, such as shops, hotels, restaurants and gas stations, receive lots of cash payments. These businesses will regularly deposit the contents of their tills at the bank, usually at a branch nearby. Sometimes they use the services of a secured money transport firm.

10.1 The counter deposit

With a direct counter deposit, the amount of money offered is counted in the presence of the depositor. The number of notes per denomination is itemised on a special form or keyed into a terminal. If cheques are also presented, these too are checked and totalled. After approval the bank makes a deposit slip and credits the account of the depositor.

10.2 The money transporter

Where large amounts need to be deposited at the bank, it is more efficient to use the services of a professional money transporter. This service is commonly carried out by a security firm. In this case, the money transporter delivers the money and cheques to the bank in a cash-box, which is locked by the depositor. The receiving bank branch also has a key so that it can open the cash-box to process its contents. At least two different individuals at the bank will have to count the cash to ensure accuracy and prevent fraud. This will increase the bank's operating costs.

10.3 Advantages and disadvantages of cash receipts

The main advantage of cash receipts is the mere fact that everyone has access to this type of payment. On the other hand, holding large amounts of cash is unsafe and handling cash collections is quite expensive. Banks will, generally, charge a substantial fee for cash collection services. In addition, cash does not generate interest income, which will stimulate companies to deposit cash with their banks as frequently as possible.

11
List of payment and collection instruments

We end this chapter with a list of the various payment products. We match types of payment and collection with the most appropriate payment products, as well as mentioning the advantages and disadvantages.

Payables			
Product	Suited for	Advantages for the payer	Disadvantages for the payer
credit transfer / low value payment	– vendor payables – salaries	– cost effective – efficient	
credit transfer / high value payment	– treasury payments – urgent payments – taxes	– 'same day finality'	– more expensive
company cheque	– vendor payables	– delayed debiting of account	– more labour intensive
bank cheque	– vendor payables	– provide certainty to receiver	– instant debiting of account
documentary credit	– vendor payables – import transactions	– commercial: exporter is more willing to do business	– expensive – labour intensive – time-consuming procedures

Collectables			
Product	Suited for	Advantages for the beneficiary	Disadvantages for beneficiary
credit transfer	– accounts receivable	– efficient – cost effective	– no guarantee for collection of funds – uncertain timing of the collection
company cheque	– accounts receivable		– no guarantee for collection – time-consuming procedures – delayed crediting of account
bank cheque	– accounts receivable	– guarantee for the collection	– time consuming procedures – delayed crediting of account
direct debits	– accounts receivable – recurring receipts	– active role – fixed timing of transfers	– transfer of funds may be refused or reversed
documentary collections	– export transactions	– payment is guaranteed when documents are exchanged	– expensive – labour intensive – time-consuming procedures
cards	– shops, restaurants, gas stations etc.	– commercial: consumer friendly	– infrastructure is needed
cash	– shops, restaurants, gas stations etc.		– funds must be physically deposited at the bank – unsafe

Chapter 6
Delivery channels

Introduction

Delivery channels provide the key entry point for companies to access banks' products and services, and they facilitate data communications betweens banks and companies. Delivery channels are of increasing importance in the world of international cash management.

The primary needs met by delivery channels are in the areas of account information (account statement reporting) and payment initiation. Over the last few years, delivery channels, especially Internet systems, have become more sophisticated, combining greater product breadth and stronger self-service components. At the same time, companies increasingly need to manage working capital effectively and to incorporate delivery channels into their organisational structures and processes in a more effective manner.

Nowadays, companies can choose between four types of delivery channels: internet systems, direct link systems, desktop systems and SWIFTNet. The delivery channel that a company selects depends on a number of factors, including transaction volumes, accessibility requirements, data integration and security needs.

1
Internet systems

Although Internet banking for corporate customers has taken several years to become commonplace, it is now the primary delivery channel for companies of all sizes. Originally utilised for payment initiation and account reporting capabilities, internet systems have become more sophisticated and now offer enhanced benefits to companies.

1.1 Technical aspects of Internet systems

A company that merely wants to carry out individual payments via the Internet will not need to make major adjustments to its technical organisation. All it needs to arrange is a contract with a provider so that its PCs have access to Internet. Software is only generally required if the Internet system utilises a smart card security device, although most banks offer contact-less security devices such as a Digipass-token. Authorised staff can then access the bank's payment and reporting services from anywhere in the world, and from any PC or laptop that is linked to the Internet. Internet banking, thus, offers extensive flexibility.

If the company wants to send large numbers of payment orders from its own computer system via Internet to the bank, it must make sure that the applied format is supported by the bank's Internet banking system. For truly larger volumes of 100 payments or more on average per day, it is generally still more efficient for companies to use a direct link channel or SWIFTNet fileAct.

The communication between the bank and the company takes place via the Internet. The Internet applications are based on TCP/IP (Internet Protocol Suite) and customers can simply log in through their own internet provider.

Figure 1 gives a diagrammatic representation of the data communication between the company and the bank, and of the interaction between the various internal systems in the company's internal computer network, making use of a web-based payment system.

Figure 1   *Web-based delivery*

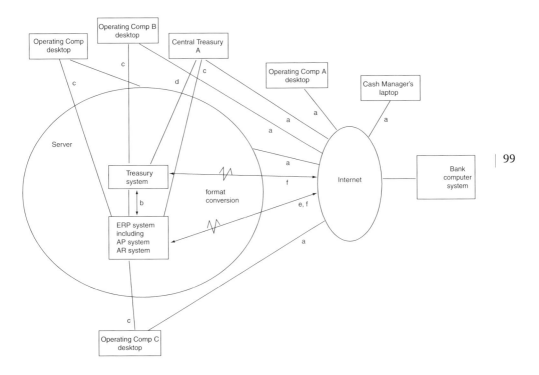

| 99

a.   All personal computers (including the stand-alone personal computer of operating company A and the laptop of the cash manager) can access internet and authorised officers can access the bank's web system from any online computer in the world.

b.   The treasury system is linked via an interface to the ERP system.

c.   Most personal computers are linked to the company's internal network and to the ERP system.

d.   The computers of the central treasury are linked to the treasury system.

e.   At many companies the ERP system will also be linked to Internet, particularly if the company engages in Ecommerce.

f.   When payment orders are delivered from the treasury system (or the ERP system) to the Web-based payment system, these must be converted to an XML format.

1.2 Applications of web-based systems

Internet payment systems now offer a wide range of applications and services, such as:

- executing payments
- import and export of payment files
- balance & transaction reporting (BTR)
- other reporting facilities
- deal initiation
- trade finance
- status reports
- on-line and personalised market information

EXECUTING PAYMENTS

Internet systems offer a wide range of payment products. Apart from low value payments, high value payments and cheques can also be initiated. Some internet systems can also take care of the central bank formalities in the case of payments between residents and non-residents.

Most electronic banking packages not only enable the cash manager to control the accounts held at the company's own bank but also those held at other banks. Before the company is able to control accounts at third-party banks via the Internet system of its own bank, mutual contracts need to be signed. The entire administrative process usually takes several months. Controlling accounts at other banks involves extra costs, as all payment orders charged to these accounts are channelled through SWIFT. The banks pass the costs charged by SWIFT on to the customer.

IMPORT AND EXPORT OF PAYMENT FILES

Payment files can be imported from the Internet systems into the ERP or treasury systems (and vice versa), thus removing a manual operation between the systems.

BALANCE & TRANSACTION REPORTING (BTR)

Internet systems allow the cash manager to view the end-of-day balances on his bank accounts. Most systems allow the company to view the accounts at his own bank as well as accounts held at other banks. This is called multi-bank reporting. Apart from the end-of-day book and value balances of the accounts included in the package, most Internet systems currently offer intraday transaction statements. A company can also obtain information on all incoming and outgoing urgent payments executed that day by logging into the Internet system.

OTHER REPORTING FACILITIES

Balance and transaction reports are usually not the only types of report that electronic banking systems can generate. Liquidity forecasts can be made with the aid of most systems while consolidated reports can be prepared in a single currency. Some internet systems can also prepare various cash pooling reports, such as shadow interest statement reports and notional pooling reports.

DEAL INITIATION

Some Internet systems include a separate module with which the company can effect short-term investment transactions or foreign exchange transactions with the bank. These were historically achieved by different systems specifically designed for these transactions, but, more frequently, deal initiation of these transactions is integrated with the cash management applications.

TRADE FINANCE

Import and Export Letters of Credit can be initiated via Internet systems, a process that previously was very paper intensive. Guarantees and collections are other Trade Finance instruments that are generally supported by Internet systems. These products were previously provided to companies in separate systems but are also being integrated with the traditional cash management applications.

STATUS REPORTS

Companies can obtain real-time information about the status of their payments. By accessing the bank's internal tracking system via the internet, the customer can largely keep track of its own payments. This saves the bank millions of euros of costs it would otherwise have incurred handling telephone inquiries.

ON-LINE AND PERSONALISED MARKET INFORMATION

Real-time information on all interest rates and exchange rates can be given via the Internet. In addition, the bank can also make a selection of the various interest rates/exchange rates and report only those relevant to the customer in question.

1.3 Benefits and constraints of web-based systems

Apart from the extensive applications, web-based systems offer a large number of benefits:

- access from anywhere
- personalisation
- single point-of-entry
- on-line client support and training
- reduced physical distribution of software

ACCESS FROM ANYWHERE

The company can access an Internet system from anywhere in the world. All the company needs is a personal computer, laptop or mobile telephone with an Internet connection. The only other condition is that security software has been installed, if applicable.

PERSONALISATION

Web-based systems can offer personalised services. This is an important marketing tool and can be used by banks for cross-selling activities. The bank can make a personalised home page for each customer. Basic examples include the storage of personal data supplied by the customer to generate personalised views or product recommendations. The bank can also select certain articles for the customer. In this case, the customer receives all information tailor-made and need not undertake its own searches.

SINGLE POINT-OF-ENTRY

Though desktop systems provide integrated payments and reporting into one system, or 'one window to the bank', Internet channels go much further. They let the client access all aspects of his relationship with the bank in one place including e.g. client support, account analysis, implementation tracking and reference material.

ONLINE CLIENT SUPPORT AND TRAINING

Companies that use the web-based systems can communicate with the bank's helpdesk through e-mail to obtain online support. In addition, the bank can provide an online training module.

REDUCED DISTRIBUTION OF SOFTWARE

Previously, with desktop systems the bank had to install one or several packages at every company. Furthermore, payment systems are periodically upgraded with a new version. In the case of the desktop systems, this involved installing one or several new systems at each and every company. With web-based systems, the bank only needs to replace the single system on the Internet. All upgrades are then immediately available for all users.

2
Direct link systems

These days banks offer companies the possibility of sending payment orders directly from their ERP systems or, in some cases, their treasury systems, to the banks' computers. Such systems are called direct link systems, open link systems, straight-through processing (STP) systems or bulk-processing systems.

Large companies simultaneously deliver extremely large volumes of diverse types of payments to a bank or clearing centre or receive extremely large volumes of payments. Normal Internet systems are unable to handle such large volumes. The direct link systems are capable of this.

2.1 Technical aspects of direct link systems

With Internet systems, companies must first adapt the information from their computer system to the bank format before they can send payment orders to the bank. With direct link systems, companies can send the payment orders in their own format directly from their own system. This can be done both from an ERP system and from a treasury system. The files containing information are converted at the bank from the company's format to the bank's format with the aid of a 'format converter'.

Communication between the bank and company generally takes place through HTTPs (Secured Hypertext Transfer Protocol), FTP (File Transfer Protocol) or via a plain dial-up number, although the latter is being phased out by most banks.

Figure 2 gives a diagrammatic representation of the data communication between the company and the bank, and of the interaction between the various internal systems in the internal computer network of the company, making use of a direct link system.

Figure 2   *Direct link delivery*

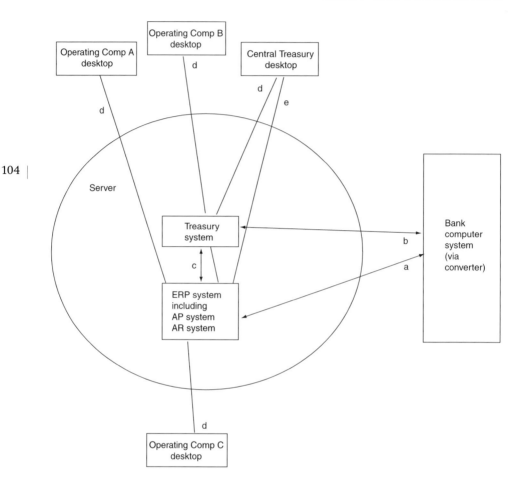

a. The ERP system of the company is linked directly to the bank's computer system. At many companies, this is the only connection with the bank. All low value payments are sent directly from the company's ERP system to the bank. The balance and transaction information is sent via a separate module in the ERP system to the treasury system.

b. In some cases the company's treasury system is also linked directly to the bank's computer. The balance and transaction information is then imported directly from the bank into the treasury system. This connection is sometimes also used for delivering high value payments from the treasury system to the bank.

c. The treasury system is linked via an interface to the ERP system.

d. All personal computers are linked to the company's internal network and to the ERP system.

e. The computers of the central treasury are connected to the treasury system.

2.2 Applications of direct link systems

Bulk processing systems generally offer fewer facilities than Internet systems or desktop delivery systems. The most important applications of these systems are:

- simultanuously sending or receiving extremely large numbers of payments
- simultanuously sending several types of payments simultaneously
- balance and transaction information

With direct link systems there is, in principle, no limit to the number of outgoing/incoming payments that can be simultaneously sent to, or received from the bank. Also, these systems make it possible to deliver several types of payments simultaneously. Apart from normal low value payments such as salary payments that are usually sent in a batch, all sorts of electronic data interchange (EDI) payments, urgent payments or other kinds of payments can be delivered simultaneously.

Direct link systems are being constantly improved and are offering a growing number of applications. These include preparing letters of credit and ordering foreign currency. In the future, direct link systems will probably be used for all transaction-related matters.

2.3 Benefits and constraints of direct link systems

We saw that the range of applications of bulk processing systems is limited to the processing of extremely large numbers of incoming and outgoing payments. It should be remembered that these systems were, in fact, designed precisely for this purpose and do not aspire to offer a wide range of applications. Even so, bulk processing systems offer companies a great many benefits. These benefits all lie in the field of efficiency and include the following:

- cost savings thanks to economies of scale
- wider choice of formats for delivering payment orders
- cost-savings because the bank can select the cheapest routing for each payment

COST SAVINGS THANKS TO ECONOMIES OF SCALE
If the company has extremely large numbers of payments processed by a single bank, it will generally be offered more favourable payment rates. All payment orders can then be handled by means of straight-through processing, which is cheaper. The bank will generally pass this cost benefit on to the company.

Companies and banks often use different file formats for their electronic messages. The most frequently used company formats are the general standards - i.e. ED-IFACT, ASC X12 and, more recently, ebXML – or the formats used by the most important ERP systems (such as SAP or Oracle). Banks, by contrast, mainly use SWIFT formats, such as the MT103. With direct link systems, these differences play no role, since the company can use its own format.

COST SAVINGS BECAUSE THE BANK OPTS FOR THE CHEAPEST ROUTING
With direct linked systems, the company will generally use a network bank or a bank with a large number of partner banks. The bank will choose the most efficient routing for each payment. First, it sorts the payments according to urgency – i.e. high value payments or low value payments – and country of destination. The high value payments will be settled via an RTGS system (such as TARGET or Fedwire). The local low value payments are sent to the local clearing house. The low value foreign payments will then be sent on to the beneficiary's country for settlement via the local clearing system. If the bank is a network bank and has a branch in the beneficiary's country, it will send the payments through its own computer network in its own file format to that branch. If the bank does not have a local (network) branch, it will send the payments in an agreed format to a partner bank in the relevant country where the payments are then settled locally.

3
Desktop systems

Desktop systems are quickly fading away as banks and companies move most of their customers towards web-based and direct links technology. We speak of a desktop system because the company itself operates the system from a personal computer. There are three types of desk top systems:

- bank specific systems
- systems developed collectively by banks
- systems developed by a third party

BANK SPECIFIC SYSTEMS
These systems are developed by the individual banks. The advantage of these packages is that they are designed specifically to provide the services of the bank in question. They often offer a wide range of applications.

In a number of European countries, such as France (Etebac) and Belgium (Isabel), the banks have collectively developed a single desktop system. This approach has a cost advantage for companies. They use the same package to control accounts and obtain account information from all banks in their own country without incurring high costs. The advantage for the banks is that the costs of developing and maintaining the packages are shared. One disadvantage is that the range of applications is usually limited because the system's range of applications is confined to those available at all banks. This may mean, for instance, that the system can only handle domestic payment orders.

SYSTEMS DEVELOPED BY A THIRD PARTY

Some independent software suppliers market their own desktop systems. One example of such an independently developed system is MultiCash, which is mainly used by banks in Germany and Austria.

3.1 Technical aspects of desktop systems

A desktop system is a software package that enables the customer to send electronic payment orders and to view electronic account statements. The package is installed on the company's internal computer network.

The information flow from the bank to the company takes place as follows. The company is assigned an electronic mailbox in the bank's computer where the bank stores all information addressed to the company. This details account and transaction information. In addition, the bank's computer can fill the electronic mailbox with market information, practical information and commercial information about its bank services. As noted, the desktop system is installed on the company's internal computer network. This means that the company can control the system from any personal computer or terminal linked to that system. Each time the company logs into the bank computer via one of the connected personal computers, the electronic mailbox is emptied and the information is sent from the electronic mailbox to the company's computer system.

The information flow from the company to the bank consists of the sent payment orders. Sometimes these are entered manually into the desktop system. Often, however, the desktop system is linked to the treasury system or to the company's ERP system. In those cases, the payment orders are not entered manually into the desktop system, but are created in the treasury system or even in the ERP system. To permit this exchange of information, the systems involved must be able to understand each other's (computer) output. Computer output is stored in a file format. If the two systems use the same file formats, there is no problem. If the computer systems do not use the same file formats, the information must be translated from one format to the other. This is done using an interface or format converter.

The communication between the bank and the company goes through the telephone network or via TCP/IP.

Figure 3 gives a diagrammatic representation of the data communication between the company and the bank, and of the interaction between the various internal systems in the company's internal computer network, where an electronic banking system is used.

Figure 3 *Desktop delivery*

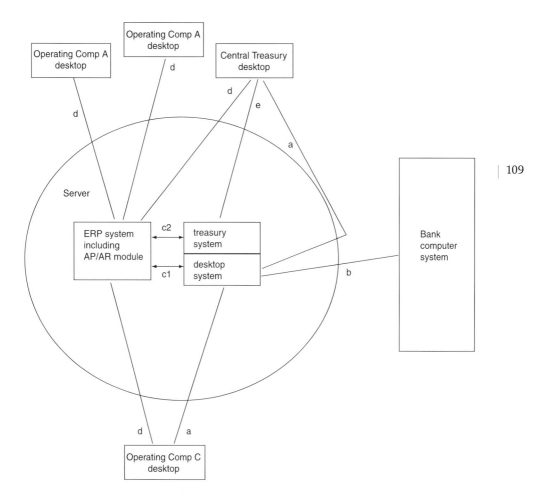

| 109

a. Once delivered by the bank, the desktop software is installed on the computer network of the company. All of the company's computers are linked to its internal network. The personal computers of the central treasury are linked to the desktop system. In addition the personal computer of operating company C is linked to the desktop system. Operating company C can thus enter its high value payments directly into the desktop system.

b. The desktop system communicates with the bank computer. The company delivers payment orders to the bank and the bank sends balance and transaction information.

c. 1. The desktop system is linked via an interface to the Accounts Payable module and to the Accounts Receivable module of the ERP system. Payment orders are read in from the AP system. Reconciliation information is sent both to the AP system and to the AR system.

2. The ERP system is also linked via an interface to the treasury system.

DELIVERY CHANNELS

*Balance and transaction information is read into the treasury system from the desktop system for liquidity reporting purposes.

d.   All computers in the network are linked to the ERP system.

e.   The personal computer of the central treasury department is linked to the treasury system.

3.2 Functionality of desktop systems

The first electronic banking systems were developed in the 1980s. The early packages could only be used for controlling accounts at the company's own bank, and for receiving balance and transaction reports on these accounts. In the following decades, the range of functionality offered by desktop systems expanded greatly. Most of this functionality is now offered by Internet systems and is described above:

- executing payments
- import and export of payment files
- balance and transaction information
- other reporting facilities
- deal initiation
- market information

3.3 Benefits and constraints of desktop systems

Electronic banking systems were developed as an alternative to sending payment orders by mail. The advantages of electronic transmission over physical mail are self-evident. It is much faster and cheaper. But desktop systems also entail a number of disadvantages. The most important of these are:

- limited accessibility
- limited capacity
- interfaces are necessary between own systems and desktop system
- different window-applications are required
- comprehensive software must be maintainted at customer site

LIMITED ACCESSIBILITY
Communication with the bank is only possible with a computer on which the desktop software has been installed, or with a computer that is linked to the company's network and has access to the desktop system. Whenever a new branch is opened, either new desktop software (known as middleware) must be installed or the new branch must be linked to the company's computer network.

Desktop systems are capable of sending several payment orders together. This is called an interchange or a batch. With an interchange, several different types of payment orders are sent in the same file. With a batch, by contrast, the payment or collection orders are of the same type. As the communication between a desktop system and the bank usually takes place via a telephone line, desktop systems are not suitable for the simultaneous processing of very large volumes of payments.

INTERFACES ARE REQUIRED

When the company wants to read payment orders directly from the AP system into the desktop system, it must make sure that the desktop system recognises the payment orders as such and is able to process them. The same applies vice versa: if the company wants to read information from the desktop system into its own computer systems, the company must build an interface between its system and the desktop system. Many ERP systems use formats that are suitable for most desktop packages. Where this is not the case, however, the company must build its own interface.

VARIOUS WINDOW APPLICATIONS REQUIRED

Desktop packages, thus, offer various applications, such as effecting payments and foreign currency transactions. Each functionality is included in a separate application. If the cash manager wants to go from one application to the other, he must start up the relevant applications separately. In addition, he will usually have to enter a password for each application.

COMPREHENSIVE SOFTWARE MUST BE MAINTAINTED AT CUSTOMER SITE

Installing new versions of desktop systems is highly labour-intensive, as the new version needs to be installed at each location within the company where an independent version of the desktop system is in use.

4
SWIFTNet

The Society for Worldwide Interbank Financial Telecommunication (SWIFT) was founded in Brussels in 1973 by 239 banks from 14 European countries and the United States. SWIFT's main tasks are:

- to maintain a communications network for banks
- to help with the creation of common standards for financial messages

SWIFTNet is the message platform operated by SWIFT. SWIFTNet consists of two system control centres (SCC), one in the Netherlands and one in the United States. These are linked to a large number of regional processors which, in turn, are linked to the participants, mainly banks. SWIFT operates a closed computer network which, unlike the Internet, is not freely accessible to everyone. The SWIFT network is one of the most secure in the world.

In 2006, more than 7,800 financial institutions in 200 countires use SWIFTNet to exchange their financial messages. They comprise members (banks), sub-members (subsidiaries of SWIFT member banks) and participants such as money traders, fund managers, security depositories, processing centres and stock exchanges. Although SWIFTNet is commonly used by banks, nowadays companies are also able to use SWIFT as delivery channel for exchanging payment information.

4.1 Types of access to SWIFTNet

To gain access to SWIFTNet, companies can choose between becoming a participant or a service participant.

PARTICIPANT
A company that becomes a SWIFT participant can communicate directly with all other SWIFT members. The company establishes a single point of access to banks and other SWIFT users. SWIFT offers two message services for companies: SWIFTNet InterAct and SWIFTNet FileAct.

SERVICE PARTICIPANT
SWIFT offers the opportunity for banks to use the SWIFT network in order to communicate with its corporate clients by establishing a Member Administrated Closed User Group, MACUG. The corporate clients that participate in a MACUG will not become SWIFT members themselves, but they are referred to as Service Participants. The bank that sets up a MACUG is referred to as the administrator of the MACUG. Being a service participant, a company is only able to communicate directly with the administrator bank through the SWIFTNet. However, companies may become service participants with several MACUGs. By doing so through the SWIFTNet they are able to communicate with several banks.

4.2 Technical aspects of SWIFTNet

A company that wants to use the SWIFT Network has to set up an interface network connection with the network. The company must ensure that its own back office systems can interface with the access software.

Messages sent through the SWIFT network need not necessarily comply with the standard SWIFT MT formats. If a company uses the SWIFTNet FileAct service, the file may be formatted according to other formats, e.g. local payment formats. This means that companies can send the payment orders in their own format directly to the SWIFTNet system (straight-through processing). If a company uses the SWIFTNet Interact service, however, messages have to be formatted according to the SWIFT MX standard.

If a company does not use the SWIFT MT-format, the SWIFT MT-encryption technology will not be operational. Messages, however, are then secured by the SWIFT-Net public key.

By using SWIFTNet, a company can be connected to several banks through one single window. Figure 4 gives a diagrammatic representation of the data communication between the company and several banks if the company uses the SWIFT-NetInterAct service, or FileAct service, or if the company is a service participant of several different MACUGs.

Figure 4

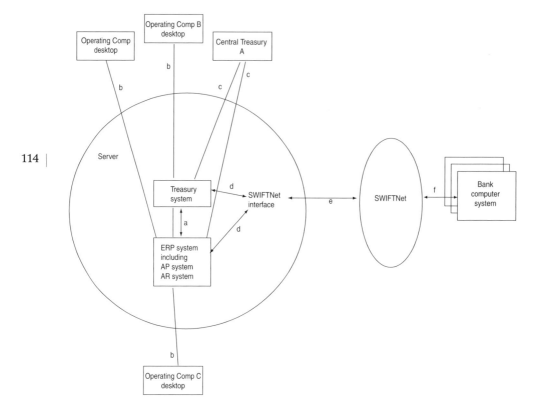

a. The ERP system is linked to the treasury system
b. The computers of the operating companies are connected with the ERP system
c. The balance and transaction information is sent via a separate module in the ERP system to the treasury system
d. The treasury system is linked via an interface to the SWIFTnet system. Payment instructions are sent via the SWIFTNet interface to the SWIFTNet system
e. SWIFT passes all payment orders through to the banks and passes balance and transaction information from the banks through to the company

4.3 Applications of SWIFTNet

SWIFTNet InterAct can be used for individual structured financial messages. SWIFTNet FileAct is used for bulk payments.

Apart from sending payment instructions, SWIFTNet services enable the participants to gain access to websites of financial institutions which are SWIFT users themselves. SWIFT Net browser exchanges are secured through the use of a strict protocol, and by the use of the secure SWIFT network.

4.4 Benefits and constraints of SWIFTNet

SWIFTNet offers the following benefits:

- single interface
- high level of security
- high level of availability
- store-and-forward message service
- non-repudiation database

ONE SINGLE INTERFACE

If a company uses SWIFTNet as a member, or joins several MACUGs as a service participant, it only has to install one computer system: the interface network connection with the SWIFT network. Once the company is connected to the SWIFT system, it is able to send messages to many different banks without having to install other computer programs.

HIGH LEVEL OF SECURITY

The SWIFT network is a closed system. Therefore, transferring messages through SWIFTNet is much more secure than through a web-based system.

HIGH LEVEL OF AVAILABILITY

The SWIFT network is very reliable. SWIFT claims it has a 99.999% service availability.

STORE-AND-FORWARD MESSAGE SERVICE

Both systems, SWIFTNet InterAct and SWIFTNet FileAct, offer a store-and-forward messaging service. This means that if a correspondent is not online at the moment the company sends the message, this message is put on hold and is delivered as soon as the correspondent is ready to receive it.

NON-REPUDIATION DATABASE

In case of a dispute, SWIFT is able to confirm that a message exchange has taken place. For that purpose, SWIFT stores all messages in a non-repudiation database.

One disadvantage of using the SWIFT network is that if a company wants to make use of the standard security protocol used by SWIFT, it has to deliver the messages in the MT format. This means that the company has to adjust its ERP system. This may involve high costs.

5
Overview of delivery channels

The following table summarizes the features of the different delivery channels.

Delivery channel	Advantages	Disadvantages
Desktop	Wide range of applications Easy to implement	Limited accessibility Limited capacity Format conversion different windows installation of middleware
Direct link	Large capacity Different products may be sent in one file and or to different bank accounts (in various countries) No need for format conversion Lower fee per item	Limited functionality Difficult to implement
Web-based	Most wide range of applications Easy to implement Accessible from anywhere Tailor made information (personalisation) One window On-line client support and training Reduced physical distribution of middleware	
SWIFTNet	Single interface (if the company is a member or joins several MACUGs) Very secure Very reliable Store- and forward message service Non-repudiation database	

6
Security

One of the most important aspects when sending information is security, particularly when financial information such as payment orders or electronic balance is included. The security of delivery channels has two areas of concern:

– access control of the systems at the company and at the bank
– security of messages sent between the company and the bank

Figure 5   *The different security aspects of a payment order* | 117

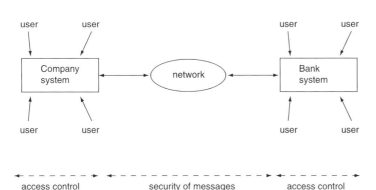

6.1 Access control

In order to restrict access to payments systems, users have to be identified and authenticated. This can be done by presenting something a user knows (for example a password), or something a user possesses (for example a smart card), or a combination of the two (smart card with PIN-protection). Nowadays, biometrics can also be used (for example a fingerprint).

Within the payment system, the system manager can usually define individual user profiles. A user profile defines what tasks each user is allowed to perform, or to which data a user gains access.

An example set of tasks are:

- viewing market information
- opening account statements
- creating payment orders
- authorising payment orders
- sending payment instructions to the bank

After successful identification and authentication, it is ensured that each user exclusively has access to those tasks and data which he or she is authorised to use.

6.2 Security of messages

The messages, which are sent between the company and the bank, include payment orders from the company to the bank and the transmission of balance and transaction information from the bank to the company. The security services that play a role here are discussed in the next sections.

The following four security services are desirable when sending messages between the company and the bank:

- authentication;
- data-integrity;
- non-repudiation;
- confidentiality.

AUTHENTICATION
When the bank receives a payment order, it wants to be sure that this particular payment order originates from one of the bank's customers. In other words, the bank wants to verify that the sender really is who he says he is. This is called authentication. The authorisation service is considered as the most important safety service.

DATA-INTEGRITY
When the bank receives a payment order, it wants to be sure that the payment order remained complete and unchanged after it was sent out by the company. This is called data-integrity.

NON-REPUDIATION
When the bank processes payment orders for customers, it wants to be sure that the customer cannot deny the sending of the particular payment instructions. This is called non-repudiation.

Payment orders and messages containing balance and transaction information often contain sensitive information. Payment orders might for example contain information about the business associates. It is desirable to guarantee the confidentiality of this sensitive information. Confidentiality means that only the bank and the relative company are able to read the payment order and the balance and transaction information.

The four services authentication, data-integrity, non-repudiation and confidentiality can be provided using cryptography. Cryptography literally means 'secret writing' and is typically used for sending messages via a medium that is considered unsecure such as the Internet. With cryptography, a readable text can be made unreadable for outsiders. Cryptographic keys are used to encrypt and decrypt data. This data could be a payment order.

An extensive overview of the cryptography used by sending payment orders is provided in Chapter 15, 'Cryptography'.

| 119

Chapter 7
The payment process

Introduction

The processing of payments is a complex matter. At the most basic level, the client sends a payment instruction to a bank which inputs this into its payments system. The bank then sends the payment instruction on to 'clearing and settlement institutions' for further processing – unless the beneficiary also banks with it, in which case this is not necessary.

Processing payments across national borders, or between different currencies, however, makes the process even more complex. It is also true that euro payments between euro countries, which are currently not supported by a pan-European payments system, can have more complications than pure domestic payments. There are a few systems, like Euro1, STEP1 and STEP2, which may grow into Europe wide clearing systems. Furthermore, the initiative to launch a Single Euro Payments Area (SEPA) in 2008 – 2010, a clearing infrastructure for euro transactions, will improve matters. But foreign currency transactions will still be processed using a correspondent bank.

1
How the bank accepts and reads a payment instruction

The bank transfers the information on the payment instruction to its electronic payments processing system. In the case of paper instruments, the bank can either key in the relevant information, or make a digital copy which is automatically fed into the system. When the client is using an electronic banking system to transfer the payment instruction, the information can be entered directly into the bank's computer system. Of course, the bank's computer should be able to read the payment instructions. This means the format used by the sender should be converted to the bank's format. This is called format conversion. Companies can choose between various systems for sending their payment information electronically to the bank. They can do so via desktop systems, direct link systems, the Internet and SWIFTNet. These systems are called delivery channels.

Next the bank checks the identity of the payer before processing the instruction. This is called authentication, and the type of verification depends on the payment instrument used. With credit transfer orders on paper and cheques, the bank will check the signature. With debit card transactions at the point of sale, the payer's PIN (Personal Identification Number) suffices. With credit card payments at the point of sale, the payer signs a sales slip. Where delivery of a payment instruction takes place via data communication, codes are used to check its authenticity automatically. Each instruction or batch of instructions must be accompanied by an acceptance code or transaction code, which serves as a kind of electronic signature. Customers use standardised software applications to generate the codes.

The bank will also check whether the payer's cash balance or credit facility is sufficient to make the payment. If it is not, payment will be automatically refused and bank staff will decide how to handle the payment request. They may decide to execute the payment order, in which case the bank allows an overdraft position.

2
The clearing process

In order to execute the millions of payments executed daily between different banks, the financial industry has established specialised institutions variously called multilateral clearing institutions, clearing centres or automated clearing houses. In general, those clearing institutions perform the following functions:

- sorting of payments and calculation of the ultimate claims for settlement
- sending information on the settlement claims to the settlement centre
- exchanging relevant payment information for all individual transactions between the payers' and the beneficiaries' banks

With most clearing institutions, incoming and outgoing payment instructions from participating banks are sorted and matched. The clearing institution nets each bank's outgoing and incoming transfers, and calculates a net amount to be paid or received. It relays this information to another entity, the settlement institution. The participating banks are only liable for the resulting net amounts. When the settlement claims are calculated on a net basis, the clearing system is called a net settlement system. This is different from a gross settlement system, where all transactions are processed individually and settled on a gross basis.

While only the net amounts are settled, the clearing institution supplies receiving banks with details of all their clients' underlying transfers. Using this information, they will credit their clients' accounts accordingly. With direct debits, the clearing institution sends details of underlying transactions to the payers' banks, which then debit their clients' accounts.

Following is an example of a calculation of settlement claims on a net basis.

EXAMPLE

| 123

Banks A,B and C send the following payment instructions to a clearing institution:

payer	payer's bank	amount transferred	beneficiary	beneficiary's bank
Client A	A	USD 100	Client U	C
Client B	B	USD 200	Client V	A
Client C	C	USD 150	Client W	B
Client D	A	USD 200	Client X	B
Client E	B	USD 200	Client Y	C
Client F	C	USD 350	Client Z	A

It is clear that some payments partly offset each other. One payment, for instance, concerns the transfer of USD 100 from bank A to C, while another concerns the transfer of USD 350 in the opposite direction from bank C to bank A.

First, the clearing institution totals all incoming and outgoing transfers for each bank. Then the clearing institution calculates the net transfers resulting from all outgoing and incoming payments for each bank:

bank	outgoing transfers	incoming transfers	Net transfers
Bank A	USD 300	USD 550	+ USD 250
Bank B	USD 400	USD 350	- USD 50
Bank C	USD 500	USD 300	- USD 200

The clearing centre now sends information on all separate transfers to the receiving banks as well as information on the net transfers to the settlement institution. The information that the ACH sends to the central banks consists of no more than three net payment obligations.

3
The settlement process

Settlement is the final exchange of funds between the banks concerned. In the settlement process, a valid claim from the beneficiary is discharged by means of a credit transfer from the payer's bank to the beneficiary's bank. Under a net settlement system, settlement operations are completed on a net basis, provided that the net paying banks hold enough liquidity on their settlements accounts (mostly with the local central bank), or collateral, to cover the required transfers. Since only the netted amount is to be settled, the payers' banks need less liquidity compared to gross settlement systems.

Following is a picture of the settlement transfers that would occur if all payments in the above example were settled on a net basis.

Figure 1   *Settlement on a net basis*

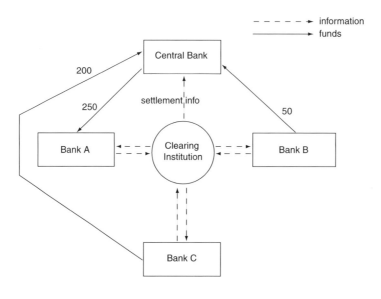

The figure shows that the central bank only has to execute three settlement payments. Once the central bank has transferred the settlement amounts, it advises the banks of these payments.

A disadvantage of the net settlement system is that the participants run a systemic risk. In other words, there is a risk that one bank's failure to meet its settlement obligations may have a knock-on effect, making others unable to meet their settlement obligations. If, for instance, bank C fails to meet its settlement obligations, bank B may also be unable to do so.

If large sums are involved, such a failure might cause significant liquidity or credit problems, and possibly even threaten the stability of financial markets. In 1974, the Herstatt Bank caused just such a crisis when it could not meet obligations resulting from foreign exchange transactions. In the domino effect that followed, several other banks collapsed. Since then systemic risk has also been known as the Herstatt risk.

In many cases, transfers processed through a net settlement system are settled on the next working day, or sometimes even after two working days. Some clearing centres, however, work on a same-day basis. These clearing centres specify a cut-off time, after which incoming payments will no longer be processed for same-day settlement. This cut-off time is usually linked to the cut-off time of the organisation responsible for settlement. Payments received too late for same-day settlement are set aside for processing on the following working day. EURO1 is an example of a same-day system.

4
Alternative ways of processing payments

Some payments are not processed in the ways described above. If the payer's and the beneficiary's bank are one and the same, payments are processed within the bank itself. This is referred to as an 'in-house' arrangement.

Additionally, some payments are processed on an order-by-order basis. These are not processed through clearing institutions, but through special real-time gross settlement (RTGS) systems.

4.1 In-house arrangement

Sometimes, the payer's bank and the beneficiary's bank are one and the same. We refer to this as an in-house arrangement. With an in-house arrangement, all phases in the payment process occur within a single bank.

4.2 RTGS systems

Payments that have to be processed immediately are sent by the payer's bank to the receiver's bank on an order-by-order basis through a specific system. This system passes each payment instruction individually to the central bank, with the instruction to debit the payer's account at the central bank in favour of the beneficiary's account, regardless of any other payment instructions. This is done immediately after the system has received the payment instruction and the transfer is settled in a few minutes. These systems are the so-called real-time gross settlement (RTGS) systems.

Processing electronic transfers through RTGS systems is very expensive. Therefore, these are principally used for high value payments between banks or corporates in the financial markets that require timely settlement. Note, incidentally, that the size of the transfer is not important. A transfer of USD 1,000 can be a high value payment as well as a payment of USD 10,000,000.

Many central banks in Europe, the United States and, to a lesser degree, in Asia operate RTGS systems for high value payments.

With RTGS settlement the participating banks must have sufficient funds in their account, or overdraft facilities, with the settlement bank for each separate payment order. Failing that, the single payment order may be cancelled or put on a waiting list. Once the payment order has been accepted by the settlement bank, settlement is final and irrevocable.

With RTGS systems, all transfers are settled individually through the central bank. The central bank, therefore, needs information on all individual transactions and can in many cases also pass on relevant payment details to the beneficiary. Some central banks do not provide sufficient room in their transaction messages, which is why the payer's bank may feel the need to advise the beneficiary's bank bilaterally for each separate payment.

Using a net clearing system is much cheaper than using a RTGS system. Therefore, low value payments between banks within a single country are often cleared through a net clearing institution.

Following is a table which shows the main advantages and disadvantages of processing a transfer through a RTGS system compared with a net clearing system.

	Net settlement clearing systems	RTGS systems
Types of payments	low value payments	high value payments
Advantages	-low transaction costs -relatively few liquidity needed	-same day settlement
Disadvantages	-settlement after one or two working days (with exceptions) -systemic risk	-high transaction costs -much liquidity needed

5
Local and cross-border transfers

The processing of payment orders across international borders differs from doing so within one country. In banking practice, the routing of transfers is primarily determined by where the accounts are maintained. For this reason, banks make a distinction between:

- local transfers
- cross-border transfers through a correspondent bank
- remote local payments
- transfers via international clearing systems

5.1 Local transfers

A local transfer is a transfer between two accounts in the same country in the local currency. The account holders may be residents or non-residents.

In each country the national clearing institution only settles transfers in the local currency. US dollar transfers are settled in the United States, transfers in British pounds are settled in the United Kingdom, etc. Until the Single Euro Payment Area (SEPA) is established in 2008 - 2010, the national clearing institutions in various euro countries will still mainly handle transfers in euros. Settlement of local transfers will usually take place at the national central bank where the participating banks maintain an account. The following diagram shows a local transfer within a country with a central clearing institution.

Figure 2   *Routing of a local payment through a local clearing centre*

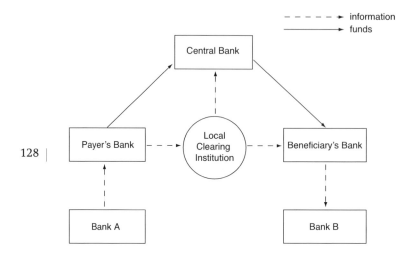

128

Some countries are divided into separate regions, each with its own affiliate of the central bank and its own clearing centre. In the United States there are 12 different regions, each with their own regional central bank and their own automated clearing house (ACH). All ACHs are connected and act as a single clearing house for inter-regional transfers. Settlement takes place at the Federal Reserve Bank in New York.

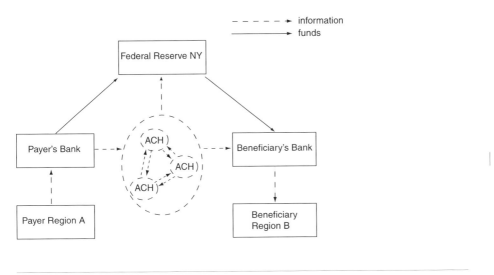

5.2 Cross-border transfers through a correspondent bank

A cross-border transfer is a transfer between two accounts held in different countries or a transfer between two accounts in the same country but in a non-local currency. Cross-border transfers are executed via 'correspondent banks' or international clearing institutions rather than local clearing institutions.

Most large banks have an extensive network of correspondent banks. A correspondent banking relationship normally involves two banks holding accounts with each other, denominated in the currency of the country where the correspondent bank is located. An account held by a local bank with a foreign correspondent is usually called a 'nostro account' or 'our account' by the local bank, while the same account is known to the correspondent as a 'loro account' or 'their account'. So, whether an account is called a 'nostro account' or a 'loro account' depends on the point of view of the bank in question.

Non US-banks hold their US dollar accounts with US banks. A German bank's dollar account, for instance, is a 'nostro account' to the German bank and a 'loro account' for its US correspondent. If the German bank wishes to make a payment in US dollars, it will ask its US correspondent to debit its dollar account for the amount in question. Conversely, US banks will hold their euro accounts with banks in one or more euro countries. If a US bank wishes to make a payment in euros, it will ask one of its correspondents in the euro countries to debit its euro account.

EXAMPLE

Bill Smith, a US citizen, is staying in France. He has opened a euro account and a USD account at Caisse d'Epargne in Paris.

1. The first payment that Bill wants to make is a transfer from his euro account to his French landlord's account at Crédit Mutuel. In daily practice this is considered to be a local payment, because both parties have an account in France and the transfer is denominated in euros. The transfer can be settled by the national clearing institution of France.

2. Next, Bill wants to pay his subscription to Newsweek. To this end, he has a USD amount transferred from his USD account at Caisse d'Epargne to the USD account of Newsweek Inc. at JP Morgan Chase in New York. This is a cross-border transfer, because Bill has his account in France while the Newsweek account is held in the United States. The transfer is made in USD, and must be cleared and settled in the United States.

3. Bill also wants to transfer an amount in euros to his friend Heidi, who lives in Berlin. This is also a cross-border transfer as Heidi has a euro account at a German bank in Berlin.

4. Finally, Bill wants to transfer an amount from his USD account to the account of Chester, a fellow American who has an account at BNP. This, too, is a cross-border payment. After all, though the two French banks are both members of the central French clearing institution, this institution does not process any USD transfers. The USD payment must be cleared in the United States.

130

Figure 4   *Routing of a cross-border payment using a correspondent bank*

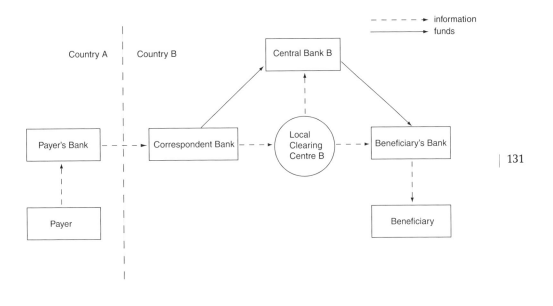

The routing of a cross-border payment using a correspondent bank is a relatively high cost and time-consuming procedure. As a result, banks have explored ways to speed up the correspondent banking system while reducing its costs. This upgrading process is commonly referred to as 'enhanced' correspondent banking. Enhanced correspondent banking systems all make use of special, or preferential, relations between banks, and are based upon agreements between the participating banks on common formats, or formatting arrangements for file transfers between different countries. The club arrangements described in the next section are an example of this.

5.3 Remote local payments

Many multinational corporations (MNCs) open non-resident accounts abroad, often at a foreign bank. Suppose a French MNC opens a USD account at Citibank in New York, a GBP account at Barclays in London and a euro account at Deutsche Bank in Germany. The MNC can operate these accounts with the aid of various banks' electronic banking packages. The payments they make directly from these accounts are fed directly into the local clearing system. The accounts, however, are controlled remotely, which is why we refer in this case to 'remote local payments'.

Figure 5   *Routing of low value 'remote local payments'*

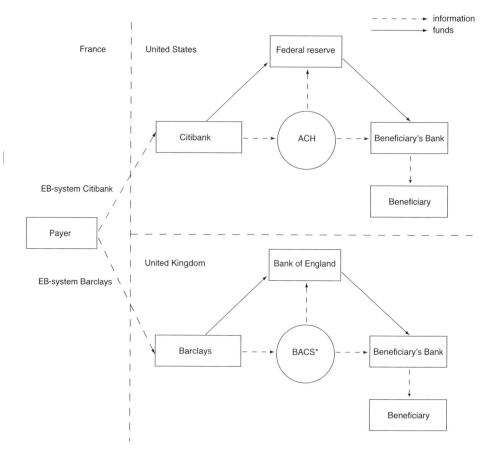

* ACH and BACS are the multilateral clearing systems for low value payments in the US and the UK.

One disadvantage of this procedure is that the MNC needs separate electronic banking packages for all non-resident accounts. International banks have found the following solutions for this:

- club arrangements
- network banks

5.3.1 Remote local payments through club arrangements

One type of enhanced correspondent banking is the 'club' arrangement. This consists of agreements between a group of banks (one or more in each country) that provide one another with indirect access to the domestic clearing system in which each participates. Sometimes these arrangements operate in real-time and use proprietary harmonised standards, enabling the 'club' banks to transfer funds directly between their customers' accounts. An example of this model is IBOS, in which several European and American banks, including ING Bank, Banco Santander and Bank of New York, participate.

Figure 6   *Routing of low value 'remote local payments' through a partnership or club arrangement*

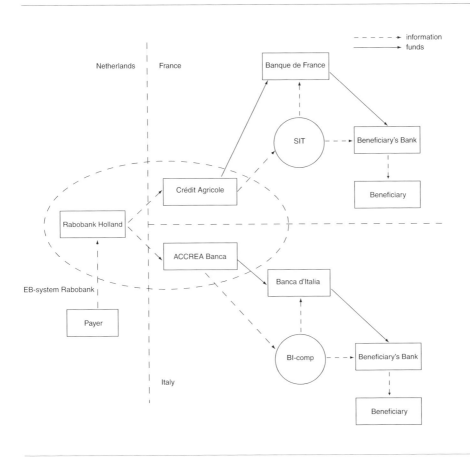

Banks participating in such partnerships offer clients the opportunity to open accounts at their partner banks. Clients can operate these accounts using the electronic banking package of their own (local) bank.

5.3.2 Remote local payments through international network banks

Another variant of this model is the 'in-house' arrangement. In this case, a large network bank with international branches or subsidiaries becomes a member of relevant local clearing and settlement systems in different countries. In this way, the bank can route international transfers through its in-house network, and enter them into the country of destination's local clearing system. Large global banks such as Citibank, Deutsche Bank and ABN AMRO use this model.

Clients of these network banks can open accounts at relevant international branches, rather than with different local banks. The network bank's electronic banking package can access these accounts, and make either local or remote local transfers.

EXAMPLE

Xenia SA wants to make a USD transfer to a US supplier. Xenia banks with ABN AMRO Bank in France. The cash manager of Xenia has opened a non-resident account at ABN AMRO New York. He can access this non-resident account with ABN AMRO's electronic banking package. Xenia's cash manager now instructs ABN AMRO via electronic banking to carry out the USD transfer, and to charge this transfer to its USD account. ABN AMRO New York then first charges the account that Xenia BV holds with it, and then sends a transfer instruction to a clearing institution in the United States of which both ABN AMRO New York and the beneficiary's bank are members. Xenia's cross-border transfer is now processed as a local transfer.

Figure 7 *Routing of low value 'remote local payments' through an international network bank*

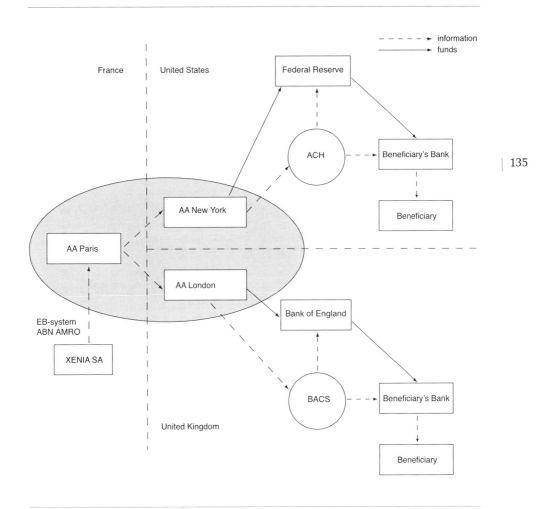

5.3.3 Cross-border payments through an international clearing system

Since the beginning of the 1990s, authorities and banks in the European Union have made strenuous efforts to improve the efficiency of international credit transfers. The need for such an improvement became even more apparent following the euro's introduction in 1999. New systems were developed to facilitate fast clearing and settlement of international euro payments. One example is TARGET, the clearing and settlement system of the European Central Bank and the national central banks of the EU countries. Other examples are the Euro Banking Association's two clearing systems, EURO1 and STEP1, respectively for high value and low value payments. Settlement takes place at the European Central Bank.

6
Differences between local and cross-border payments

Besides the differences in clearing and settlement arrangements, there are several practical differences between local payments on the one hand, and cross-border and remote local payments on the other hand. This explains why a non-local (i.e. cross-border or remote local) payment is generally less easy to process and settle than a local payment. We will consecutively discuss:

- reporting obligations to the central bank
- exchange charges and foreign exchange risk
- different payment infrastructures
- float
- exchange control regulations
- other risks associated with cross-border payments

6.1 Reporting obligations to the central bank

Monetary authorities use international payments data to calculate their national balances of payments. The balance of payments provides an overview of a country's the imports and exports. The monetary authorities make a formal distinction between domestic and foreign payments when preparing the national balance of payments. They distinguish between:

- domestic payments, where both the paying and the receiving parties are residents of the same country
- foreign payments, where either the paying or the receiving party is a non-resident of a country

All foreign payments are included in the balance of payments on a cash basis, including outgoing foreign payments for imports and incoming foreign payments for exports.

If an individual or company is not officially registered in the country in question, the term non-resident is used. In other words, resident status does not depend on the nationality of the parties but on their place of permanent residence. A resident of a country is either a natural person (consumer) registered in the register of

136

births, deaths and marriages, or a legal person (company) registered in the public register.

Consumers and most small and medium-sized companies operate primarily within their own countries. Consequently, they mainly use the international payment services offered by their domestic banks. However, many internationally active corporations, such as MNCs, will either hold foreign currency accounts at their local bank, or local currency accounts with banks in countries where they are active.

There are two types of accounts: resident accounts and non-resident accounts.

RESIDENT ACCOUNTS

A resident account is an account held by a resident of a country at a resident bank in the same country. A resident account may be denominated in local currency or in a foreign currency. Holding a resident account in a foreign currency at a local bank has the benefit that the client does not need to buy and sell the currency in question each time it pays or receives funds in that currency. However, a Dutch client with a dollar account at a Dutch bank does not have direct access to the local clearing system in the United States. So the client's bank will still need to use a US bank or branch for credit transfers to and from the United States, which is costly and time-consuming.

NON-RESIDENT ACCOUNTS (OFFSHORE ACCOUNTS)

A non-resident account, or off-shore account, is an account held by a non-resident with a resident bank. A non-resident account is almost always dominated in the local currency of the resident bank, such as a dollar account with a bank in the United States. Such an account gives the client direct access to the US clearing system.

In many countries, transactions between residents and non-residents have to be reported to the central bank. Reporting obligations differ from country to country. Some countries, such as the USA and the UK, do not require any central bank reporting. But others, such as Germany and France, require all international transactions above a certain amount to be reported.

6.2 Exchange charges and foreign exchange risks

When a local payment takes place, the parties involved mainly use the local currency. With non-local funds transfers, payments are often conducted in a currency that is foreign to at least one of the parties. Either the payer will exchange the amount payable from his own currency, or the beneficiary will exchange the amount received into his own currency. Sometimes the currency used is foreign to both parties, so both will have to make an exchange to, or from, their own currency at some point. These currency exchanges obviously have costs. Additionally, parties exchanging currencies also run foreign exchange risks because exchange rates may fluctuate between the contract's agreement and final payment.

When a payment in euros takes place between two euro countries, there is obviously no foreign exchange risk.

6.3 Different funds transfer infrastructures

Funds transfer infrastructures differ from one country to the next. Consequently, account number formats vary from one country to the next. Some countries, such as Germany, use separate bank sorting codes. Furthermore, there is a great difference between the number of digits and / or letters that make up an account number. For example, an account held at the Dutch Postbank can have as few as seven digits, while an account held with a bank in France has 23 digits and letters. These variations in account number formats make it very difficult, even impossible, to verify if an account number is viable and to which country and bank the number belongs.

Banks in several European countries – including all EU countries – have implemented the international bank account number (IBAN) in order to improve the speed and efficiency of cross-border credit transfers. IBAN consists of a two-letter country code and a two-digit check code, followed by the bank branch code and the original bank account number. Banks of the associated European countries have undertaken to use IBAN for their international payments, and clients making cross-border transfers are obliged to include IBAN in their payment instructions.

A growing number of companies within Europe are using a standard format for the delivery of cross-border or remote local transfers. This format is called the International Payment Instruction (IPI). An IPI is a form containing structured payment information, which is attached to a form being sent to a foreign country in order to facilitate international funds transfers. The IPI is filled in beforehand by the beneficiary who sends it to the debtor. The debtor uses the information on the form to instruct his bank to make the transfer and also fills in the missing details. The creditor's IBAN, as well as his bank's SWIFT address, must always be printed on an IPI. Thanks to the distribution of IPIs and pre-printed IBANs, international transfers can be handled faster. Delays due to errors and incomplete data are avoided.

6.4 Exchange control regulations

When international transfers are executed, the parties involved have to take account of the exchange control regulations both in their own country and the other party's country. In many countries in Central and Eastern Europe, Asia and Latin America, international transfers are still subject to restrictions. A common rule in many of these countries is that funds may not be transferred out of the country unless related to an underlying trade transaction.

Moreover, currencies in some countries cannot be freely exchanged against other currencies.

6.5 Float

Sometimes, the book date on which the payer's account is debited is one, or more, days earlier than the date on which the beneficiary's bank account is credited. In other words: the banks involved retain the amount of the transfer for processing during a short period of time. This is called 'banking float', or more commonly 'float'. Generally speaking, banking float is more common with cross-border payments than with local payments. But in countries with less developed financial infrastructures, banking float may also occur with local payments. Banking float does generally not exist with credit transfers between two accounts held with the same bank, as is the case with network banks. We will now give an example cross-border credit transfer where banking float occurs.

EXAMPLE

On day 1, Christian Flior S.A., a French importer, gives a payment instruction to his bank in France to transfer EUR 100,000 to the euro account of Fine Flagrances Ltd. in Ireland. On day 1, the French bank debits Christian Flior's euro account.

On day 2, the French bank actually transfers EUR 100,000 to the beneficiary's bank in Ireland by issuing a payment instruction through the TARGET system. Since the TARGET system is a real-time gross settlement system, the euro account of the French bank at the Banque de France (the central bank of France) is directly debited. Also, the euro account of the beneficiary's bank with the Bank of Ireland (the central bank of Ireland) is credited immediately.

Also on day 2, the beneficiary's bank credits the EUR 100,000 to the euro account of Fine Flagrances Ltd.

In this example there is a one day banking float, earned by the payer's bank in France. The banking float may be for technical or procedural reasons, which make it impossible for the French bank to send the payment instruction earlier than on day 2.

Banks may also generate additional income by applying a different value date from the date on which they make the entry on behalf of the customer's account into their bookkeeping system. The payer's bank may cease to pay interest one or two days before the book date, and the beneficiary's bank may only pay interest one or two days after the book date. This practice, called value dating, differs from country to country, and is subject to arrangements made between banks and their clients.

6.6 Other risks associated with non-local payments

Apart from foreign exchange risks, parties involved in non-local payments run other risks, such as debtor risk and banking risk. For example, there is a risk that the debtor or the debtor's bank will fail to pay on time. These risks also exist with local payments, but they are more difficult to manage if the parties are located in different countries and are subject to different legal systems. Also, creditors sometimes run a political risk, i.e. the risk that the authorities will delay, or even prohibit, payment due to political upheavals or financial problems. Banks have developed special products to mitigate these risks, such as documentary credits and export credit insurance.

7
SWIFT

The huge growth in international payment volumes since the 1960s has left banks with rising costs, as well as difficulties in processing these payments rapidly and efficiently. Responding to this challenge, several European and US banks got together and decided to set up an automated message transmission system linked to the banks' own computers. As a result, the Society for Worldwide Interbank Financial Telecommunication (SWIFT) was founded to establish a network for interbank communications. This so-called SWIFTNet network is commonly used by banks, with the main service they employ called SWIFTNet FIN.

7.1 The MT standard of a SWIFTNet FIN message

SWIFTNet FIN is a service that enables banks and clearing and settlement institutions to exchange messages that are formatted with the highly secure SWIFT MT-standards. SWIFT messages that are formatted accordingly use a very complex code.

All SWIFT messages are standardised, so that participating banks can quickly communicate with the network and process incoming messages directly into their automated systems. SWIFT messages are mostly used for cross-border payments through correspondent banks and high value payments processed through RTGS systems.

Each SWIFT message comprises specific fields detailing the sending and receiving parties, value date, amount and other information. Each field begins with a number, for example: 52A for 'ordering bank'.

When a SWIFT message includes more than one currency, the ISO codes of these currencies have to be specified (USD for US dollars, EUR for euros, etc). Furthermore, SWIFT has developed so-called BIC codes (Bank Identifier Code) which are also recognised by ISO. The BIC code system is a global standard for identifying individual banks when using telecommunications. The BIC codes used by the head offices of four major international banks are:

- ABN AMRO Bank: ABNANL2A
- Deutsche Bank: DEUTDEFF
- Citibank: CITIUS33
- J.P. Morgan Chase: CHASUS33

The first four letters form the bank code, the consecutive two letters the country code (NL = Netherlands, DE = Deutschland/Germany, US = United States) and the last two characters the office location code (2A = Amsterdam, FF = Frankfurt, 33 = New York).

SWIFT messages are defined by the letters MT (message type), followed by three numbers. These messages are categorised as follows:

- MT 100 series for transfer instructions and cheques on behalf of clients
- MT 200 series for transfer instructions on behalf of banks
- MT 300 series for treasury transactions
- MT 400 series for documentary collection transactions
- MT 500 series for securities transactions
- MT 600 series for precious metals and syndication transactions
- MT 700 series for documentary credits and guarantee transactions
- MT 900 series for special messages, such as daily statements, debit and credit advice notes

All message types ending with 99 are 'free messages'. The sending party is not bound by any specific standard when sending these types of messages. They can fill in any text they wish.

A SWIFT message consists of several fields. These contain information about the sending and the receiving bank, the sending and receiving customer, the amount transferred, etc. Each field has a standard numeric prefix, such as '50' for sending customer and '59' for receiving customer.

7.2 Example of SWIFTNet FIN messages

Gianni Angelo from Milan has received an invoice for USD 5,443.99 from his supplier, Killy SA in Paris. Gian Angelo requests his bank, the Banca Commerciale Italiana (BCI) in Milan, to transfer this amount to Killy SA's account at the BNP in Paris. The account number is 20041 01005 050001M026 and the account statement should quote the following description: 'payment of invoice no. 559661'.

Because BNP and BCI do not maintain a USD dollar account with each other, the payment will have to be routed through their respective correspondents in the United States. The BCI uses its own branch in New York, with reference number 8861198-0706. BNP's correspondent is the Bank of New York in New York. The transfer charges will be split between the payer and the beneficiary.

The following SWIFT messages will be sent:

- MT 103 from BCI Milan to BNP Paris
- MT 202 from BCI Milan to BCI New York
- MT 910 from Bank of New York New York to BNP Paris

The transfer between BCI New York and the Bank of New York is carried out through the local clearing system. The banks involved do not send each other SWIFT messages. BCI New York sends the information to the local clearing house (in this case: CHIPS), and when clearing has taken place the clearing house in turn sends the information to the Bank of New York. The clearing house also sends settlement information to the Federal Reserve Bank.

Figure 8   *SWIFT messages used with a cross border payment using correspondent banks*

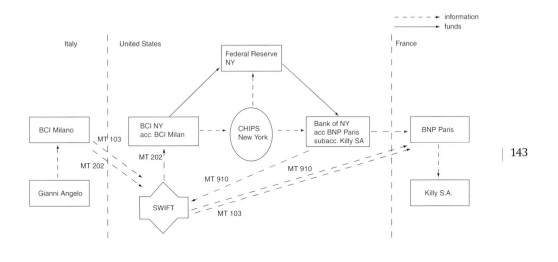

7.2.1 MT 103 from BCI Milan to BNP Paris

A MT 103 (single customer credit transfer message) is a SWIFT message containing a transfer that a bank executes on behalf of its customer. In this message the receiving bank is requested to credit the beneficiary's account with a certain amount. In our example, it is a message from BCI Milano to BNP Paris stating that the account of Gian Angelo at BCI Milano will be debited in favour of the USD account of Killy S.A. at BNP Paris, and that the transfer will be executed by the correspondent banks of itself (BCI New York) and of BNP Paris (Bank of New York).

Description	Format
Sender	BCITITMM
Message type	103
Receiver	BNPAFRPP
Message text:	
Reference sender	:20:8861198-0706
Bank operating code	:23B:CRED
Value date/currency/amount	:32A:990610USD5443,99
Remitting customer	:50K:GIAN ANGELO MILAN
Remitting bank	:52A:BCITITMM500
Remitter's correspondent	:53A:BCITUS33
Receiver's correspondent	:54A:IRVTUS3N
Receiving bank	:58A:BNPAFRPP
Receiving customer	:59:/2004101005050001M026 KILLY SA PARIS
Transfer information	:70:/RFB/INVOICE/559661
Charges specification	:71A:SHA
End of text	

7.2.2 MT 202 from BCI Milan to BCI New York

An MT 202 (general bank transfer) is an instruction from a bank to another bank to transfer funds. In this case, it is a cover payment instruction from the BCI Milano to BCI New York, ordering the transfer of an amount from its own account at BCI New York to the Bank of New York in favour of BNP Paris.

Description	Format
Sender	BCITITMM
Message type	202
Receiver	BCITUS33
Message text	
Transaction Reference Number	:20:597240
Reference to message MT 103	:21:8861198-0706
Value date/currency/amount	:32A:990610USD5443,99
Account with bank (receiving party)	:57A:IRVTUS3N
Receiving bank	:58A:BNPAFRPP
End of message	

7.2.3 MT 910 from the Bank of New York New York to BNP Paris

An MT910 (confirmation of a credit) is a message from a bank to its correspondent that they have credited the correspondent's nostro account. In this case it is a message from Bank of New York to BNP Paris stating that is has credited the account of BNP Paris at Bank of New York. BNP Paris has already been informed of the ultimate beneficiary (Killy S.A.) through the MT 103 message.

Description	Format
Sender	IRVTUS3N
Message Type	910
Receiver	BNPAFRPP
Message Text	
Transaction Reference Number	:20:GH45952-4587
Cross Reference to message MT 103	:21:8861198-0706
Number their account	:25:3373733
Value date/currency/amount	:32A:990610USD5443,99
Remitting bank	:52A:BCITITMM
Intermediary party (remitter's correspondent)	:56A:BCITUS33
End of text	

This MT 910 message is followed by an account statement in the form of a MT 950 (statement message).

7.3 Member Administrated Closed User Groups

SWIFT offers the opportunity for banks to use the SWIFT network to communicate with their corporate clients by establishing Member Administrated Closed User Groups (MACUGs). Corporate clients that are MACUG members will not become SWIFT members themselves, but are referred to as Service Participants. The bank that sets up a MACUG is referred to as the administrator of the MACUG.

By using a MACUG, banks can access treasury centres of large MNCs anywhere in the world. They do so through the secure and reliable SWIFT network, and do not have to develop a network of their own. Corporate clients use the SWIFT network to communicate not only with the administrator, but also with all other SWIFT users by way of the administrator.

8
SEPA

Since 2002, 12 of the 25 member states of the European Union are using the euro as the common currency for cash payments. As a result, consumers, businesses and governments can use the same bills and coins throughout the euro area. However, cashless payment systems and products are still organised on a national basis. The introduction of the euro as the single currency of the euro area will only be completed when a Single Euro Payments Area (SEPA) has been established. This is an initiative of the European Payment Council (EPC), which represents the major European banks and banking associations. They have defined the following mission:

"SEPA will be the area where citizens, companies and other economic actors will be able to make and receive payments in euro, within Europe, whether between or within national boundaries under the same basic conditions, rights and obligations, regardless of their location."

The main objective of SEPA is that consumers, businesses and governments will be able to make cashless payments throughout the euro area from an account anywhere in the euro area using a single set of payment instruments as easily, efficiently and safely as they can make payments today in the domestic context. SEPA can be especially advantageous for businesses, as they will no longer have to deliver payment files in different local formats for each country where they want to transfer money.

In order to achieve this objective, the European banking industry is committed to offer SEPA-scheme compliant instruments for credit transfers, direct debits and card payments. Common rules have been defined for two uniform transaction services:

- SEPA Credit Transfer (SCT)
- SEPA Direct Debits (SDD)

The new common rules will guarantee transparency of pricing, which means that the practice of deducting charges from the principal amount will come to an end and transaction costs will be charged separately. Credit transfers will be subject to a maximum guaranteed execution time of three days. The scheme will permit the end-to-end carrying of remittance data on a structured and unstructured basis. The direct debit scheme is based on uniform rules for collecting payments in euro throughout the SEPA area.

In addition, a common framework will apply to card payments. This will enable European customers to use cards to make payments cash withdrawals in euro throughout the SEPA area with the same ease and convenience as in their home country.

The European banks will deliver the first SEPA products to their customers from January 2008. The EPC is convinced that a critical mass of transactions will naturally migrate to these products by the end of 2010. National products may remain for some time after 2010 but they will gradually disappear through the operation of market forces and network effects.

148 | To facilitate Pan European transactions different Pan European Automated Clearing Houses (PE-ACHs) will be established with the capability to accept payment instructions from any European originator to any European beneficiary. The EPC has defined common scheme rules for a PE-ACH. The first PE-ACH compliant clearing house is the EBA who currently offers Pan European clearing services through their STEP2 service.

The geographic scope of SEPA is euro payments in the 25 EU countries plus Liechtenstein, Norway and Switzerland.

C
Core Cash Management Activities

Chapter 8
Cash balances management

Introduction

The liquidity management of a company consists of two primary components: cash balances management and funds management. The objective of cash balances management is to have a clear picture of the company's total current available balances – for both today and the very near future. The constant flow of money in and out of the company means that available balances are changing continuously. Every day the firm's cash positions change, resulting typically in surpluses or deficits in one or more currencies. The treasurer's objective is to avoid, as far as possible, debit and credit positions in different accounts in the same currency. Achieving this requires 'shifting' balances between the various current accounts.

1
Cash balances management goals

Cash balances management's objective is to optimise the use of available funds and maximise net interest. This essentially involves the day-to-day management of all balances during a period of time. It requires minimising overdraft positions and maximising the use of funds by taking into account the different currencies, as well as the legal and tax frameworks of the jurisdictions where the company operates.

All of a company's bank accounts are used by the payables and receivables departments to conduct normal business. At the end of each day these transactions generate a final value balance. Cash balances management aims to optimise the use of available funds. The cash manager can achieve this objective in different ways:

- avoiding non-earning credit balances on zero-interest or low-interest accounts (idle balances)

- avoiding expensive debit balances (overdrafts), particularly through what is typically expensive unplanned current accounts funding (note, in some markets, this uncommitted funding can be an efficient way for the cash manager to cover short-positions, but the uncommitted nature generally makes it unsuitable as a contingency funding resource)
- concentrating balances to create a single overall position per currency which will facilitate investment

2
Cash management tools

The cash manager can use the following instruments for day-to-day cash balances management purposes:

- current accounts
- cash concentration
- information / balance reporting tools

CURRENT ACCOUNT

A current account is the most basic cash instrument. In and out-bound transactions occur across the account generating an end-of-day position. A current account allows the holder immediate access to the available balance. All transactions are executed from this account. The company's account structure is the system of all its current accounts. The sum of the balances on all these accounts is the company's total cash position. The cash manager's primary responsibility is to manage this total position.

In most countries a current account is allowed to be overdrawn up to a certain amount. The extent of any overdraft depends on the company's creditworthiness. In countries where a current account is not allowed to be overdrawn, a separate account has to be opened with a credit facility. This facility helps to facilitate transactions, particularly when available balances are not sufficient to process transactions. If no credit facility has been arranged, outgoing payments may be blocked.

CASH CONCENTRATION

For simplicity, the optimal structure for many companies would be to have only one account. This scenario would enable the cash manager to understand the cash position relatively easily, without having to aggregate the positions of multiple accounts. But this is an unrealistic utopia for most cash managers. Even within a single country, most companies operate with multiple entities and therefore multiple accounts for organisational, tax, and legal reasons. This makes the assessment of the total cash position much more cumbersome. To be able to achieve one position per currency, the cash manager may choose to actually move the funds into a single physical location offering the most preferential legal and tax environment, as well as a beneficial investment environment. The cash manager can make use of techniques such as urgent transfers between bank accounts or, alternatively, he can also ask the bank to zero balance funds to one location or even use notional pooling.

INFORMATION

An electronic banking system provides the bank account holder with most of the information he is looking for: e.g. opening, closing booked and value balances, as well as the detailed information about underlying transactions. The latter can | 153 generally be provided at the end of the day or even during the day. Electronic banking systems consist of either the application of a software package supplied by the bank or a URL through the internet. Both allow the cash manager to send electronic payment instructions to the bank, receive account information from the bank, and import and export this information from and into its own accounting and treasury systems.

The bank accounts, the concentration of funds and the information reports on these activities provide the cash manager with all the basic tools he needs to successfully achieve his primary cash management goals.

3
The day-to-day operational activities of cash balances management

To achieve the primary objectives of cash balances management, the cash manager carries out the following daily activities:

- determining the current balances of all of the company's accounts
- fine-tuning outgoing payments
- performing cash concentration transactions - manual high-value, sweep transactions and / or automated zero balancing transactions

3.1 Compiling a cash position statement

To determine the required internal transfers, the cash manager draws up a forecast of the end-of-day balances of all of the company's accounts. To this end, he prepares a cash position statement for each account. In these statements, the cash manager forecasts the end-of-day balances of each individual account. The cash manager compiles the cash position statement on the basis of:

- the electronic bank statements of the current accounts (electronic balance and transaction reporting – BTR)
- forecasted payments and receipts

In most cases, the cash manager reviews the bank statements of all current accounts first thing each morning. He does this for each currency in which the company trades. The following key data points are detailed on the statements:

- the opening balance
- transactions entered during the day
- closing balance

A bank statement of a EUR account is shown below (figure 1). This concerns the group account of a parent company.

Figure 1   Bank statement June 9th

	(EUR)	book date	value date
opening book balance 8/6	1,000,000		
value balance 8/6	800,000		
accounts receivable	+900,000	9/6	10/6
accounts payable	−400,000	9/6	8/6
retransfered deposit	+1,000,000	9/6	9/6
high value payment	+800,000	9/6	8/6
settlement forward transaction	+2,000,000	9/6	9/6
cheque payed cashed under usual reserve	+600,000	9/6	12/6
closing book balance 9/6	5,900,000		

For interest related purposes, the cash manager will look at the value balance. The value balance in the above example on 8/6 is EUR 800,000. But the cash manager now wants to forecast the value balance for today (9/6) in order to determine what amount he should deposit or must replenish. The objective is to deposit or finance the entire value balance in the money market. How, then, does he compute the value balance of 9 June? This depends on the following components:

1. value balance on 8 June.
2. items on the bank statement of 9 June with value date 9 June.
3. items already entered with value date 9 June.

4. items that are entered on (or even after) 10 June with value date 9 June (forecast items).

ITEMS ON THE BANK STATEMENT OF 9/6 WITH VALUE DATE 9 JUNE
The bank statement contains the following items with value date 9/6:

-   re-transferred deposit EUR 1,000,000
-   forward transaction settlement EUR 2,000,000

ITEMS ENTERED EARLIER WITH VALUE DATE 9/6 (FIGURE 2)
The EB system gives information on items entered before 9/6 with a value date of 9/6. This could be the following items, for instance: | 155

-   incoming debtor payments (accounts receivable) of EUR 1,000,000, entered on 8 June with value date 9/6
-   cheque settled by the bank on 4 June for EUR 400,000, value date 9/6

FORECAST TRANSFERS WITH VALUE DATE 9/6
Finally the cash manager must take into account transactions effected during the day that will influence the value balance. Every day the cash manager attempts to collect information about the outgoing and incoming payments with a value date of today but which are not yet shown on a bank statement.

For instance, the cash manager may receive information daily from the creditor accounts department about the planned creditor payments (with entry date one day later, but value date today). Or the financial director may give him information on large investments that are to be paid today by means of a high value payment. In his planning for that day, the cash manager also includes transactions scheduled for the previous day but not yet effected. And finally, as noted, the operating companies may also communicate transactions to him during the course of the day.

In our case, the cash manager is confronted with the following income and expenditures with value date 9/6:

-   un-received non-recurring urgent payment, expected on 8/6 at EUR 500,000
-   outgoing creditor payments by electronic transfer of EUR 500,000, entry date 10/6 (from A/P system)
-   outgoing creditor payments by cheque of EUR 300,000 (sent 1 June)
-   scheduled tax payment at 9 June of EUR 1,500,000
-   outgoing high-value payment in connection with purchase of Canon Printer of EUR 900,000

In addition, during the day, the following transactions are reported by two operating companies:

- operating company A: tax payment, value date 9 June, of EUR 1,000,000
- operating company B: operating company B: salary tape, entry date 10 June / value date 9 June, of EUR 400,000

The above transactions result in the following forecast for the value balance of 9 June:

Figure 2 *End-of-day balance forecast for June 9th*

Balance Forecast			
(EUR)		**Book date**	**Value date**
800,000	**value balance 8/6**		**9/6**
	on balance statement 9/6:		
+1,000,000	retransfer of deposit	9/6	9/6
+2,000,000	settlement of forward transaction	9/6	9/6
	booked earlier		
+1,000,000	accounts receivable	8/6	9/6
+400,000	incoming cheque payments	4/6	9/6
	not yet shown on account statement:		
+ 500,000	'overdue' high-value payment	9/6	9/6
−500,000	accounts payable by electronic transfer	10/6	9/6
−300,000	accounts payable by cheque	11/6	9/6
−1,500,000	tax payment	9/6	9/6
−900,000	Canon international / hvp	9/6	9/6
−1,000,000	tax payment operating company A	9/6	9/6
−400,000	salaries operating company B.	10/6	9/6
1,100,000	**Forecast end-of day book balance**		**9/6**

For the cash manager's purposes, the value balance is much more important than the book balance. The book balance of 9 June in the above example was EUR 5,900,000. However, if the cash manager were to deposit an amount of EUR 5,900,000 in the money market, the value balance would become strongly negative, i.e -/- EUR 4,800,000. The account would then be heavily overdrawn for interest computation purposes and the cash manager would accordingly have to pay debit interest.

3.2 Fine-tuning of payments

When compiling the cash position statement, the cash manager often looks one or several days ahead. If he foresees a liquidity deficit on any of these days, he can try to delay less critical outbound payments to a later date. Bank loan repayments or tax payments cannot generally be postponed. Salaries, too, must be paid on time or generate legal repercussions. But there may be some creditor payments that can wait a day or two. The cash manager will have to explore the opportunities for postponing payments in consultation with the purchasing department.

3.3 Performing cash concentration transactions

In order to understand the overall position of a company, a cash position statement must be drawn up for all current accounts. This includes all accounts of the parent company and all accounts of the operating companies where cross-funding is permitted or preferential from a tax versus cost perspective. To facilitate this, the cash position statements of the accounts of the operating companies are often compiled by local cash managers and sent to a central treasury.

What happens now that a value balance has been forecast for all accounts? One of the primary objectives of cash balances management is to optimise the overall interest result for all of the company's current accounts. The cash manager can now achieve this by transferring credit balances in low-interest accounts to accounts with debit positions, achieving effectively a self-funded position. The contra account for this purpose is the current account of the central treasury. These transfers must be effected on a 'same-day value' basis.

Many cash managers no longer carry out such 'sweep transactions' manually. Most banks now offer to automatically sweep balances from the operating companies' accounts into a master account. This is commonly known as zero balancing, target balancing or automated balance transfer. Sometimes the sweep transactions are not physically carried out. Instead, the balances of all accounts are simply added up for interest computation purposes. This is typically referred to as notional pooling. In both cases there is a single value balance for the entire group at the end of the day.

When the cash manager has determined the group's overall value balance, he can then deposit any excess funds into the money market. Higher returns are generally achieved in the money market versus the return offered by a current account. If the group balance shows a deficit, the cash manager can try to borrow money from the bank for one day or a longer period if necessary.

3.4 Cut-off times

The cash manager should always check the balances of all of the company's accounts before the cut-off times for the various currencies. The cut-off time is the deadline for sending payment instructions to the bank.

A problem may occur if the company's treasury department closes before the local cut-off time of a certain currency. This will happen if, for instance, a treasurer based in Europe is in charge of a USD account in New York. In this case amounts may still be received in the USD accounts after the cash manager has gone home. The cash manager is then no longer able to sweep the account, or place the excess funds in the money market.

In such cases accurate forecasting is even more important, as the cash manager can then already take account of anticipated incoming payments in his sweep transfers or money market transactions.

4
Evaluation of Cash Balances management

The cash manager must periodically evaluate the performance of his cash balances management activities. As the effectiveness of cash balances management largely depends on the quality of the company's account structure, as well as its ability to forecast accurately and concentrate effectively net cash positions, he will want to evaluate these cash balances management activities from time to time. The central question to be answered is: to what extent has the overall interest result on all current book balances been optimised?

The performance can be checked by examining the movements of the various value balances. It is important that none of the following situations have occurred in relation to any of the currencies in question:

– simultaneous debit and credit positions (without notional pooling). If one subsidiary of the firm has credit balances and another one has a debit balance, they should lend and borrow from each other. Unfortunately, where

cash management is not optimised, you still see companies in the situation of one subsidiary going to the market for one investment while another one is borrowing.
- credit positions in local accounts and accounts with low credit interest rates.
- debit positions in 'expensive' accounts.

To establish whether any of these situations have occurred, the cash manager must review the balance movements of each account over the period under evaluation. On the basis of his findings and the interest terms for the various accounts, he can calculate the costs incurred as a result of any mismatches.

Figure 3   *Total current book balance movement*

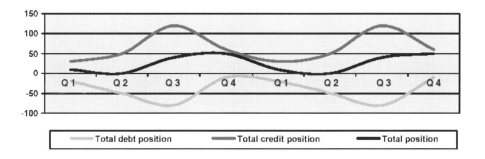

The figure above, for example, shows a case where, in general, no major credit and debit positions occurred simultaneously. In this case the cash manager has done a good job.

The review can also provide an accurate picture of the quality of the periodic sweep actions agreed with banks. If improvements are possible, the cash manager can use these results to make new sweep arrangements with the banks.

Further, the cash manager should, periodically, evaluate the account and cash pool structure. In doing so, he will ask himself the following questions:

- are all existing bank relationships necessary?
- have all accounts, where possible, been incorporated in a cash pool?
- can any accounts be closed without hindering operations?
- are the account terms still competitive?

- are the pools still effectively managed?
- do we receive the most accurate information from our banks on movements on the accounts?

These questions will help the cash manager to improve the performance of balance management, setting the scene for better fund management.

Chapter 9
Cash concentration

Introduction
161

Global companies have cash balances on different bank accounts, at different banks, in different currencies and often even in different time zones. The corporate cash manager is responsible for controlling these balances, with the goal of optimising interest results and the use of excess cash. The cash manager does so by funding deficits internally and investing net surplus positions in the market. Toward this end most companies physically concentrate the cash balances in one place, giving them a much better handle on liquidity positions that were previously dispersed across geographies. Although cash managers can move balances manually, banks have developed sophisticated methods to automatically concentrate, offset or even convert balances to achieve one balance position each day. These methods are called 'cash concentration' or 'cash pooling' and are the focus of this chapter.

1
The basic concept of cash concentration

There are many different forms of automated cash concentration, but the concept of cash pooling is based on the idea that all value balances in the same currency are concentrated. This offers the advantages of:

- tighter control on group balances
- improved interest results because credit balances offset debit balances
- no idle balances on subsidiary accounts
- balances that can be invested or funded at more favourable rates in the money market

The example below shows the impact of cash concentration on interest results.

Suppose a company holds the following four accounts at one and the same bank:

account	debit interest rate	credit interest rate	balance	interest amount (annual basis)
operating company A	7%	4%	+500	+20
operating company B	7%	4%	−400	−28
operating company C	7%	4%	+700	+28
operating company D	7%	4%	−200	−14
total				6

The debit and credit interest rates are identical for all accounts. Two accounts are in credit and two accounts are in debit. The bank charges a debit interest rate of 7% and pays a credit interest rate of 4%.

We see that the total interest income on an annual basis is 6.

What would be the interest result if the company were able to concentrate all balances in one account on the same interest conditions as all the separate accounts?
This is shown below.

account	debit interest rate	credit interest rate	balance	interest amount (annual basis)
operating company A	-	-	0	0
operating company B	-	-	0	0
operating company C	-	-	0	0
operating company D	-	-	0	0
master account	7%	4%	600	+ 24

The interest income rises spectacularly from +6 to +24.

Why does the interest income in our example increase by 18? Before the balances were concentrated, the company's total credit balance was 1200 (operating company A plus operating company C), and the total debit balance was 600 (operating company B plus operating company D). By concentrating the balances, the debit balances are completely eliminated because the company is no longer required to borrow 600 from the bank at a rate of 7% and lend the same amount to the bank at 4%, effectively losing a margin of 3% on debit and credit balances. By pooling all balances, the company realises 3% more on the offsetting balance of 600, which is exactly the interest gain of 18.

1.1 Physical sweeping and notional pooling

Banks offer companies various methods of cash concentration to automatically offset debit and credit balances on current accounts.

A cash pool is a group of current accounts in the name of one or more companies and a master account. The master account is usually in the name of the central treasury, and the other accounts are called 'operating accounts' or 'sub-accounts'. Balances can either be physically concentrated on the master account or can be notionally concentrated for interest calculation.

A cash pool with all accounts located in the same country is a domestic or 'in-country' cash pool, while one that includes accounts held in several countries is called a 'cross-border' cash pool.

A diagram of a cash pool is shown below.

Figure 1   *Cash pool*

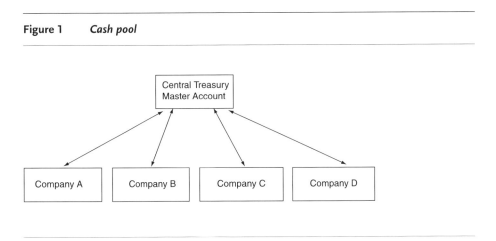

There are two types of cash pooling, physical sweeping and notional pooling.

2
Physical sweeping

With physical sweeping, balances on all operating accounts are automatically moved by means of automatic concentration transactions or 'sweeps'. The central account, also called 'master account', serves as the cash concentration account, and in most cases the operating accounts are set in a zero position and all value balances are booked on the central account. The sweeps take place automatically with same-day finality.

Sweep transactions can happen in two ways: upstream transactions and downstream transactions. Upstream transactions are automatic transfers of credit balances from operating accounts to the master account, while downstream transactions are automatic transfers of balances from the master account to operating accounts.

There are two types of sweeps:

- end-of-day sweeping
- intra-day sweeping

END-OF-DAY SWEEPING

With end-of-day sweeping, sweeps are carried out only at the end of the day, after all other transactions have been executed for the operating accounts. This means that the exact total balance, only known at the end of the day, will be reported at the start of the next day. Treasurers, however, want to invest or fund the net balance position before the end of the day when the money market is closed, so they must make a forecast of the expected net balance for the day. They do this by correcting the opening balance of the day with all planned incoming and outgoing payments with a value date that same day.

INTRA-DAY SWEEPING

With intra-day sweeping, balances are transferred during the working day and before the end of the day. This may be done by banks for several reasons:

- they need to move the funds from one bank to another before the clearing is closed
- they need to move the funds from one country to another using SWIFT rather than their internal booking process
- the company wants the sweeps booked and reported the same day

Intra-day sweeps are often carried out through the bank's payments process; as a result they may be affected when delays and other problems occur in the payments process. End-of-day sweeps are generally error-free because they are executed in a separate internal booking process.

2.1 Frequency and size of the automatic sweeping transactions

Various alternatives are available for the size and frequency of sweeps:

- regular (daily or weekly) sweeps:
  - zero balancing
  - target balancing
  - constant balancing
- ad hoc sweeps:
  - trigger balancing

2.1.1 Zero balancing

With zero balancing, operating accounts are periodically swept to a zero balance. If this takes place daily, the operating accounts will always show a zero value balance.

There are two alternatives to zero balancing: target balancing and constant balancing. With both types, a certain opening balance is made available to the sub-accounts of the cash pool each day, so that the operating companies can still make payments from these accounts.

2.1.2 Target balancing

With target balancing, the value balances of the sub-accounts are swept to the master account every day. At the same time, transfers are made in the opposite direction from the master account to the sub-accounts in order to maintain the target balances for the sub-accounts. The book date is 'today' and the value date is 'tomorrow', so with this method the book balance of the sub-account is always in credit but the value balance is always zero.

EXAMPLE

Mediflex is an operating company of Europharma. The account of Mediflex is included in the cash pool of Europharma. The central treasurer of Europharma has agreed with the controller of Mediflex that the sub-account of Mediflex must always have a minimum book balance of EUR 70,000.

On 1 September the value balance on the account of Mediflex is EUR 140,000. The account of Mediflex is now swept at the end of the day for EUR 140,000, thus reducing the value balance to zero.

At the same time, an amount of EUR 70,000 is transferred in the opposite direction with book date 1 September and value date 2 September. The value balance of Mediflex thus remains 0 on 1 September, but there is money in the account, so that Mediflex can make outgoing payments on 2 September.

2.1.3 Constant balancing

With constant balancing, the sub-account balances are swept every day, such that the pre-agreed minimum balance always remains on the account. In other words, only the 'surplus' balance is swept, so the sub-account always shows both a book and value balance equal to the constant balance amount. As soon as the balance of a sub-account drops below the constant balance level, it is supplemented from the master-account by means of a downstream sweep transaction.

EXAMPLE

The account of Sanor is a sub-account of the cash pool of Beladyn Inc. The sub-accounts are swept according to the 'constant balancing' method. The constant level is USD 50,000.

On 10 October the account of Sanor shows a value balance of USD 125,000. At the end of the day, the account is swept for an amount of USD 75,000, leaving a value balance of USD 50,000.

2.1.4 Trigger balancing

'Trigger balancing' means the sub-accounts are swept only when their balances exceed a pre-determined level, so the frequency of sweeping is irregular. The level of the trigger is set for both credit and debit balances. A sub-account, for example, is swept automatically when there is a credit balance in excess of EUR 50,000, and replenished when there is a debit balance in excess of EUR 50,000.

Trigger balancing is often used for accounts with only a limited number of transactions, and its purpose is to reduce sweeps and the related operating costs.

2.2 Mono-bank sweeping and multi-bank sweeping

So far we have discussed physical sweeping between accounts held at one bank, but some banks have developed sweeping services that move balances automatically between accounts held at different banks. This service, known as 'multi-bank sweeping' or 'multi-bank cash concentration', is of interest to companies that use one bank as their cash concentration bank, but use others (whether in the same country or in different countries) for payments, collections and other services.

With this service the cash-concentration bank checks balances on sub-accounts held with the other banks using SWIFT MT940 or MT942 messages. It then creates a transfer request using a SWIFT MT101 message, to move the funds to the master account. The payment instruction is executed by the receiving bank and, as a result, the funds are transferred to the cash-concentration bank in a domestic or international transfer. As we have seen with mono-bank cash concentration, different sweeping options can be used, such as constant balancing to maintain a working balance on sub-accounts or trigger balancing to avoid sweeping of small amounts.

Multi-bank sweeps are executed through the local clearing process or, in case of cross-border transfers, through the correspondent banking process. This means that the sweeps will normally be initiated before the end of the day, so it will be more difficult to achieve a zero balance on sub-accounts.

2.3 Sweeping of book balance or value balance

We now know that sub-accounts can be swept in different ways, but which of the two types of balances are transferred, book or value balances? The book balance represents the legal relationship between the bank and the customer, whereby the cash held on account belongs to the customer and is at the customer's free disposal. The value balance is the sum on which the bank pays or charges interest.

2.3.1 Sweeping the book value

If the book balances of the sub-accounts are swept, the sweeping operation includes all items stated in the book balance at the time of sweeping, irrespective of the value date. In other words, items with a value date in the future are also swept, such that both the value and book balances of the sub-accounts are always zero. This is referred to as 'zero balancing with forward sweeping'.

2.3.2 Sweeping the value balance

When the value balance is swept, the sweeping operation exclusively includes those items with the value date 'today' or earlier. With this form of sweeping, known as called 'zero balancing without forward sweeping', the value balance on the account is always equal to zero. Items with a value date in the future, such as collections from customers, remain on the sub-accounts; so the book balance is not always equal to zero.

2.4 Interest settlement with zero balancing

Two kinds of interest settlement can be distinguished with zero balancing:

- interest settlement between the bank and the company
- interest settlement between the participants in the cash pool

2.4.1 Interest settlement between the bank and the company

With zero balancing, the interest settlement between the bank and the company is generally simple: the value balance on all sub-accounts is zero, so the bank does not need to set interest conditions on the sub-accounts. It simply calculates interest on the value balance of the master account. The same applies to target balancing: cash balances are maintained on the sub-accounts, but the value balance on these accounts is always zero. Consequently, the bank does not need to pay or charge any interest on these accounts.

With trigger and constant balancing and other types of non-daily sweeps, there will generally be value balances on the sub-accounts. In these cases, the bank can apply interest conditions to the sub-accounts and settle accordingly.

2.4.2 Interest settlement between the participants

As we saw, the bank only settles interest on the balance of the master account, which is the sum of the interest due on the balances originating from the sub-accounts. The operating companies are entitled to receive interest on the credit balances they have provided to the central treasury, and likewise, are obliged to pay interest on debit balances. How then, does the central treasurer re-allocate the interest that the bank pays or charges in respect of the master account to the various operating companies?

Each sweep can be seen as an internal loan from one account holder to another. For tax reasons, the central treasury must keep a record of these internal loans, which take place between the treasury and the operating companies, in an internal account administration. This places an administrative burden on central cash managers, and it constitutes one of the main disadvantages of physical sweeping.

The treasury periodically calculates the interest to be settled in relation to the internal loans and pays or charges the relevant amount to the operating companies. The tax authorities, however, will insist that internal interest rates are in line with the going market interest rates (rates which an operating company would have gotten if it had placed the balance with a local bank in their home country). This is known as pricing 'at arm's length'.

Cash managers can relieve the administrative burden in various ways. First, many modern treasury systems can administer internal loans by making use of electronic transaction reporting from banks. Sweep transactions are marked on electronic bank statements with a sweep code, allowing treasury systems to identify and select entries as sweeps and export them to the company's internal-loan management system.

As an additional service, some banks can perform this task for their customers by keeping track of balance sweeps and reporting at regular intervals (usually once a month) the 'shadow balances' of the different subsidiaries. This service is often referred to as 'shadow administration'. In addition, the 'inter-company interest', which is the interest based on the shadow balances, can be calculated, reported and booked.

2.5 Credit facilities with zero balancing

The bank usually extends a credit facility related to the cash pool. The following facilities are available:

- overnight limit for the master account
- intra-day limit for the sub-accounts

2.5.1 Overnight limit for the master account

If the company and the bank have agreed on a credit facility for the master account, it is allowed to be overdrawn up to a certain amount on an overnight basis. When the debit balance is exceeded, the customer must replenish the deficit during the day or request the bank's approval for a temporary limit excess. The company is then allowed to replenish the debit balance the next day or even later. In daily practice, however, sweeps are usually executed even if this would result in a higher debit position than allowed under the overnight limit.

2.5.2 Intra-day limit for the sub-accounts

When a bank assigns an intra-day limit to the participating accounts, these accounts may be overdrawn up to a certain amount during the day. This is generally needed when the sub-accounts are zero balanced. As we have seen before, sub-accounts will start the day with a zero balance. With an intra-day credit facility, the participants can now make payments provided that the intra-day limit is not exceeded. An overnight limit is not necessary because all sub-accounts always have a zero balance at the end of the day.

2.6 Example of zero balancing

Following is a numerical example of zero balancing, the interest rates on the master account are more favourable than for most sub-accounts. The interest gain generated by the cash pool is partly attributable to these more favourable rates and, as we saw earlier, partly to the fact that credit balances are offsetting debit balances.

A company holds the following four accounts at one and the same bank:

account	debit interest rate	credit interest rate	balance	interest amount (annual basis)
operating company A	8%	3%	+500	+15
operating company B	9%	2%	−400	−36
operating company C	8%	3%	+700	+21
operating company D	7%	4%	−200	−14
total				−14

We see that, in total, the company must pay an interest amount of 14.

What would be the result if the company managed to concentrate all balances on the master account? The interest conditions for the master account are identical to those of operating company D (credit interest 4%, debit interest 7%). This is shown below.

account	debit interest rate	credit interest rate	balance	interest amount (annual basis)
operating company A	n.a.	n.a.	0	0
operating company B	n.a.	n.a.	0	0
operating company C	n.a.	n.a.	0	0
operating company D	n.a.	n.a.	0	0
master account	7%	4%	600	24

We see that the company's interest income rises even more spectacularly than in the example at the beginning of this chapter, namely from −14 to +24, an improvement of 38.

In the example at the beginning of this chapter, the improvement of 18 was obtained assuming that the interest conditions were equal for all accounts. The improvement of the interest result has increased so much because there now is a difference in the rates applied to the operating accounts and the master account, with the master account having the most favourable rates.

This is illustrated in the following figure:

Figure 2   *Zero balancing, situation before and after sweeping*

Before sweeping

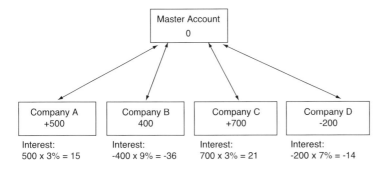

With sweeping

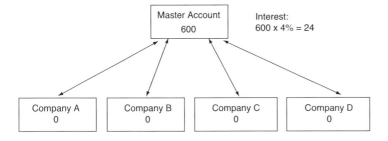

3
Notional pooling

With notional pooling all balances in the same currency are left on the various participating accounts, but the bank agrees to calculate interest on the overall net balance. In contrast with zero balancing, no cash balances are actually transferred with this method.

Zero balancing and notional pooling lead to an identical improvement of interest results, but there are some significant differences between them. Let's look in greater detail at the interest settlement method used with notional pooling.

3.1 Interest settlement with notional pooling

The following interest rates are applied within a notional pool:

- interest rate for the total cash pool
- interest rates for the sub-accounts

3.1.1 Interest rate for the total cash pool, applied to the net balance

The bank and the company agree on the interest rate for the entire pool. The interest income or charges are calculated daily, based on the total pool balance. How this total interest balance is allocated to the master and sub-accounts depends on the interest rates for the sub-accounts, which are set by the company.

3.1.2 Interest rates for the sub-accounts

The company determines the debit and credit interest rates for each sub-account. The bank pays interest on each account (in the case of credit balances) or charges interest (in the case of debit balances) based on these rates. The central treasury can set the rates so that the local managers of the participating accounts are encouraged to manage their liquidity for the good of the company as a whole. For example, relatively high credit and debit rates can be applied to get local cash managers to increase credit positions and avoid debit positions.

The company can also set the interest rates on sub-accounts to zero, with the bank paying interest only on balances on the master account. As with physical sweeping, central cash managers themselves must decide how the interest is re-allocated to the sub-accounts. As with zero balancing, tax authorities insist that arm's length pricing is used.

What amount does the bank pay into the master account if the interest rates for the sub-accounts are not set at zero? The bank first calculates the total amount of interest to be paid on the entire pool, since part of this total amount has already been paid (or charged) to the sub-accounts, the amount to be paid to the master account is calculated by deducting (or adding) the interest already paid (or charged) to the sub-accounts. After these corrections, the interest payment into the master account represents the net pool benefit, which is equal to the margin on the offset between the credit debit balances. This benefit can be paid out to the participating companies using a certain allocation key, such as the profit contribution of the operating company.

3.2 Credit facilities with notional pooling | 173

As with zero balancing, the bank may extend a credit facility related to the cash pool. Again, the following facilities may be granted:

- overnight limits
- intra-day limits

OVERNIGHT LIMIT

An overnight limit can be attached to the pool as a whole, and the bank will allow the net pool balance to be in overdraft to the agreed maximum amount. This means that an individual account can be in overdraft to this maximum amount plus the net credit position on the other accounts in the pool. In other words, surplus positions on accounts in the pool allow other accounts in the pool to go into overdraft. This umbrella credit facility is usually called 'balance compensation'.

In order to control the use of credit by individual operating companies, an additional 'sub-limit' can be attached to an operating account, which is an overnight limit for each individual account. The bank will check credit positions on individual accounts against the 'sub-limit' as well as the overall pool limit.

INTRA-DAY LIMITS

As with a zero balancing pool, intra-day limits may also be set for all participating accounts.

3.3 Example of notional pooling

Following is an example assumes the same company as in the zero balancing example, but in this case no sweeping of balances occurs and the pooling benefit is settled on the group balance.

A company holds the following four accounts at one and the same bank:

account	debit interest rate	credit interest rate	balance	interest amount (annual basis)
operating company A	8%	3%	+500	+15
operating company B	9%	2%	−400	−36
operating company C	8%	3%	+700	+21
operating company D	7%	4%	−200	−14
				−14

We again see that, in total, the company must pay an interest amount of 14, based on the individaul account balances.

What would this picture look like if the company had set up a notional pool? Suppose hat the interest conditions on the cash pool are equal to that of operating company D (credit interest 4%, debit interest 7%).We assume that the same conditions apply to all operating accounts. This is shown below.

account	debit interest rate	credit interest rate	balance	interest amount (annual basis)
operating company A	8%	3%	+500	+ 15
operating company B	9%	2%	−400	− 36
operating company C	8%	3%	+700	+ 21
operating company D	7%	4%	−200	− 14
total individual settlements				−14
pool	7%	4%	+600*	(+24)*
pool benefit settlement on master account				+38

*Fictitious notional net pool balance and fictitious pool interest.

The pool benefit is now the difference between the total of the individual settlements (-14) and the calculated pool interest (+24), i.e. + 38, which is the same as in the earlier zero balancing example. In this example, the pool benefit of + 38 is booked to the master account.

This is illustrated in figure 3.

Figure 3   *The result of notional pooling*

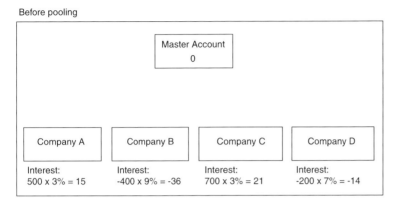

Before pooling

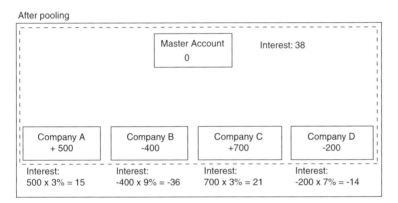

After pooling

3.4 Cross-currency notional pooling

So far we have discussed notional pooling of balances in a single currency, but some banks also offer notional pooling of balances in different currencies. This service, called 'cross-currency notional pooling', works generally in the same way as single-currency notional pooling, but interest results are affected by two additional factors: daily movements of currency exchange rates and varying interest rates on different currencies.

To make its notional pooling calculations, the bank notionally converts the balances in each currency to a chosen base currency. This calculation is made daily, based on current exchange rates. The bank then calculates the compensated balances in the pool, which is used to calculate the pool benefit using interest spreads for each currency. We can best illustrate this by using a simplified example based on full offset.

EXAMPLE

A company has accounts in euros and US dollars:

Total balances in euros:	800 credit
Total balances in US dollars:	480 debit
Credit interest rate:	EONIA -/- 100 bps
Debit interest rate:	Fed Funds + 150 bps
Exchange rate:	EUR 1 = USD 1.2

The bank makes its notional pooling calculation in three steps:

Step1: Notionally calculating balances in base currency (euros).

Balances in euros	800
Balances in US dollars (euro equivalent)	480 : 1.2 = 400

Step 2: Calculating the 'offset ratio'.

Offset ratio credit balances:	800 / 400 = 50%
Offset ratio debit balances:	400 / 400 = 100%

Step 3: Calculating interest benefit using interest spreads by currency.

Interest benefit credit balances: 800 x 100 bps x 50% = 4
Interest benefit debit balances: 400 x 150 bps x 100% = 6

Total pool benefit = 10

Although the calculation is more complex, we see that the same principle applies to both cross-currency notional pooling and single-currency notional pooling: the company avoids an interest disadvantage because it has credit and debit balances at the same time. In the case of full offset the bank returns the interest margin on the compensated balances. Unlike single currency notional pooling, however, the returned interest amounts on debit and credit balances may not exactly match because interest rates vary by currency.

There are two possible methods of providing interest benefit:

- partial compensation
- full compensation

PARTIAL COMPENSATION

In most cases the bank will provide a pooling service based on partial offset, especially when less liquid currencies are involved and the operating accounts are held in multiple countries. Notional pooling with partial offset, also called 'cross-currency interest optimisation', is beneficial to the company because it can enhance its interest results.

FULL COMPENSATION

When the bank is dealing in highly liquid currencies and is able to offset debit and credit balances in its solvency report to the central bank, they may be able to provide full compensation. This allows the company to run the cross-currency notional pool as one position. It avoids investment and funding transactions in each individual currency as well as foreign currency swaps to manage opposite liquidity positions in different currencies.

3.5 Accounting aspects of notional pooling

How should a company report the balances in a notional pool in its corporate balance sheet? Should all credit and debit balances be reported separately (gross reporting) or can the company report the net balance in the pool (net reporting)? The answer to these questions is very much driven by the accounting rules applicable in the country where the company publishes its financial statements. Under the new International Financial Reporting Standards, reporting of the net pool position is subject to restrictions. Companies unable to meet these criteria may decide to reduce the opposite positions in a notional pool on the day of reporting by executing one or more manual sweep transactions.

4
International cash pools

Traditionally, cash pools were operated within a single country, but with the introduction of the euro cross-border cash pooling has grown steadily. Today, cross-border cash pools – those which include accounts located in several different countries – are commonplace in Europe.

4.1 A simple cross-border zero balancing pool

As an example, let's look at a Dutch multinational corporation (MNC) with four operating companies in different euro countries, Belgium, Germany, France and Italy. The MNC sets up a zero balancing cash pool comprising the central treasury's account in the Netherlands plus the accounts of the four operating companies. All accounts are maintained at different local branches of a European bank and, therefore, can be automatically swept. At the end of each day, the balances of the operating companies are zero, and the central cash manager can either invest any net balance on the master account in the euro money market or fund any deficit. A schematic representation of this international cash pool is given below.

Figure 4   *Simple international cash pool*

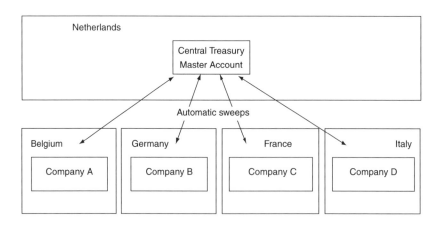

The international cash pool shown above portrays an ideal situation because operating companies hold their accounts with a branch of a European network bank. This has the advantages of:

- complete and fully automated concentration of funds
- one service desk to support the European cash pool
- a 'one stop shop' for all cash management arrangements including harmonised pricing

4.2 Overlay structure, zero balancing

In many cases, however, the accounts of foreign operating companies are maintained with different local banks. Some companies do not want the inconvenience of changing bank relationships, while other companies have local needs that are best met by local banks. An overlay structure effectively links local banks to the liquidity services of an international network bank.

Each operating company opens an 'overlay account' with the local branch of a network bank, while maintaining its existing account with the local bank. The operating companies continue to use accounts at their local bank for payments and collections, but each day before the local cut-off time (the closing time for sending in payment instructions) for inter-bank transfers, the balances on the local accounts are transferred via the local clearing system to the overlay accounts at the network bank. Once the balances are on the overlay accounts, they can be automatically swept across borders into the cash pool's master account.

The diagram below shows an overlay structure based on zero balancing.

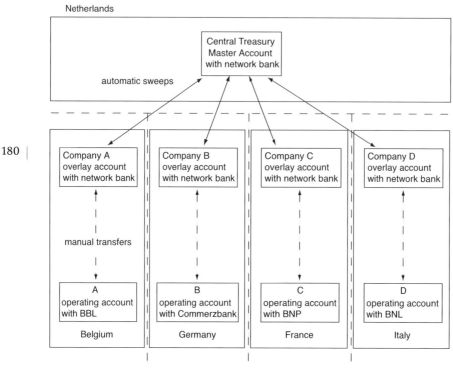

Figure 5   *Overlay structure / pure zero balancing pooling*

Netherlands

Central Treasury
Master Account
with network bank

automatic sweeps

180

Company A
overlay account
with network bank

Company B
overlay account
with network bank

Company C
overlay account
with network bank

Company D
overlay account
with network bank

manual transfers

A
operating account
with BBL

B
operating account
with Commerzbank

C
operating account
with BNP

D
operating account
with BNL

Belgium

Germany

France

Italy

With this structure, the balances with the local banks can be transferred daily to the overlay bank by:

- making a transfer through the company's electronic banking system (when using overlay accounts a multi-bank payment instruction, a SWIFT MT101 message, can be issued)
- giving a standing order instruction to the local bank
- using automated multi-bank sweeping

The last option can be used if the overlay bank is able to provide a fully automated sweeping service that moves surplus balances from third party banks into the overlay bank.

4.3 Overlay structure, multi-entity pooling

Most MNCs have different legal entities operating in different countries, and for tax reasons, these companies may want to avoid co-mingling of funds between legal entities and keep balances on separate bank accounts. This can be achieved by establishing a notional pool on top of the cross-border sweeping structure. The participating entities can open non-resident accounts in the country where the cash is centralised, which are then included in a notional pool, with their balances being swept to the non-resident accounts on a daily basis.

Figure 6 *Overlay structure, Multiple Legal Entity Pooling* | 181

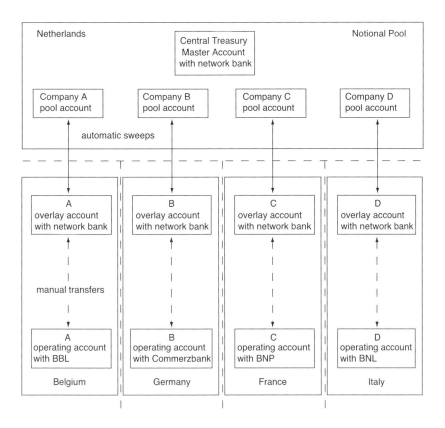

4.4 Building global pooling structures

Since the introduction of the euro in 1999, many MNCs have established cross-border cash pools in euros, and they are now looking to extend these pooling structures to include additional countries and currencies. There are three approaches to global cash pooling:

–   include euro accounts outside the euro area
–   include other convertible currencies
–   link US dollar accounts outside Europe

4.4.1 Euro accounts outside Europe

The euro is increasingly being used as a transaction currency in new EU member states, such as Poland, the Czech Republic and Hungary. Euro accounts in these countries may be connected to the euro pool in Western Europe by multi-bank sweeping (when the accounts are held with in-country banks) or zero balancing (when the accounts are held with a pan-European bank).

4.4.2 Other convertible currencies

Companies are looking for a 'total solution' for their liquidity management, which includes ways to control their euro balances and their balances in other currencies, such as US dollars, British pounds , Swiss francs, Swedish krona, Polish zloty, Czech koruna, Hungarian forint, Australian dollar and Hong Kong dollar. There are three types of account structures for these currencies:

–   in-country accounts
–   single currency-centre model
–   multi-currency centre model

IN-COUNTRY ACCOUNTS
Traditionally, companies have kept foreign-currency current accounts with local banks in their own countries, but this type of account is often inefficient in terms of transaction costs, cut-off times and liquidity management. Transaction costs are generally higher outside the home country of the currency and the cut-off times are earlier. Still, many companies prefer these local accounts because of the service provided by local banks.

SINGLE CURRENCY-CENTRE MODEL
In the single currency-centre model, all current accounts are kept in the home country of the currency; for example, US dollar accounts in the United States, Brit-

ish pound accounts are kept in Britain and Swiss franc accounts are held in Swit-zerland. Transaction costs are significantly lower and cut-off times more attractive because the accounts are located in the same country as the local clearing centre. However, liquidity management is still difficult because the corporate treasurer has to manage different liquidity positions in many different countries.

MULTI-CURRENCY CENTE MODEL

In this case all foreign currency accounts are held in one international financial centre, such as London or Amsterdam, with the advantage of all liquidity posi-tions being held in one place. This enables the treasurer to settle foreign exchange (FX) transactions easily, execute FX-swaps at lower costs and possibly integrate all currency accounts into one cross-currency notional pool. The downside is that the transaction costs of making and receiving payments are higher than with the sin-gle-currency centre model. This may be acceptable if the volume of cross-border payments is limited or if competitive prices have been negotiated with the cash-concentration bank.

For companies with substantial transaction volumes, it is more attractive to apply the single-currency model for all domestic and cross-border initiated payments. However, they can still achieve the liquidity benefits of the multi-currency centre model by using physical sweeps to move the funds from the single-currency centre to the multi-currency centre. A few large banks offer these sweeping capabilities in multiple currencies, which allows for a structure that can both reduce transac-tions costs and optimise liquidity.

4.4.3 Linking US dollar accounts outside Europe

Many MNCs doing business across multiple regions operate US dollar accounts in North America, Europe and Asia, and, increasingly, they are looking to set up a global structure for their liquidity management, whereby dollar balances are con-centrated in one location. For US companies this may be New York or Chicago, and for European companies this may be London or Amsterdam. This will have the ad-vantage of integrating the global dollar position with balances in other convert-ible currencies. A few large banks with global networks are able to physically sweep local dollar balances into one location, sometimes even providing a true end-of day zero-balancing service. This simplifies treasury operations extensively and helps the company to fully centralise and optimise liquidity management.

5
Checklist for setting up a cash pool

In this section we look at the most important issues that a company must consider before setting up a cash pool.

Key questions that treasurers or central cash managers should ask themselves are:

- What is the purpose of the cash pool and is a cash pool suitable for my company?
- Which accounts should be included in the pool?
- Should sweeping be manual or automatic?
- What obstacles must I overcome to set up a cash pool in the local environment?
- Should the pool use physical sweeping or should it be notional?

5.1 Purpose of the cash pool

The cash manager must define the purpose of the cash pool and decide whether it makes sense for the company. Broadly speaking, cash pooling can serve two purposes:

- it gives the cash manager a better understanding of and control over the balances of an MNC's operating companies
- it improves the MNC's interest result

In practice, many companies are more concerned with cash control than with improved interest results.

Whether a company can benefit from cash pooling depends on the company's own operations and policies. Treasurers and cash managers also need to ask:

- Does the company regularly have substantial balances on several accounts at the same time?
- Are the operating companies prepared to have their balances moved to a centrally regulated cash pool or to maintain their main balance at the cash concentration bank of the parent company?
- Is the company able and willing to meet the requirements imposed by the central bank and/or legal authorities?
- Can the organisation cope with the additional administrative work?
- Do the revenues from the cash pool outweigh the external and internal costs?

5.2 Which accounts must be included in the cash pool?

When setting up a cash pool cash managers must decide which accounts are to be included. It's not always necessary to include all of the company's accounts in the pool, especially if accounts have relatively small transaction volumes and balances, because the costs of inclusion may be greater than the benefits. They should consider the costs of transfers to the central account and the credit interest paid on the local account compared to the interest achieved in the cash pool.

5.3 Manual or automated pooling?

Various sweeping options are available: automatic sweeping, manual draw downs and manual replenishments.

5.3.1 Automatic sweeping

With automatic sweeping, bank systems are set up so that sweeping can be executed without human intervention. Sweeps take place every day without interruption, saving an enormous amount of time for the corporate treasury. Automated sweeping can also include back-valued transactions, guaranteeing that the value balance of the sub-accounts is always zero. After the initial set up, the company can leave the management of balances to the bank, with only periodic evaluation of pooling settings.

5.3.2 Manual draw downs and replenishments

Alternatively, sweeping can be done by the companies themselves, but normally this is a manual process in which cash managers periodically check all the accounts and create funds transfers as and when appropriate. Sometimes manual sweeping is performed by the bank or by the cash manager of the various operating companies. Manual sweeping by the bank may take place in less developed countries, where local banks may not have fully automated pooling systems. In this case, the risk of manual sweeping is clear: balances may not be under the control of the cash manager, who will then be unable to invest the funds or use them for lending to subsidiaries with deficits. It will also be more difficult to achieve a true zero balance because sweeping of back-valued transactions is no longer possible.

5.4 Obstacles to setting up cash pools

In many countries local monetary or fiscal regulations make it difficult or even impossible to set up local cash pools or have local accounts participating in cross-border cash pooling.

5.4.1 Monetary regulations

Common monetary restrictions include:

- solvency or capital adequacy requirements
- cash reserve requirements
- reporting obligations
- prohibition of certain types of cash pools

SOLVENCY REQUIREMENTS
Central banks impose solvency requirements on the banks for outstanding credits, including debit positions in current accounts. These solvency requirements mean that the bank must maintain a certain percentage of equity against credits, usually 8%. Since equity is more expensive than debt financing, this requirement leads to higher costs for the banks, which they usually pass on to clients through debit interest rates. When a bank sets up a notional pool, and the central bank does not allow the debit and credit balances of a group of operating companies to be netted against each other for solvency reporting purposes, then the bank will suffer an interest loss. In this case, it is required to maintain a certain percentage of its shareholders' equity against the debit positions, but does not receive interest on the debit position by way of compensation.

CASH RESERVE REQUIREMENTS
Banks are sometimes required to maintain a certain reserve at the central bank against the funds entrusted to them; this is called a 'cash reserve requirement'. Some central banks pay no interest on these reserves, while others may pay interest below the market rate. With notional pooling, the bank has to maintain more cash reserves than with zero balancing, so the bank has to charge the resulting loss of interest to the company.

REPORTING OBLIGATIONS
A number of central banks require the reporting of transfers between resident accounts and non-resident accounts. Although in many cases the bank can assist the client, this usually leads to an extra administrative burden for the company when using physical sweeping.

PROHIBITION OF CERTAIN TYPES OF CASH POOLS

In some countries certain types of cash pools are prohibited. For example, US regulatory authorities do not allow cash pools comprised of accounts maintained in different states, and both the United States and Japan prohibit notional pooling.

5.5 Fiscal regulations

Tax aspects also play a role when setting up cash pools. A few of these aspects are mentioned here:

- interest deductibility
- withholding tax
- transfer pricing
- thin-capitalisation legislation
- controlled foreign corporations legislation

INTEREST DEDUCTIBILITY

The interest paid to banks is not tax deductible in all countries, and in some countries the interest paid to non-banks is not deductible or is only partly deductible. This may be a problem in cases where sweeping leads to inter-company loans.

WITHHOLDING TAX

Many countries levy advance taxation on interest paid, called 'withholding tax'. Tax treaties between most industrialised countries usually enable companies to recover this tax, but sometimes the company must wait a certain period of time before receiving the refund. It always involves an extra administrative burden.

TRANSFER PRICING

We saw that zero balancing involves the mutual extension of inter-company loans between the central treasury and the participating operating companies. Interest is paid on these inter-company loans, and tax authorities expect the going market interest rates to be applied to them. If a MNC uses its own internal rates of interest for inter-company loans, it's known as 'transfer pricing', which is illegal in most countries.

THIN-CAPITALISATION LEGISLATION

In most countries 'thin capitalisation' legislation limits the risk of tax-paying entities having their balance sheets eroded. This is often done by setting a limit on the equity/debt financing ratio, and this legislation plays a particular role with sweeping.

Some countries have introduced Controlled Foreign Corporations (CFC) legislation, which prevents companies from transferring profitable activities, particularly financial activities, to low-taxation countries. CFC legislation requires parent companies to add any revenues from a financial centre in a low-taxation country to its taxable profit. A company considering locating the master account in a tax haven must take possible CFC legislation into account. This legislation is particularly strict in Japan, the United States and the United Kingdom.

5.6 Physical sweeping or notional pooling

188 | The company must make a choice between physical sweeping and notional pooling, which each have certain advantages and disadvantages. The importance of these depends on the country where the pool is set up and the financial circumstances of the company.

5.6.1 Advantages of physical sweeping over notional pooling

With notional pooling, the individual accounts can show overnight debit positions, so an overnight facility must be arranged either for each account separately or for the entire pool. In the latter case, cross guarantees must be issued between all participating operating companies. With zero balancing, no overnight limits are necessary for the sub-accounts.

Notional pooling is forbidden in a number of countries.

We saw that the costs incurred by the solvency requirements for current-account debit positions are higher with notional pools than with physical sweeping, when the central bank does not allow off-setting of debit and credit positions for solvency reporting. The banks pass on these higher costs through for notional-pool interest rates.

To avoid the higher solvency requirement, banks oblige the entities participating in a notional pool to issue mutual guarantees, but these are not necessary with zero balancing pools.

We saw that some central banks require banks to maintain reserves at the central bank against the funds entrusted to them. These costs are higher with notional pooling, and they are reflected in the credit and debit percentages applied to the pool.

5.6.2 Advantages of notional pooling over zero balancing

Since no sweeping transactions take place with notional pooling, no internal current-account administration is necessary, and it's administratively simpler than physical sweeping.

With notional pooling, the participating operating companies retain full control over their own accounts, which may be why local subsidiaries are more willing to co-operate with a notional pooling system than with physical sweeping.

In many countries, sweep transactions between a resident account and a non-resident account must be reported to the central bank, but, of course, this does not apply to notional pooling.

The banks charge costs for executing the sweep transactions, but these costs are avoided with notional pooling.

Physical sweeping gives rise to inter-company loans between the central treasury, on the one hand, and the participating operating companies on the other. These inter-company loans must be stated on the balance sheet, possibly with an adverse impact on certain balance sheet ratios. However, with notional pooling accounting issues may also arise because it is not always possible to report the net balance of a notional pool in the corporate balance sheet.

The table below sums up the respective advantages of physical sweeping and notional pooling:

Advantages zero balancing	Advantages notional pooling
no overnight limits are necessary for the sub-accounts	no internal current account administration is necessary
notional pooling is forbidden in a number of countries	operating companies retain full control over their own accounts
no extra costs incurred in connection with solvency requirements	no reporting requirements to the central bank for sweeps
no need for mutual guarantees to avoid the higher costs of solvency requirements	no transfer costs for sweeps
lower costs for central bank reserve requirements	no impact on balance sheet ratios

Chapter 10
Investment management

Introduction

Once maximum efficiency has been achieved in balance management, the treasurer can turn to the management of excess cash or cash shortages. The aim is to achieve the best possible return on invested liquidity while minimising the funding cost on debits. A reliable cash flow forecast is crucial to enable the company's cash balances to be managed with a longer horizon than several days.

The daily cash flows from the operational or commercial side of the firm will naturally result in daily balance fluctuations. This will occur in various currencies across different current accounts in different jurisdictions. The cash manager's challenge is to achieve the highest possible return on these balances.

Investment, also referred to as fund management, concerns the placement of the company's liquidity positions in the market. Investment management consists, on the one hand, of determining the movement of the future liquidity positions and, on the other, of depositing positions through the money market on the most favourable terms possible - all within the investment policy of the firm.

1
The objectives of investment management

The objectives of investment management are to:

- assure that there is sufficient liquidity in order to meet the company's current and future financial obligations
- optimise the interest results on short-term liquidity positions to minimise the carrying cost of excess cash
- protect the company against sudden interest rate fluctuations

To achieve these objectives the fund manager should have an overview of the individual account balances results in several short or long positions in different currencies to the net position of the company. This can be achieved by automatic concentration structures supplied by banks, or by manual wire transfers, currency conversion, or physical swaps. The cash manager invests these balances in different instruments depending on the profile and characteristics of the firm's balances and predicted cash flows.

2
Defining an investment strategy

The selection of investment instruments depends on the company's treasury policy. This policy translates the firm's liquidity, risk and return profile into a rule to be followed when investing.

A treasury policy describes in detail what the treasurer can and cannot investment in. Policies are sometimes either incomplete or extremely rigid. For example, a policy might authorise investment in deposits with an AA-rated bank but not in AAA-rated money market funds (See also chapter 16). This type of inconsistency should be minimised within a treasury policy. Inconsistencies can result in under-utilisation of available instruments, confusion and ambiguity.

Liquidity investment is a trade-off between liquidity, risk and return. In general terms, a firm can only achieve a higher return than the inter-bank rate if more risk is taken. As invested funds are required to be liquid - which is mostly the case for operational cash balances for most firms - longer term instruments are not an option and yield enhancement is difficult to achieve.

Designing the short-term investment strategy that best matches a company's risk profile typically involves a three-step decision-making process:

1. Determining how a company chooses an optimum mix of liquidity, risk and return
2. Deciding whether an 'outsourced' or 'do-it-yourself' investment style is appropriate
3. Categorising the excess cash positions into different maturity buckets with different investment parameters

2.1 Balancing liquidity, risk, and return

The corporate treasurer must consider three key factors: liquidity, risk and return, which need to be balanced and traded off against each other. What is the desired trade-off between these factors?

2.1.1 Liquidity

The ability to turn at least some of the investments quickly into cash, often within the same day, is generally crucial. Failure to do so can cause the company to default when critical cash payments cannot be met. The need to consider how quickly an instrument can be liquidated, if required, and the associated cost, is a very important consideration when choosing an investment instrument.

EXAMPLE

To unwind a three months deposit after one month can be very costly and jeopardise the return of the deposit completely. This is only the case in an appreciating market; when rates are declining the result is positive. Often a more liquid instrument may be more appropriate.

This example shows clearly the need for accurate forecasting, and matching maturities, when making liquidity decisions. Good forecasts depend on the quality of cash-flow forecasting, as well as sophisticated understanding of the impacts of financial activities such as capital expenditure or acquisitions.

2.1.2 Risk

Appetite for risk when choosing a strategy is arguably the most important variable factor. When dealing with cash investments, the most important variable to consider is the attitude towards capital preservation. Another key risk variable to consider is counterparty risk. This risk can be mitigated by having a maximum risk rating per counterparty. Operational and other risk factors should also be taken into consideration. Levels of risk may be restricted by lenders. Shareholder, rating agency, and corporate objectives will also influence risk appetites. Of course the higher the risk the higher the potential return and potential loss of principal.

2.1.3 Return

Generally, a higher level of return will correspond to a higher level of risk or illiquidity. The need to balance return versus risk is a constant battle. One question to ask is: Should our company make its money by investing its excess cash or should it re-inject its cash in its core processes? By improving the return on excess cash, the treasurer helps to reduce the company's total cost of capital. This should be a primary argument for seeking an appropriate return within the predefined liquidity, risk and return profile of the company.

2.1.4 Choosing the optimal mix

The emphasis placed on each factor is a matter of risk appetite as determined by a company's management. The treasurer usually advises that risk is the primary concern, with liquidity second and return tertiary. A company's assets and its ability to meet its ongoing financial obligations must never be jeopardised for the sake of a marginal improvement in return. The potential for having insufficient liquidity is nearly always too high.

Meanwhile, a variable range of considerations will dictate the risk appetite. In many treasuries the board or a committee of senior management will determine the company's approach to the various investment options and formulate an investment policy. The investment policy or treasury policy generally describes the acceptable instruments, maturities, currencies and counterparties for short-term investment transactions.

Most treasury policies have capital preservation as the primary consideration. Therefore most investment policies are very restrictive and conservative. Most policies do not allow high risk and illiquid instruments. The consequence of this prudent conservatism is a lower overall return on the overall excess cash position. In order to enhance the return on the cash investment, it may be worthwhile to explore the use of alternative instruments such as futures, which are negatively correlated with mainstream financial markets. Alternatively, making use of asset management funds with specific investment expertise, economies of scale and large portfolio effects may be an attractive alternative. As an added benefit due to the economies of scale, these funds typically achieve a much higher diversification ratio compared with individual investment portfolios. As a result, the overall return may be improved without increasing the overall risk profile or becoming illiquid.

2.2 Selecting an 'outsourced' or 'do-it-yourself' investment style

In a world where the efficiency of all areas of companies is keenly scrutinised, treasurers need to make the best possible use of their excess cash. Success here depends on a well-designed and appropriate investment strategy which must be professionally executed. This is especially true when trying to optimise the return of the company's cash position. The treasurer may need to consider taking incremental measured risk to increase the probability of generating excess, or above-bench-mark, returns.

When investing excess liquidity there are two primary alternatives. On the one hand, the company executes the investment strategy itself (active/ do-it-yourself management style) without involving any external skills and resources. On the other hand, the company outsources liquidity investments completely to a professional third party. This is known as a 'passive / outsourced' investment style.

An 'outsourced' solution means that the company asks a professional third party, e.g. an asset manager, to manage the company's cash position. This can be done through the use of money market funds or enhanced cash funds, or through a seg-regated account. With a segregated account, the professional manager takes the company's investment policy, and uses his expertise to manage funds within the policy's guidelines. In all cases, the investor will benefit from the expertise of the market, economies of sale and the professionalism of the asset manager. For this expertise, the company must, however, pay the asset manager a fee.

In the case of a 'do-it-yourself' approach, the company designs a strategy that it be-lieves best represents the company's liquidity, risk and return profile. This has the advantage of greater flexibility and intimacy with the day-to-day cash flows of the firm. This, however, comes at the expense of maintaining a full investment team.

Deciding between the 'outsourced' or 'do-it-yourself' approaches depends on many factors including cost, control, diversification, expertise and return. In many cas-es, the company may decide that a combination of the two best fits its needs. It will make its own investments but will use money market funds and enhanced cash funds, for example, to increase diversification. By adopting this style, the overall blended return of the investment portfolio will be higher without increas-ing the overall risk rating.

2.3 Categorising cash into time buckets

When a company has excess liquidity, the cash typically comes from diverse sourc-es and future uses. Generally, most of the cash results from the company's daily core operations. More may be generated from disinvestments or other corporate fi-nance related transactions.

We must also look at the various future uses of the excess cash. Cash can be used for supplier payables, dividends or repayment of debt, as well for corporate fi-nance-related activities such as acquisitions. At a certain point in time, a company may find itself flooded with free cash. It will look at how the cash can be best utilised to improve its balance sheet. The board may decide to pay a super dividend, or use the cash to start a share buy-back programme, or to spend the cash on the early retirement of bonds. It is clear that the different sources, and future use of the cash will determine the company's options for employing the excess. When determining the different characteristics of the total cash position, we typically see three distinct categories of cash:

- short-term (operational)
- medium-term
- long-term cash (core)

This is an important step in determining the appropriate investment strategy.

SHORT-TERM CASH
Daily fluctuating, or short-term operational, cash is designated for daily cash management and must be available instantly. Daily fluctuating cash must therefore be highly liquid. It is traditionally invested in deposit accounts, but a high yield current account might provide a more convenient option in some situations.

MEDIUM-TERM CASH
Medium-term cash, which is not required for between a few days and three months, has stability that allows it to be invested for a longer period. This, however, remains relatively short-term, primarily invested in weekly deposits or short-term money market funds. A key determinant is guaranteed availability at short notice.

LONG-TERM CASH
Long-term cash is available for investment for periods of more than three months. These funds can, typically, be invested across a wider range of instruments. A longer time horizon allows for more strategic placement. It frees the treasurer to focus on above-money market returns. Normally, companies keep this cash to a minimum because investment returns are unlikely to match the carrying cost of cash.

The following graph shows how the three time buckets comprise the total excess cash position of a company. If clarity can be determined for the different time buckets, the company can deploy its operating and excess cash more strategically. Of course, a constant evaluation of the categorisation is crucial to assure that the treasury keeps making the right investment decisions.

Figure 1   *The composition of the excess cash position*

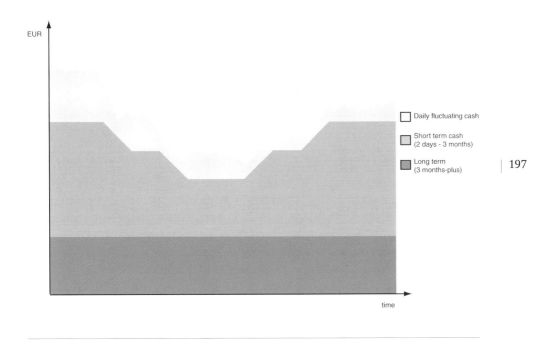

EUR

Daily fluctuating cash

Short term cash
(2 days - 3 months)

Long term
(3 months-plus)

time

3
The day-to-day decision making process of fund management

Once the investment horizon has been identified, the cash manager first has to draw up a liquidity forecast to determine the time horizon of his investment or funding decisions.

Then, he has to decide on the terms of the transactions he wants to conclude.

Finally, he has to decide what kind of instruments he wants to invest in or will use to cover a shortfall. The selection of investment instruments depends on the company's treasury policy. This policy translates the firm's liquidity, risk and return profile into a rule to be followed when investing.

3.1 Drawing up liquidity forecasts

Based on accurate and reliable cash flow forecasts of the operations and cleared balances on accounts, a treasurer should be able to identify the total balances accessible for a company to invest. Operational balances in the same currency can either be concentrated – automatically or manually – from a variety of group companies to form a single bucket of cleared balances for investment. As mentioned earlier, this can be achieved by employing cash concentration techniques such as sweeping or notional pooling. Alternatively, the treasurer can invest a number of smaller balances in different locations, although this can create execution risk, missed self-funding opportunities, and attract additional reconciliation costs.

Armed with accurate and timely balance information from his bank and own back offices, the cash manager should be able to make the appropriate decision as to how such surplus funds should be utilised. In nearly every instance, his goals are firstly to reduce total borrowing costs and then to maximise interest income.

A liquidity forecast is a best estimate of the company's future liquidity positions. The liquidity forecast provides a picture of the company's expected financial position in the coming period.

The cash position statement is a liquidity forecast for only one day. To make a liquidity forecast, the fund manager needs information from the various areas within the company, as well as balance positions reported by the bank. The departments that supply the most essential information on future money flows are:

- the sales department, which reports on expected receivables
- purchasing department, which reports on planned payables
- the different operating companies and subsidiaries, which report onspecific in- and out-going flows
- the corporate finance department, which can give a forewarning of 'extraordinary' events
- the treasury itself, which reports when certain loans mature for re-financing and when certain interest payments for debt are scheduled

The information which the treasury receives from its bank to compile an accurate forecast should contain the following information:

- daily balances in all accounts
- effected payments (incoming and outgoing)
- maturity dates of current investments such as deposits and money market loans

After having determined the expected balance, the cash manager should know the expected positions for each currency, and whether he has an overall net liquidity surplus or deficit. The liquidity forecast should allow him to estimate how long these surpluses or deficits will remain.

All this information contributes to an ongoing process, leading to an accurate forecast and enabling the treasurer to allocate the excess cash into different maturity buckets. This allows for the most efficient deployment of the various cash positions as previously discussed.

3.2 Determining the term of the cash investments/borrowings

The terms of the different instruments a cash manager can use to invest cash surpluses or cover cash shortfalls, are dependent on:

- the duration of the company's liquidity surpluses or deficits
- the extent to which the cash manager wishes to be able to dispose of the liquidity (flexibility)
- the difference in interest rates between the various terms (yield curve)

THE DURATION OF THE LIQUIDITY SURPLUSES AND DEFICITS
With the help of the liquidity forecasts, the cash manager can estimate how long the liquidity surpluses or deficits will last. In principle, the cash manager will match the timing of the investments, or funding, to the term of these positions.

FLEXIBILITY
Sometimes the cash manager is not certain of the outcome or timing of the liquidity forecasts. Unexpected events often happen in the course of a treasurer's and cash manager's day. In such cases, the cash manager needs to make certain that there is an adequate funding buffer of investments with a higher liquidity profile. This means the full investment portfolio is easy to liquidate - turn into real available cash. If this is the case, you will find a strong bias away from long-term deposits. If, for example, some of the funds will be used for a dividend payment within six months, this amount can be invested for a matching term. This, of course, will only be done if it does not weaken the company's ability to meet its financial obligations. Unwinding a six-month deposit before the due date can be very costly and generate a negative net return.

Where the company does not have a full treasury operation, and the return is more of a tertiary objective, the company may rightly adopt convenience as the primary driver of its investment decisions. Instead of placing funds in instruments that require a daily roll, the company will simply leave excess cash in its high yield current account. By adopting this instrument, the cash manager achieves a near-market return, but will achieve immediate access to its invested liquidity with minimum effort on his own part.

The yield curve is a graphic representation of the return set against an investment horizon. It indicates the relationship between the various terms and the related interest rate yields. Normally, the longer the term the higher the yield. This is generally the case, but not necessarily an absolute rule. The shape of the yield curve can change quickly.

200 | The short term yield curve is primarily driven by the central bank's interest rate policy in the country in question. Expectations that a central bank will raise rates quickly will appear in the yield curve. If it is the expectation the central bank will, for example, raise the rates by 25bps in two months time, the difference in yield of two and three month rates will show this difference. The rate increases are, in this case, already priced into the market.

Depending on market expectations of future interest rates, clients can select investments with longer or shorter maturities – always considering primarily the company's own cash flow forecasts.

The following example shows how the cash manager can use his interest rate outlook as a basis for the term of money market transactions.

EXAMPLE

A cash manager sees that his liquidity position allows him to place a deposit for a period of six months. Additionally, he knows that the current three-month interest rate amounts to 3.20% and that the six-month rate is 3.40%.

However, the cash manager expects the central bank to raise interest rates in one or several steps in the very near future, thus pushing up the three-month interest rate to 3.75%.

In line with his interest outlook, he will opt for a three-month deposit. His return on the first three months will then be 3.20%. The return he expects to generate over the following three months is 3.75%. The 'average' over the total period of six months is thus 3.475%, while a six-month deposit would have yielded 3.40%. Of course, the treasurer in this case is betting against the market. If the market anticipated that the rate would be 3.75% in three months, this would be factored into the curve. If the treasurer is wrong and rates do not move, he will have sacrificed 20 bps over the period.

The cash manager's decision regarding the term also depends on his risk 'appetite'. A cautious cash manager would, in the above case, simply settle for the six-month deposit with a guaranteed return of 3.40% over the entire investment horizon.

3.3 Choosing the appropriate Instrument for investing

The range of investment opportunities is greater than ever. While low-risk deposit or money market investments remain the primary destination of excess cash, there is a growing range of alternatives for investing excess for relatively long periods of time. It is now possible for the treasurer to leverage the full capabilities offered by large financial services groups in order to achieve the optimum trade-off between liquidity, risk and return. Any investment strategy must be drawn up in accordance with the corporation's guidelines and stated investment objectives.

When investing excess cash, various types of instruments can be used. All instruments serve a different purpose and have different characteristics. The cash manager can choose between the following investment opportunities:

- deposits
- near-banking deposits
- money market paper
- banker's acceptances
- money market mutual funds

3.3.1 Deposits

A deposit is a loan. One party deposits money with another party for an agreed term and at an agreed rate. The deposit rate is usually close to the interbank rate and higher than the interest rate on a current account. The lender takes on the risk of the other party, generally another bank in the case of a deposit placed by a bank.

The interest rate of a deposit is fixed during its term. As a result, neither party is exposed to interest rate risk during the term of the deposit. A company can place deposits with its bank in different currencies and for different terms. The minimum term for a deposit is one day (call deposit or overnight deposit), except for the US, which sets a minimum term of seven days by regulation for it's domestic market. Typical deposit periods are one, two and three weeks and one, two, three, six and 12 months.

Deposits are generally not traded by banks in the US money market. When banks in the United States borrow funds for short terms from non-banks, they issue short-term financial instruments called certificates of deposit. US banks can also participate in the Fed Funds marketplace which is restricted to banks.

3.3.2 'Near banking' deposits

Companies and governments sometimes lend money to one another directly. These transactions take place outside the normal banking system and are sometimes referred to as 'near banking' deposits. Basically, the investor assumes the role of a bank in such cases. Near banking deposits are almost always executed with the help of a broker.

When placing a near banking deposit, the investor must make sure the debtor is creditworthy. Otherwise, he runs the risk of late payment or non-payment (credit risk).

3.3.3 Structured deposits

A structured deposit is essentially a combination of a deposit and an investment product, where the return depends on the performance of some underlying market rate. Like regular deposits, a structured deposit is principal-protected. But instead of providing a fixed interest rate, the return of a structured deposit is variable.

The underlying market rate can reflect variables ranging from a currency rate to a commodity price; from a share price to an interest rate. The investor gives up (a part of) his deposit coupon, which the bank uses to buy options for the client. If the options are in the money at the expiry date, the investor will receive a payout.

An example of a structured deposit is the 'Tower Deposit'. A Tower Deposit is a deposit offering an above market return if a particular exchange rate remains within a certain bandwidth, and a lower than market return if it moves outside these bands. The rates depend on the term of the deposit, the range width and the minimum rate. The lower than market return can be as low as 0%. The investor decides on the term of the deposit and the range he expects the exchange rate to remain within.

If the excange rate falls on or outside the range, the client receives the minimum rate.

A P&J plc fund manager has EUR 10 million which he wishes to place on deposit for the coming four months. He would normally receive 2.70% p.a. on a fixed deposit for this period. The current EUR/USD spot rate is 1.20. The fund manager expects no significant movements in EUR/USD rates over the four months and wishes to benefit from this view. He is willing to accept a lower return if his view on the EUR/USD rate is incorrect.

The return of the Tower Deposit will be 6.00% if the EUR/USD spot rate remains between 1.18500 and 1.27500 throughout the reference period. If the range is broken, the client receives a lower return of 0.5 %.

3.3.4 *Money market paper*

Money market paper is a negotiable short-term bond. The maximum term is two years in the euro money market and, typically, 270 days in the US money market, because issues of 270 days or less in the US money market are exempt from registration. Depending on the issuer, we can distinguish between:

- Commercial paper, issued by companies, lower government and institutions and
- Certificates of deposit, issued by commercial banks

The following bonds are unique to the US money market:

- Treasury bills, issued by the Federal government
- Municipal notes, issued by municipalities
- Federal Agency short-term securities, issued by federally sponsored agencies e.g. The Farm Credit System

If an investor buys commercial paper, he runs a credit risk. Therefore, it is crucial that the investor has reliable information on the quality of the issuing organisation. To meet the investors' information requirements, issuers of commercial paper generally apply for a rating at one or more of the well-known rating agencies such as Standard & Poor's, Moody's and Fitch I.B.C.A. These institutions assess companies and express their opinion of the company's quality in a fixed letter-figure combination known as the 'rating'. Companies often stipulate in their treasury policy that the treasurer or cash manager may exclusively invest in securities of companies with a certain minimum rating, e.g. A1-P1 (this indicates a good short-term rating both at Standard & Poor's and Moody's).

Money market paper can be traded during the applicable term. This gives the investor the advantage that he can sell the paper if faced with a sudden cash shortage. A downgrade in the creditworthiness of the issuer, however, logically decreases both the price and the ability to liquidate the paper.

3.3.5 Banker's acceptances

A banker's acceptance is a bill of exchange which has been accepted by a bank. A bill of exchange is a piece of paper bearing a payment instruction. A company may send a bill of exchange to the customer who, by signing the paper, enters into an obligation to pay. Sometimes, the company also requires the bill of exchange to be accepted by a bank. This means that the signature from a bank is added to it. If the bank accepts the bill of exchange, it acts as guarantor of the payment. The bill of exchange is then called a banker's acceptance. Banker's acceptances can be traded in the money market. Generally speaking, they are comparable to certificates of deposit.

3.3.6 Money market mutual funds

Money market mutual funds or cash funds are investment funds that invest in money market instruments. The advantage of using such funds is that cash is not tied up for a fixed term and can be accessed at any time. On retrieving their investment, investors get back the initial capital invested and the return realised over the investment period. Given that these funds strive to return the principal plus interest, they are often referred to as stable Net Asset Value funds (stable NAV funds).

Another advantage of money market funds compared to, for example, an investment in commercial paper or a near banking short-term loan is the diversification of risk. A money market fund portfolio manager invests in a wide variety of short-term money market instruments which are collectively owned by all investors in the fund. The allowable money market investments are stated by a prospectus and in some countries by regulation.

The risk of a money market fund collapsing is many times smaller than the riks of one individual counterparty defaulting on its obligations. Last but not least, it is a convenient instrument. This is because of the fact that a company can make arrangements with its bank to ensure that any surpluses in its current accounts are automatically swept to the bank's money market fund or, vice versa, that debit balances are eliminated.

3.3.7 Products for covering a cash shortfall

In the case of a liquidity shortfall, the cash manager can use an overdraft facility on the company's current account, or can choose between taking a money market loan or issuing money market paper.

MONEY MARKET LOANS

A company can borrow money from a bank. If the term of this loan is short, the loan is referred to as a money market loan. The terms vary from one day up to two years. The interest rate is fixed during the term of the loan and is usually much lower than the interest rate which a bank charges on a current account overdraft.

COMMERCIAL PAPER

A company which wants to raise money can issue commercial paper. In order to do so, it must set up a commercial paper programme. Banks operate as the arranger of commercial paper programmes. As such, they prepare prospectuses and notify the central bank of the programme. The prospectus must not only contain information about the company, but also the maximum amount that may be issued must be mentioned.

The bank also plays the role of broker (issuing and paying agent). In this capacity the bank is not exposed to any debtor risk. This risk lies with the buyer of the commercial paper.

Once a commercial paper programme is set up, the issuer can ask the bank to look for investors, whenever he needs funds. The amount of the issue, the term and the yield are set by the issuer.

After the investment horizon has been identified, an appropriate strategy can be defined to optimise each bucket. We will now consider the different investment products available. Taking the previous section into consideration and factoring in the heterogeneity of the excess cash, we will consider a portfolio of different investment products which can meet the company's specific investment horizons. Such an investment portfolio can give the company a blended return, while meeting its liquidity requirements and risk appetite.

3.4 Determining the liquidity investment portfolio

When the investment horizon is identified an appropriate strategy can be defined to optimise each bucket. We will now consider the different investment products available. Taking the previous section into consideration and factoring in the heterogeneity of the excess cash, we will consider a portfolio of different investment products which can meet the company's specific investment horizons. Such an investment portfolio can give the company a blended return, while meeting its liquidity requirements and risk appetite.

Figure 2   *Investment products in the money market*

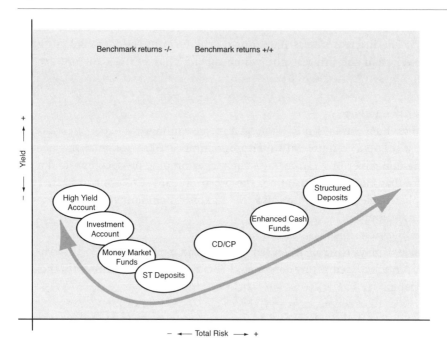

The above picture reflects a typical risk versus value primarily for short-term and medium-term cash products. It is clear from the illustration that risk and return are generally positively related to each other. But when investing overnight balances, additional factors must be considered – the operational risk, transaction settlement costs, monitoring costs and booking accounting costs. Small incremental yield can quickly be consumed by higher transaction monitoring costs and booking accounting costs. For example, a high yield current account may earn marginally less than an equivalent overnight deposit, but once transaction and reconciliation costs are factored in, the high yield current account may generate a net benefit. For example, a high yield current account can provide a near-market return without requiring any actions by the cash manager. By comparison, overnight deposits involve significant activities, particularly back office exercises such as booking entries and reconciling investment and redemption, as well as the interest. Consequently, the net benefit of the placement may be quickly eroded. This is especially true if the cash manager executes deposits daily.

We have seen that the following factors determine the investment portfolio:
- the liquidity risk and return profile
- the size of the forecast liquidity surpluses or deficits
- the different time buckets
- the degree of convenience desired

As seen in the previous sections, most companies are very risk adverse and, as a result, the treasury policy will not allow the fund manger to enter certain products. For most companies, liquidity is the most important variable. This is particularly true if the company is not flush with excess cash. As a result, a company will not enter into long-term (more than several months) investment contracts without having the possibility to freely unwind the transaction. What is possible depends on the cash flow forecast, its accuracy and how the excess cash is divided across the different time buckets.

The following example shows how an investment portfolio can be constituted, taking into account the above considerations.

EXAMPLE

P&J plc has excess cash of 50 mio EUR, 10 mio is really excess operational cash, another 15 mio can really be considered as long or core cash and will probably be used at the end of the year as a dividend payment. The rest of the cash is available for a couple of weeks up to several months. The investment manger of P&J plc has decided, which is heavily dictated by its treasury policy, to keep 80% of the total balance liquid. He has constructed the following portfolio:

- 10mio EUR is parked on a high yield current account, providing the convenience he is looking for;
- 25mio EUR is invested in an overnight money market fund
- 10mio EUR is invested in an enhanced yield fund
- 5mio EUR is invested in a six-month deposit till the end of the year

The high yield current account (HYCA) is convenient for the investment manager and means that he need not to be worried if funds stay in his bank account because the balance on the HYCA will automatically receive competitive remuneration. The money market fund provides him with investment diversification and the funds are redeemable daily until the 12 p.m., which is important should he need more cash during the day. The enhanced yield fund provides him with an opportunity for a higher yield, although the fund provides him with liquidity with a short notice period. The six-month term deposit provides him with an extra yield pick-up which has a positive effect on the portfolio's total return. Of the total portfolio, only

10% is illiquid. A secondary benefit of such an investment approach is that the total portfolio is low maintenance, has a minimum AA risk rating, and gives a good blended return. Depending on the allocation per instrument, the blended return should beat overnight market benchmarks.

This example shows clearly the benefit of keeping some funds liquid in case of unforeseen expenditures or inaccurate forecasts. Not all information that reaches the cash manager from the various departments and units is equally reliable. Consequently, actual income and expenditure can vary to a greater or lesser degree from forecast income and expenditure. This, of course, varies by business and by volume and predictability of cash flows.

4
Evaluating investment management

As with the other cash management disciplines, the cash manager must evaluate the investment management performance regularly. The central question to be answered is whether interest income on surpluses has been maximised and interest charges on deficits minimised – while maintaining adequate liquidity to support operational needs. Additionally, the cash manager will want to establish whether the period in question contained any days where a liquidity deficit forced the cancellation, or postponement, of planned activities.

During the evaluation of investment management, the cash manager will make the following analyses:

- an analysis whether the investment strategy is still adequate and does it still service its purpose?
- an analysis whether the liquidity, risk and return profile still are appropriate?
- an analysis whether how successfully liquidity forecasting has met with actual liquidity positions?
- an analysis of the current book balances to confirm that all liquidity positions have been deposited or replenished in the money market
- an analysis of the term and timing of investment transactions to find out whether investments and loans have been effectively staggered (i.e. spread out over time)
- an analysis of the current interest result set against the optimal interest result (calculated retrospectively)
- an analysis of the performance of the total investment portfolio against the required benchmark.

These analyses enable the cash manager to establish whether his forecasts and/or investment decisions were correct. The cash manager performs a daily evaluation of the cash position statements. Every day he assesses whether large forecast payments (both incoming and outgoing) have actually been realised. If not, he will 'shift' these to the next day.

If the evaluation shows the following results, the cash manager knows he has done a good job:

- no material deficit or surplus liquidity positions in current accounts
- a good and balanced diversity in the investment portfolio which is in line with treasury policy and with the current liquidity risk and return profile

If the evaluation shows that one or more of the following situations have occurred, he knows that certain changes are required in the coming period:

- large debit or credit balances in current account
- all deposits and/or loans have extremely long, or short, terms
- many deposits or loans with the same maturity date

The cash manager must then try to trace the causes of this sub-optimal performance. Possible reasons are:

- errors in liquidity forecasts
- mis-interpretation of liquidity forecasts
- inaccurate interest outlook
- investments in wrong products or bad debtors

If this is done periodically, the cash manager will be able to finesse the cash management process to make it as effective as possible.

Chapter 11
Cash flow management

One of the corporate treasury's core tasks is to manage the company's cash flows. These are the funds flowing into and out of the company, as well as between the company's subsidiaries. As we know, multinational corporation (MNC) cash flows occur at any moment in time, and happen in different currencies on different bank accounts and in different countries. Corporate treasury must orchestrate this logistical process in such a way that transactions happen at the right time, in the right place and at minimum costs.

In this chapter, we look at options available to the company to improve its control of cash flow. We discuss various ways of reducing the costs of payment processing, especially the costs related to cross-border payments and to inter-company payments. Transaction costs can be reduced not only by reviewing and pushing down bank fees, but also by changing the structure of the cash flows, i.e. by routing international payments through offshore accounts, and by netting-off inter-company payables and receivables. The company can also realise cost savings by centralising its transaction processes into 'Payment' or 'Collection Factories'.

1
Cash flow management: definition, objectives and instruments

Cash flow management comprises the management of the company's payment flows, both with third parties and between its entities. This includes settlement of transactions in bank accounts, as well as through internal accounts managed by the company itself.

The objectives of cash flow management are:

- to minimise the internal and external costs of the payment flows
- to control the timing of the transactions in order to optimise the company's liquidity position

The following types of cash flows can be distinguished:

- outgoing payments:
    - vendor payments
    - tax payments
    - payments of social security contributions
    - payments to utility companies
    - payroll payments
- incoming payments:
    - collections from customers
    - tax repayments
    - subsidies
- treasury payments
- inter-company payments

The company's cash flows can be visualised in a cash flow structure. A simple cash flow structure is shown in the following diagram.

Figure 1   *The cash flow structure of a company*

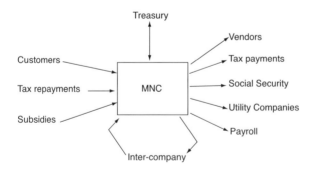

A company has the following three options to reduce its transaction costs and to improve its control:

- cost saving measures within the existing cash flow structure
- changing the cash flow structure
- changing the internal organisation

2
Saving costs within the existing cash flow structure

The company can reduce the payment costs in various ways without adjusting the existing cash flow structure. These measures include:

- negotiating lower payment charges
- reducing bank float and value dating
- substituting expensive payments products for more cost effective instruments
- reducing internal handling costs
- collecting fast and paying late

2.1 Negotiating lower payment charges

The costs that banks charge for payment services are negotiable to a limited extent. Payment products are increasingly becoming 'commodities'. This trend is already well-established in the United States and Western Europe and is now spreading to other regions. Prices have been driven down by fierce competition and competitive charges apply to everyone buying these services, with only limited scope for price variances.

A treasurer is, therefore, well advised to check regularly whether the company is still paying the going market rate. Another important factor is the manner in which payment services are purchased – at decentralised level by the operating companies, or at centralised level by the corporate treasurer. Companies that opt for centralised purchasing can often benefit from lower rates.

2.2 Reducing bank float and value dating

Bank float is the time that a transfer is 'in transit' – the time lapse between the moment that the payer's account is debited (book date) and the moment that the beneficiary's account is credited (book date). Bank float particularly affects international payments involving more than one bank. When several banks take part in a transfer, it is often very difficult to ascertain which bank is still 'sitting' on the money.

To avoid bank float, companies can try to avoid international payments, i.e. by using offshore accounts. However, bank float can also occur in domestic payments processes, depending in which countries the payments are made. Often, all inter-company payments are entrusted to a single bank, so that the cash manager can negotiate zero float conditions for inter-company payments.

Banks may also apply value dating, when an amount transferred only starts earning interest one or more days after it has been posted to the account. Value dating is traditionally used by banks to compensate for transaction services, enabling them to apply lower transaction fees.

Value dating can often be influenced by the customer. In many countries, banks can reduce or switch off value dating when the company prefers to pay transaction fees. Under the new rules of the Single Euro Payments Area, which will be effective from 2008 onwards, value dating can no longer be applied by banks transferring euro payments across the euro area. In some countries, however, value dating practices may not always be clear and transparent. Therefore, it is recommended to investigate how banks handle value dating and to use reputable banks which are able to offer efficient payment services.

2.3 Substituting expensive payment products with cost effective instruments

The company must select the correct payment instrument for each outgoing and incoming payment. In general, the cash manager will select the payment method with the lowest costs, the fewest manual operations and the highest reliability (particularly in terms of timing and value dating).

The company will seek to avoid expensive and inefficient payment products such as:

- incoming cheques
- cash payments
- manual transfers

and may want to replace these payment instruments with efficient payment products such as:

- direct debits: where the payor signs a statement (direct debit mandate) allowing the company to debit automatically the debtor's account. This will give the company full control on the date of payment;

- high value payments: we know that these payments are credited to the beneficiary's account on the same day (and with the same value date). High value payments offer an efficient method for urgent payments, but are generally too expensive for ordinary vendor payments.

In short, it is important to establish which instrument is used for each type of payment, and then to find out whether an alternative payment product is cheaper, or gives tighter control in terms of payment timing.

2.4 Reducing internal handling costs

The internal costs of preparing and delivering payment instructions, and processing collections, are often significantly higher than the external costs. Companies are using electronic banking connections to deliver payment instructions and to receive information about receivables. In order to minimise processing costs, these electronic banking systems must be connected to the Accounts Payable system and the Accounts Receivable system. In addition, it is critical that the information between the client's applications and the bank can be exchanged fully automatically. This is called 'Straight-Through Processing' (STP). The more automatic the process is, the lower the costs will be.

Electronic banking technology and industry standardisation have been developed extensively in the last couple of years, enabling companies to establish automatic interfaces with virtually every accounting or enterprise resource planning system. The biggest challenge now is to achieve a high degree of standardisation of remittance information. This is the information in the payment instruction needed for the receiver to automatically identify which client has paid which invoice. Software companies have developed systems which enable companies to almost automatically reconcile outstanding receivables and incoming receipts.

2.5 Collecting fast – paying late

Additional savings can be achieved by speeding up the collection of receivables and not paying outstanding debts until this is economically and commercially needed.

Outgoing payments should be made not before the payments are due according to the agreed terms of payments, or before the day deemed acceptable by the company doing business with the supplier. It is critical to organise the payments process in such a way that it facilitates these 'just in time' payments.

Companies with effective working capital processes can substantially reduce their borrowing requirements, or increase their excess liquidity positions. This helps to minimise the company's interest charges, or maximise its interest income.

3
Changing the company's cash flow structure

Another way of realising cost savings is to make changes in the company's cash flow structure. To assess the possibilities for cost reduction, the company should create an overall view of its most important cash flows. The following cash flows must be made visible:

- inflows and outflows of each operating company
- inter-company flows, domestic and cross-border
- cross-border flows with third parties
- separate flows in the most important currencies (i.e. USD, EUR, GBP etc)

Once the company has an accurate picture of the cash flow structure, it can explore the various opportunities for changing the routing of payment flows to achieve additional cost savings. We distinguish between:

- changing the routing of cross-border cash flows, and
- changing the routing of inter-company cash flows

3.1 Changing the routing of cross-border cash flows

Cross-border payments are relatively expensive due to higher transfer fees and bank float. For Western Europe this will change when the Single Euro Payments Area is implemented in 2008 – 2010. This will create a Europe-wide clearing infrastructure, allowing cross-border payments in euro to be processed as domestic payments at domestic rates with zero float. However, cross-border payments in other currencies will still be processed through the correspondent banking system.

To reduce transfer costs, companies may consider replacing cross-border payments with local transfers. We will look at incoming and outgoing cross-border payments successively.

3.1.1 Incoming cross-border payments

A company receiving many export orders from many different customers in a given country will be faced with a large volume of incoming cross-border payments from that country. It will not always be possible, or desirable, to pass the costs of the cross-border transfers on to the customers.

One solution is to open a non-resident or 'offshore' account in the country in question. If such an account is mainly used to receive incoming payments, it is called a collection account. The cash manager will open the offshore account with a local bank, or a foreign branch of its own bank in the export country.

Customers in that country can then transfer money via the local clearing system, and at the lower local rates, to the exporter's local account. The incoming amounts collected in this manner can then be periodically transferred (automatically or manually) to the central account, which the company maintains with its cash concentration bank in its home country. As a result, the company will only be charged the higher costs of a foreign transfer when the funds are swept to the home country.

3.1.2 Outgoing cross-border payments

Some companies need to make many payments to suppliers abroad. If these payments are made from a bank account in the home country, the resulting cross-border payments will often be conducted through a correspondent bank. To avoid the high costs of such cross-border payments, many companies open an offshore account abroad in the country of the beneficiary. The payments to the beneficiaries in that country can then be made out of this account. The payment instructions are delivered to the foreign bank using an electronic banking system. These 're-mote local payments' will be processed through the local clearing system in the country of the beneficiary.

3.1.3 Examples of changing the routing of cross-border cash flows

We will now give two examples where the routing of cross-border cash flows is changed.

The first example concerns a French company with suppliers and customers in the UK. Initially, the French company does not have a non-resident account in the UK. Both the French company and its suppliers invoice in GBP. In the cash flow structure of the French company, we see parallel cross-border payment flows in GBP going in opposite directions. This is shown in the figure below.

Figure 2   *Cross-border cash flows of a French MNC to and from the UK*

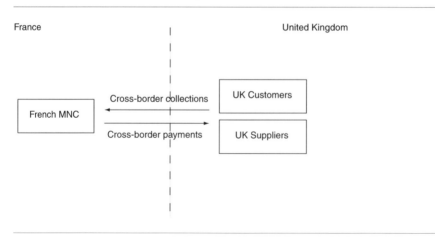

To save costs the French company can decide to open a non-resident account in the UK. This account can be used to receive local payments from customers and to make local payments to suppliers. From time to time, the central treasury will have to fund the offshore account, or transfer excess cash to the company's bank in France. A diagram of the company's cash flow structure now looks as follows:

Figure 3   *Routing cash flows through an offshore account*

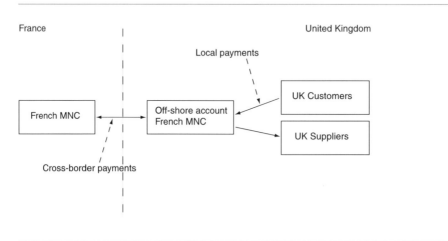

By re-routing the cross-border payment flows, the French company will benefit from the following advantages:

- the French company pays local rates in the UK for its outgoing and incoming transactions;
- reduced bank float: incoming payments are received earlier, outgoing payments can leave later, resulting in improved liquidity and enhanced interest results;
- better service to local customers, they can pay to a local account, which is easier and cheaper;
- better commercial position for the French company, showing a 'local face' in the UK market.

In our second example, the Japanese company Cyber Tech sells its computer hardware through operating companies in various countries around the world such as Germany, Italy and the United Arab Emirates (U.A.E.). Invoicing takes place in USD. All operating companies have a USD account with a local bank in the country where they operate.

Figure 4   *Cross-border USD payments to USD accounts held with local banks*

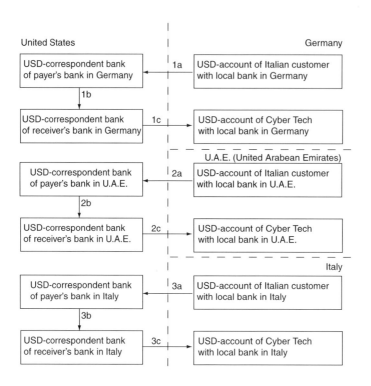

Local customers in these countries send payment instructions to their local bank, which then instructs their correspondent bank in the United States through SWIFT to move dollars to the correspondent bank of the beneficiary (receiver's) bank (arrows 1a, 2a and 3a). The correspondent bank of the payer's bank transfers money through the US clearing system, usually CHIPS, to the correspondent bank of the beneficiary's bank (arrows 1b, 2b and 3b), which then sends a SWIFT message to the beneficiary bank informing it that the funds have been received (arrows 1c, 2c and 3c). The local bank of the payer sends a SWIFT message to the local bank of Cyber Tech asking it to credit the funds to Cyber Tech's account (not pointed out in the figure).

The above method for collecting USD payments is quite common, but it has two disadvantages:

- complicated routing makes payments error-prone and expensive, as every transfer goes through the correspondent bank system and borders have to be crossed twice each time
- USD balances are spread over the USD accounts maintained by Cyber Tech operating companies with local banks, making it more difficult for Cyber Tech to manage its USD liquidity

The company now decides that all operating companies must maintain an account with one and the same bank in the United States. All operating companies now open an offshore account in their name with e.g. ABNAMRO Bank in New York. The new cash flow structure looks as follows:

| 221

Figure 5   *Cross-border USD payments to offshore accounts with ABN AMRO Bank*

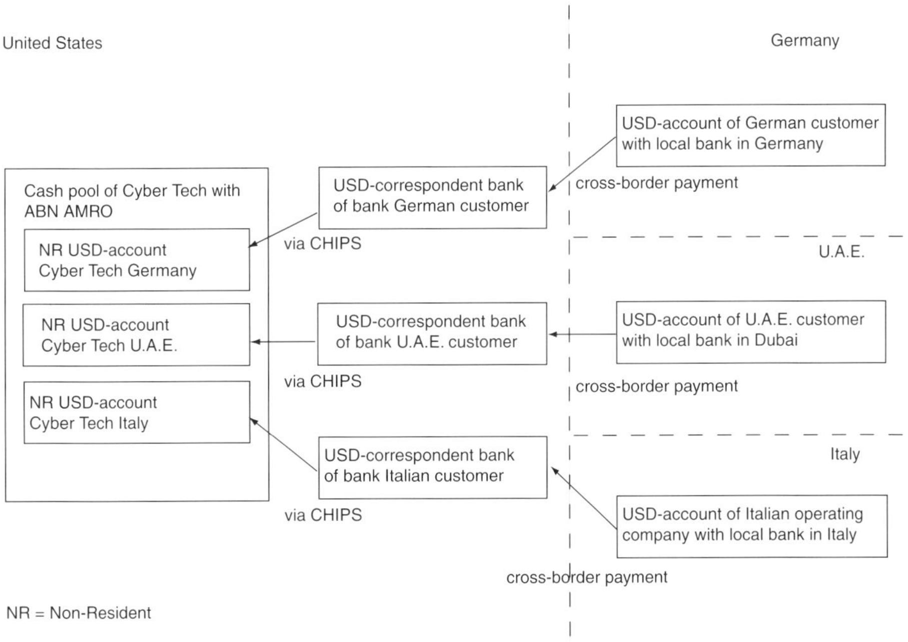

NR = Non-Resident

After the transfer instructions are delivered by the customers and their local banks, the routing of the payments is now much shorter. The transfers can now take place in just two steps, from the customer's local bank to the correspondent banks and from the USD-correspondent banks with a local transfer to ABN AMRO. The transfer only crosses the border once. The Cyber Tech companies no longer need to engage the services of a correspondent bank and so avoid the related costs. This solution is also beneficial from a cash balances management perspective. All USD cash balances are concentrated in New York and the accounts are included in the same cash pool. The overall balance can be automatically swept every day to an interest bearing account, to a money market fund or be deposited in the US money market.

Customers have the advantage of being able to give simpler payment instructions. However, they do not realise any cost savings as they still need to use their own correspondent banks and pay the costs of these services. These costs can only be reduced when Cyber Tech decides to collect its receivables in local currency and use local collection accounts.

We can conclude that a company should open an offshore account in the country where the respective currency is cleared if its operations involve very large volumes of transfers in that currency. If the volume of these transfers is small, then the company must look at the value of the individual transfers, and the costs of the cross-border payments, to decide whether an offshore account makes sense.

Figure 6   *When to use offshore accounts*

Number of cross-border-payments	Amounts transferred	
	Low	High
High	off-shore account	off-shore account
Low	Account in home country	Off-shore account or account in home country

3.2 Changing inter-company cash flows

Inter-company payments are payments between two business units of a single company. The volume and values involved can be substantial, particularly at large MNCs. The business units of MNCs often deliver services and products to each other, giving rise to mutual debts and receivables that must be settled by means of inter-company payments. Many of these inter-company transfers are cross-border payments. If such cross-border payments are conducted through the traditional correspondent banking infrastructure, there are often opportunities for major cost reductions.

A company can lower the costs of inter-company payments by settling the transactions on internal current accounts or by settling the transactions in a multi-currency centre.

A company can also set up a netting system.

3.2.1 Settling through internal accounts

A company can set up an internal system of current accounts to effect inter-company payments. Many enterprise resource planning systems have this capability. The internal transactions are settled through these internal accounts without any money actually being transferred via the bank. One disadvantage of this system is the effort to set the system up and maintain it. However, the savings on transfer charges may outweigh the extra administrative workload and costs, particularly if the company has large volumes of cross-border payments.

3.2.2 Settling through a multi-currency centre

Alternatively, a company can channel all its inter-company transactions through external bank accounts. However, these bank accounts are now held in one country. Many large international companies operate multi-currency accounts in London or Amsterdam. They have set up accounts in the name of their subsidiaries – these accounts are combined in different cash pools per currency.

Often these companies have negotiated very competitive rates for the transactions and transfers with zero float. Funds can now be moved quite easily and cheaply between subsidiary accounts. In most cases, the companies have decentralised administrations and decentralised payments initiation. The subsidiaries initiate payment transactions using the electronic banking system of the bank operating the multi-currency centre, and they can monitor their balances and transactions through the same system.

4
Netting

Netting is an important method to optimise cash flow and working capital management of a company. It comprises the administrative off-setting of reciprocal cash flows, after which only the computed net cash flow is actually settled. This should not be confused with netting used in inter-bank clearing systems where inter-bank payments are off-set against each other. When we speak of netting here, we refer to the process of off-setting payment flows between companies or between different business units of a company.

Two forms of netting are distinguished: bilateral netting, between two parties, and multilateral netting, between a larger number of parties. With bilateral netting, one of the two parties keeps the administrative records. With multilateral netting, the company usually sets up a separate unit, called the netting centre. This unit collects, orders and nets all inter-company obligations as far as possible. Sometimes the netting function is outsourced to a bank or other service provider.

Apart from the settlement of inter-company commerce, the following internal transactions can also be effected through the netting system:

- intra-group loans
- interest payments
- dividends
- investments
- commission payments

In addition, it is possible to streamline external transactions through a netting system when large numbers of reciprocal transactions happen with certain external parties. In agreement with these parties invoices could be logged into the netting system and settlement of the net amounts can be done on the same day as for the internal settlements.

4.1 Example of netting

The following example shows the impact that netting can have on the cash flows of a MNC. The company has various business units delivering goods to each other, with each company issuing an invoice in its own local currency. First we give an overview of the inter-company payments that can be expected before the company changed over to a netting system. In the figure below we see that there are nine different inter-company cash flows in four different currencies.

Figure 7   *Inter-company cash flows before netting*

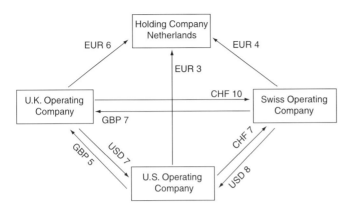

We will now see how a netting system can reduce the volume and the value of these payments. The netting centre processes all inter-company payments and compresses these into a single payment per participant. Net payers make a single settlement payment to the netting centre in their local currency, while the net recipients are paid out in their local currency by the netting centre.

The table below shows the cash flow values before netting (gross payments and receipts) and after netting (net payments and receipts) with all transactions converted into euros.

Figure 8   *Cash flow values before and after netting (in euros)*

	All amounts in euro				Gross payment	Net payment
	NL receives	U.K. receives	U.S. receives	SW receives		
NL pays	–	–	–	–	–	
UK pays	6	–	5.6	6.7	18.3	1.2
US pays	3	7.1	–	4.76	14.8	2.8
SW pays	4	10	6.4	–	20.4	9
Gross receipt	13	17.1	12.0	11.4	total: 53.5	
Net receipt	13		0			total: 13

The above netting of inter-company payments leads to the following settlement transactions in the respective foreign currencies:

Figure 9   *Inter-company cash flows after multilateral netting*

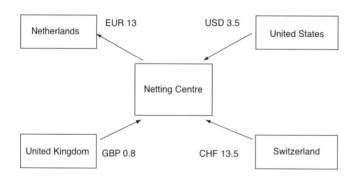

Applied exchange rates:

EUR/USD   1.2500
EUR/GBP   0.7000
EUR/CHF   1.5000

4.2 The benefits and costs of netting

Setting up a netting system can yield significant benefits for the company. However, these have to be weighed against the costs of operating the netting system.

4.2.1 Benefits of netting

The advantages of netting are:

- reduction in transaction costs
- alleviation of administrative workload
- reduction in foreign exchange costs
- intangible benefits

REDUCTION IN TRANSACTION COSTS
Netting will substantially reduce the number of payments that the participants must initiate in connection with inter-company payments to one transaction in each netting period. In our example, the number of transactions decreases from nine to only four transactions, which means a reduction of more than 50%. The total value of the transactions decreases from EUR 53.5 to EUR 26.0, also leading to a reduction of more than 50%. The lower value of the payment flows will reduce the loss of interest from value dating and bank float.

ALLEVIATION OF ADMINISTRATIVE WORKLOAD
Netting will reduce the costs of managing inter-company payables and receivables. Instead of creating a payment for each individual invoice, subsidiaries can now view their outstanding payables and receivables in the netting system and, when they have given their approval, only one physical transaction will have to be processed. This means less work to send payment reminders and reconcile incoming payments with outstanding receivables.

Back office activities in relation to foreign exchange transactions will also be eliminated at operating company level. In addition, all inter-company payments take place at fixed times, providing more certainty as to when transactions occur. Though delays in inter-company payments have no impact on group liquidity, they can still lead to unbalanced positions at subsidiary level.

In the example, we saw that the operating companies had to buy foreign currencies. In total nine transactions had to be executed. Netting will centralise all foreign currency transactions at the netting centre and reduce the number of transactions substantially. This will reduce operating costs at the subsidiary level and
concentrate foreign exchange activity in the centre, which will be more specialised and capable of negotiating competitive rates with the banks.

INTANGIBLE BENEFITS
Netting will also create some less obvious benefits. These are not always clearly vis-
ible, but they are often just as important for the company as the tangible benefits.
The most important additional benefits are:

- stronger payment discipline among participants
- standardisation of inter-company payments
- improved liquidity forecasting
- better internal communication between subsidiaries

4.2.2 Operating costs of netting

The most important costs of operating a netting system are management costs and
system costs.

MANAGEMENT COSTS
There are different ways to manage a netting process. Companies can choose to operate the netting system in-house through the treasury team or the accounting department. This will require resources and create an operational risk, i.e. exposure
to specialised manpower. Alternatively, the company can outsource the netting operations to a bank or another service provider. The fees paid to the external service
provider are usually lower than the costs of internal handling, while operational
risks will be much smaller.

SYSTEM COSTS
System costs can be quite different, depending on the type of netting system used.
Still, many companies are using spreadsheets, keeping the system costs very low
(but operational risk very high). However, the management costs will be substantially higher, especially because no automated interfaces exist with the company's
back-office systems. Alternatively, companies may use enterprise resource planning systems to operate netting. This would resolve the interfacing issue, but
would still create relatively high management costs.

Banks and third party service providers are increasingly offering web-based netting systems, which are easily accessible for all subsidiaries and relatively low cost to operate. They can also be linked to general ledger systems, decreasing internal management costs.

4.2.3 Weighing up the advantages and disadvantages

A feasibility study must be carried out to establish whether the potential benefits outweigh the operating costs. The outcome of such a study will vary from one company to another, depending on e.g. the following factors:

- number of foreign operating companies with cross-border payments
- number of inter-company payments
- countries where the participants are located
- current invoicing method
- number of currencies used
- extent to which the company has already streamlined its inter-company payments

4.3 The netting cycle

The company will organise a periodic netting cycle, e.g. once every week or month. A netting cycle typically spans five to seven days. Below, we have listed the various actions that can be identified from the beginning of such a cycle, six days before the actual netting on day x, until the reconciliation just after the netting.

EXAMPLE OF A NETTING CYCLE

1. Day x-6: The participants (operating companies) deliver the invoices to the netting centre;

2. Day x-5: The netting centre sorts the invoice data according to participant, currency type and nature of the payment and enters these in the netting system;

3. Day x-4: Provisional pre-calculation of netting and reporting of this pre-calculation to the participants. Opportunity for participants to make adjustments;

4. Day x-3: Second pre-calculation to determine the foreign currency to be bought/sold in the market on x-2;

5. Day x-2: The netting centre carries out the foreign exchange transactions and makes a definitive netting calculation on the basis of the effective buying and selling rates of these transactions. Next it sends a report to the participants;

6. Day x-1: Net paying participants pay the amount they owe via the local bank. The netting centre pays the resulting net amounts to the receiving participants. All transfers take place on value date x;

7. Day x: Actual netting. Banks execute the payment instructions on value date x;

8. Day x+n: Reconciliation is checked and execution problems are resolved;

5
Changing the internal organisation: the Payment and Collection Factory

In most MNCs, payments and collections are carried out by the local operating companies. They send their payment instructions to their local banks for execution. There are, however, a growing number of MNCs that have centralised payment processing in a Shared Services Centre or a Payment or Collection Factory.

A Shared Service Centre is a specialised unit which carries out certain non-core business activities for the corporation, enabling operating companies to focus entirely on their core business activities. Examples of such non-core business activities are finance and accounting, accounts payable administration, accounts receivable administration, processing payments and collections, treasury operations, centralised purchasing, human resources administration and support, IT functions and real estate management. By centralising these activities into one dedicated service unit, companies try to reduce operating costs and increase quality.

While Shared Service Centres usually handle many different functions, a Payment and Collection Factory focuses exclusively on the execution of transactions. This is one way in which large companies try to improve the management of their cash flows. When we discuss Payment and Collection Factories, you should bear in mind that the same functions can be fulfilled by a Shared Service Centre.

5.1 The Payment Factory

A Payment Factory is a central unit that executes payments on behalf of several, sometimes all, operating companies. When payments need to be executed, the local operating companies send relevant payment data via an internal network to the Payment Factory. The payment instructions are collected in a central system, which prepares a batch of payment instructions and sends this batch to the bank.

As all of the corporation's payment instructions are sent via a single channel to the bank, the company only needs one electronic interface with the bank. This is called a 'single pipeline'. The participating operating companies are often based in different countries. They are usually connected to the central system via a company-wide enterprise resource planning system. In addition to creating the single batch of payments, the Payment Factory may provide other services, such as settling inter-company payments on internal accounts, buying foreign currencies and central bank reporting of international transfers.

As we can see in Figure 10, the bank receiving the payment instructions will send these to the local branches in the country of the beneficiary for execution in the local clearing system.

Figure 10   *Routing of payables through the Payment Factory*

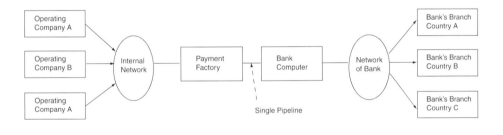

The payment factory offers the following advantages:

– reduced administrative workload for the operating companies
– reduction of transaction costs
– one bank, one interface
– concentration of foreign exchange transactions

REDUCED WORKLOAD
The operating companies do not have to make a distinction between inter-company and external payments. They can send both types of payments to the Payment Factory. In addition, the Payment Factory will handle the buying of foreign currencies needed for international transfers so that the operating companies will only pay in their own local currency.

The Payment Factory also alleviates the administrative workload of the subsidiaries by preparing the international transaction reports to the central bank in those countries where these reports are still required.

REDUCTION OF TRANSACTION COSTS

The Payment Factory is able to route the payments through the most appropriate channel. For instance, cross-border payments will be executed through in-country clearing systems to reduce transaction fees. Urgent payments will be processed via a gross settlement clearing system to ensure immediate execution, while non-urgent payments are channelled through the lowest cost clearing system.

Given the large volume of transactions, the Payment Factory will be in a position to organise the most optimal routing of the payments and negotiate competitive transaction fees with the bank.

ONE BANK/INTERFACE

The operating companies no longer need to maintain electronic interfaces with local banks. This can create significant savings because the operating companies do not have to adapt their systems to changes in electronic banking systems to ensure straight-through processing, and they will avoid electronic banking and service fees. The Payment Factory is the intermediary between the whole company and the bank, and will ensure compatibility of the external and internal systems.

CONCENTRATION OF FOREIGN EXCHANGE TRANSACTIONS

As mentioned before, the Payment Factory may be tasked with the handling of all foreign exchange transactions. This will simplify operations for the operating companies, and will enable the whole group to achieve more control of foreign exchange exposures while minimising the external costs of the currency conversions.

5.2 The collection factory

The processing of incoming payments can be centralised in a Collection Factory. Similar to the Payment Factory, the Collection Factory will usually select one international network bank to streamline its collections. Local collection accounts will be used with the network bank in the countries where the customers are located. The network bank collects all information on the incoming receipts and sends a single file containing all transaction information to the Collection Factory. The Collection Factory, in turn, splits this file into various sub-files for the various operating companies, and sends the relevant information on incoming payments to each operating company. The operating companies will use this information for reconciliation in their accounts receivable administration.

The great advantage for the operating companies is that all information on incoming payments is delivered to them on a single standard format. The company as a whole will benefit because it will achieve greater control of the receivables. This will enable the company to reduce operating costs and optimise its liquidity position

6
Evaluation of cash flow management

Many companies find it useful to evaluate cash flow management at regular intervals, i.e. once every two or three years. The starting point of this evaluation is the company's actual cash flow structure, a picture of all major cash flows by operating company, by country and by currency. The individual cash flows need to be reviewed, looking at transaction instruments used, operating costs and straight-through processing possibilities. Are the most efficient transaction instruments used? Are there ways available to reduce the transaction costs? As the payments market is changing continuously, consulting the banks is recommended when carrying out this exercise.

D
Working Capital Management and Financial Risk Management

Chapter 12
Working capital management

Introduction

In this chapter we look at the activities which the cash manager performs in managing working capital. This is a critical function because the size and composition of working capital primarily determines the company's liquidity position. An important concept with working capital is the cash conversion cycle. This cycle comprises all the steps a company uses to transform money into more money through purchasing, production and sales. The shorter the cash conversion cycle, the less money it tight up in the operational process.

1
Relevance of working capital management to the MNC

In a constantly changing business environment, companies need to focus continually on improving their operational processes to ensure an efficient supply chain. Vigilance in adapting to changing business demands can help them to improve profitability and safeguard their future place in the market. Furthermore, with senior management increasingly aware of the benefits of self-financing, treasurers and finance professionals are now, more than ever, paying closer attention to their company's 'working capital', or cash and other liquid assets needed to finance the everyday running of a business.

Chief Financial Officers (CFOs) and their treasury staff are under pressure to release liquid assets tied up in the supply chain through an enterprise-wide tightening of the 'working capital value chain'. This involves operational improvements in diverse areas, ranging from sales and accounts, to warehouse and logistics management. Treasury has a key role to play in reducing working capital requirements through active cash management – including centralising cash-flow and liquidity management – and making the business more cash-aware.

In the quest for competitive advantage, multinationals have great scope for unlocking capital trapped in physical and financial supply chains. In fact, studies show that businesses today have hundreds of billions of euros trapped in supply chains, simply as a result of inefficient working-capital management practices.

Many forces are pushing companies to reduce working capital requirements. Key among these are the renewed emphasis on growth in the corporate agenda and increased pressure from boardrooms and shareholders for more disciplined capital management. The emphasis on cash flow as a measure of performance shows the importance shareholders place on getting a competitive return on capital. In addition, a trend towards ever later payments by commercial customers has led to an increasing focus on payment terms and the reasons for late payment. Often, failure to pay or delayed payment are the result of poor client service or disputes on delivery.

Reducing working capital requirements has implications for many areas of a business, and its benefits go beyond improved working capital ratios. Improvements in operational processes that lead to a reduction in working capital also tend to reduce costs, resulting in greater operational efficiency as well as financial profits.

Poor working capital management results in a company performing below its potential and realising margins smaller than they should be. A company with poor working capital management is at a competitive disadvantage to its peers and is poorly equipped to safeguard future profits. Companies which are underperforming their peers tend to face increased capital costs. In the extreme, this competitive disadvantage can even result in defaults or can make the company an acquisition target for more efficient market participants.

The challenge here, however, is that the various departments and individuals whose day-to-day activities determine the working capital each have different, and sometimes even opposing, objectives. Ultimately, it is the responsibility of the company's management team to align the various departments – purchasing, sales, customer service, production and finance (including cash management) – so they can work together to optimise the firm's end-to-end working capital process. Focusing on working capital to optimise core processes has many advantages – in both the near and long-term.

If everyone involved in the cash conversion cycle works toward making it as efficient as possible, a company can benefit from having less working capital tied up in operational processes. Firms benefit when everyone in the company thinks in terms of cash utilisation and minimising the length of time capital is locked in operational processes. This would strengthen the company's liquidity position compared to its peers. Over the long term, many companies could enhance operations by making use of the shared services concept.

The treasurer's role in reducing working capital requirements stretches across multiple areas of the organisation, starting with the cash management function, which is where a broad working capital improvement programme can begin.

2
Net working capital

'Working capital' refers to the net working capital, which is the difference be- | 239 tween the current assets and the short-term debt capital and current liabilities.

Net working capital = current assets – short term debt

The current assets (what a company owns) consist primarily of the following items on a company balance sheet:

- inventory stocks
- accounts receivable
- cash and cash equivalents (liquid funds)

The total of the current assets is the gross working capital of the company.

The total of short-term debt capital of the company consists primarily of:

- accounts payable
- other short-term obligations, like overdrafts and other short term credit facilities

The figure below shows a company's working capital.

Figure 1   *Net working capital*

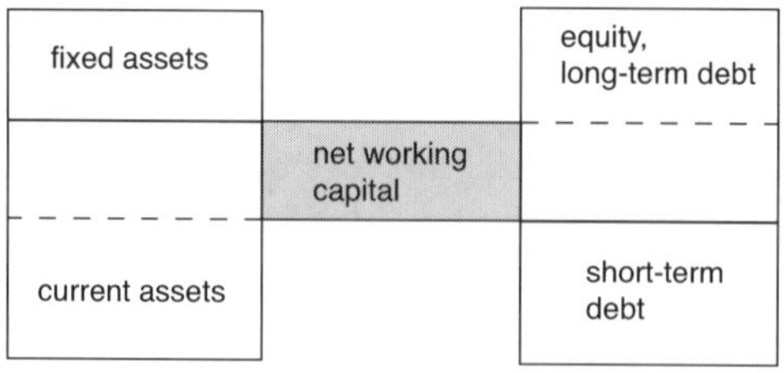

Management is responsible for determining the company's optimal level of working capital, and this decision is made by weighing up the interest costs of borrowing against the benefits of maintaining working capital. The benefits of positive working capital are:

REDUCED RISK OF ILLIQUIDITY AND SOLVENCY
A company with ample working capital has sufficient access to cash – or is able to quickly convert assets into cash – to fulfil its financial obligations in the short term.

REDUCED RISK OF STAGNATION IN PRODUCTION
If a large part of a company's working capital consists of inventory or raw materials, the company will be able to maintain a smooth production process. One caution is that this can be an indication that a part of the stock is unmarketable and can't be sold.

PREFERRED CLIENT RELATIONS
If a large part of the working capital consists of accounts receivable, the company's credit policy may be client-friendly, making it attractive to a large customer base. On the other hand, this can also indicate that a part of the corporate's clients are paying very late, or even potentially not paying the invoices at all.

BETTER ACCESS TO BANK CREDIT
Net working capital is one of the key ratios banks look at when assessing the strength of a company. Strong working capital levels are often seen as a sign of greater creditworthiness.

The disadvantage of positive net working capital is that it has an associated carrying cost. Companies, therefore, generally try to keep their working capital as low as possible, but high enough to keep production flowing smoothly. What is a sufficient level of working capital? This depends on the sector a company serves and its client base. One of the best ways to judge this is to compare a company with its peers in the sector.

The size of a company's working capital is often seen as a measure of its relative liquidity, and the composition of working capital determines a company's actual liquidity position.

Two companies may have exactly the same amount of working capital but completely different short-term repayment capacities. The following two balance sheets help make this clear:

Figure 2   *Balance sheet company A*

(x USD 1000)			
buildings	200	equity	170
machinery	70	long-term debt	220
stock	60	accounts payable	30
accounts receivable	40	short-term debt	50
cash	100		
	-----		-----
total	470	total	470

Figure 3   *Balance sheet company B*

	(x USD 1000)		
buildings	150	equity	170
machinery	50	long-term debt	150
stock	135	accounts payable	100
accounts receivable	130	short-term debt	50
cash	5		
	-----		-----
total	470	total	470

If we calculate the net working capital of the two companies, we get:

Net working capital company A = 60 + 40 + 100 - 30 - 50 = 120.

Net working capital company B = 135 + 130 + 5 - 100 -50 = 120.

Looking at the size of their working capital, the two companies appear to have exactly the same liquidity position, but we can also see key differences:

- company A has more working capital in liquid funds than company B, so A can access cash immediately, making it less reliant on customers paying their bills in a timely manner
- company A has accounts payable of 30, while company B has accounts payable of 100. B therefore has far more bills to pay in the short-term than company A, which is another weakness in B's liquidity position relative to A's

Another factor that determines a company's liquidity is the 'quality' of the balance sheet items in question. The following questions are relevant:

- How marketable are the inventory stocks? Large stocks may be due to the presence of slow-selling inventories
- What is the average quality of the accounts receivable? A large accounts receivable balance may be due to insolvent payers.
- How does this compare to industry averages?

In the above example, the net working capital position is determined by five balance sheet items. The size of the 'cash' or 'liquid funds' items (alongside the company's access to bank credit) is crucial for the company to meet all its short-term financial obligations. If the total working capital is known, the amount of liquid funds can be worked out on the basis of the other working capital components:

- accounts payable
- accounts receivable
- stocks

Note that the liquidity position increases in the following cases:

- higher values of accounts payable result from paying suppliers more slowly (using supplier credit)
- lower values of accounts receivable are achieved by persuading customers to pay more quickly
- lower stocks result from accelerating the turnover of inventory

These actions cause cash to flow faster into the company and more slowly out of the company. Assuming that companies A and B have identical sales, we can make the following observations:

- the value of company A's accounts payable is less than that of company B's, indicating that A pays its suppliers more quickly than B. Conversely, company B makes more use of its suppliers' credit, thereby retaining its cash longer and improving its liquidity position. As we will see, however, there are costs associated with supplier credit.
- the value of company A's accounts receivable is less than company B's, which means that company A has succeeded in making its customers pay faster than company B (assuming that sales of both companies are equal).
- company A has less stock than company B, which means that company A manages its stocks more efficiently, or it only purchases supplies when required.

3
The cash conversion cycle

The cash conversion cycle comprises all the steps a company uses to transform money into more money through purchasing, production and sales. The cash conversion cycle starts when the invoice received on purchase is paid. It is crucial for a company to keep its cash conversion cycle as short as possible, so it can quickly regain access to capital that can be deployed in other profitable projects. A diagram of the cash conversion cycle is given below.

Figure 4   *The cash conversion cycle*

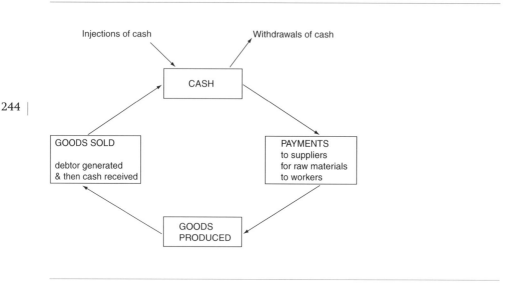

Within the cash conversion cycle we can distinguish three sub-cycles that play a role in determining the speed of the cash conversion cycle:

- purchase-to-pay cycle
- order-to-cash cycle
- stock cycle

PURCHASE-TO-PAY CYCLE

The purchase-to-pay cycle comprises the steps that a company takes to purchase materials and pay suppliers; in other words, the accounts payable policy. The figure below shows the successive steps in the purchase-to-pay cycle.

Figure 5   *The purchase to pay cycle*

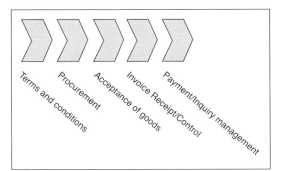

The purchase-to-pay cycle involves two areas:

-   purchasing
    -   determining delivery and payment conditions
    -   procurement, the actual ordering of goods
    -   receipt of goods, including confirmation of quality
-   accounts payable policy
    -   receipt of invoice
    -   payment
    -   inquiries regarding the status of the payment

ORDER-TO-CASH CYCLE

The order-to-cash cycle encompasses the activities of the company, from the receipt of an order until the collection of the related payment. The figure below
shows the consecutive steps in the order-to-cash cycle.

Figure 6 *The order to cash cycle*

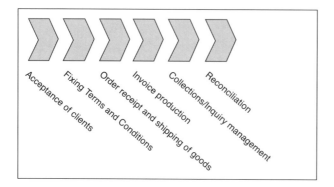

Virtually all steps in the order-to-cash cycle relate to the company's debtor policy, and the way the company takes orders from and ships goods to clients.

THE STOCK CYCLE

The stock cycle is the final component of the cash-conversion cycle, and it is defined as the average time that stocks remain within the company. The stock cycle is the time between the acceptance of raw materials and the shipping of finished goods. This comprises all the different stages in the production process, from the intake of raw materials and work in progress to the end product. The key issue for the stock manager is to determine the optimal stock levels to be maintained. The efficiency of the stock-ordering process forms a key part of the purchase-to-pay cycle.

The company aims to carry out all steps in the cash conversion cycle as efficiently as possible without negatively affecting the company's production cycles or client relations. The company's two objectives are:

1. to shorten the cash conversion cycle in order to improve the company's liquidity position
2. to realise cost savings by means of improved efficiency

4
The purchase-to-pay cycle

The purchase-to-pay cycle, as noted, includes the steps a company takes in purchasing goods and services and paying suppliers.

The two main ways of improving the purchase-to-pay cycle are by:

- paying as slowly as possible, within commercially and morally acceptable limits
- increasing the operational and financial efficiency of the company's procurement and payment process

Increasing operational efficiency can produce significant gains in the purchase–to-pay cycle, whereas paying suppliers more slowly offers only marginal gains, although it does have an impact.

The purchase-to-pay cycle, therefore, can help to accelerate the cash conversion cycle by ensuring that creditors are paid as late as possible. In this way, the cash remains at the company's disposal for as long as possible and can be used to self-finance subsequent steps in the cash conversion cycle. Obviously, the company cannot delay the outgoing payments indefinitely, because it won't want to spoil good relationships with suppliers or risk legal action. As we will see, the company can take an important step in the right direction by negotiating competitive payment terms and conditions.

Purchasing encompasses all the products and services that a firm buys from others:

- primary purchase – includes everything a company uses for core processes, such as raw materials and semi-finished and finished goods
- secondary purchase – includes goods used for non-core processes, such as stationary, computers, furniture, travel and temporary staff

The various elements of the purchase-to-pay cycle include:

- payment conditions
- procurement
- reception of goods, checking, and invoice
- payment and payment inquiry

4.1 Payment conditions

Payment conditions state when a received invoice is due for payment, and they influence the duration of the cash conversion cycle. The following arrangements are typically included in the payment conditions:

- the payment deadline
- when a payment is regarded as a 'cash' or early payment
- the discount, if any, for early 'cash' payment granted to the customer

Consider the following example.

EXAMPLE

A company has the following payment conditions:

Payment within three months, but a 2% discount for payments made within two weeks.

In this example, the customer must pay within three months of the date on the invoice. Payment within two weeks is treated as a cash payment, and the customer receives a discount of 2% on the invoice amount.

The responsibility for purchasing is naturally with the purchasing department of the company. The purchasing manager negotiates the purchasing price, the delivery date and payment terms and conditions with the suppliers. These payment conditions greatly affect the company's liquidity position. The period within which the company is required to pay is crucial. For example, a payment term of 30 or 45 days can have an enormous affect on a company's liquidity position and its net working capital. The following example shows how much a company can save if the purchaser is able to successfully negotiate extended payment terms.

EXAMPLE

A company buys EUR 15 million worth of raw materials every year, and it has negotiated the privilege of paying after 45 days instead of 30 days. The interest on bank credit is 7% (based on exact/365).

The purchaser achieves the following annualised saving for the company:

15/635 x 7% x EUR 15,000,000 = EUR 43,150.50.

Whether a purchaser can negotiate favourable delivery and payment conditions depends on various factors, including:

- the size of the company making purchases as compared with the size of the company selling goods and services – this is important because larger companies often have better bargaining positions
- the buyer's share in the seller's total annual turnover – the larger the share, the more the seller depends on this customer and the weaker its position when negotiating conditions
- available alternative suppliers – competition weakens a seller's bargaining strength

In many cases large companies can impose their own conditions on their suppliers. These will typically include generous payment conditions, with a standard payment term of, for example, three months. Smaller companies often have to accept the payment conditions of their suppliers, especially if they are highly dependent on the suppliers. This is clearly evident in the automotive sector, in which large numbers of suppliers sell to a relatively small number of car manufacturers. As a result, manufacturers can often dictate terms, and suppliers have little choice but to accept them.

4.2 The procurement process

The next step in the purchase-to-pay cycle is the procurement process. The measures that a company can take are generally aimed at achieving cost savings, especially process and administration costs. Modern procurement methods can make the stock-management process much more efficient by carefully linking procurement to sales, which reduces stock levels. This in turn helps to shorten the cash conversion cycle.

The procurement process is labour intensive by nature, and it involves the following steps:

1. Suppliers offer their range of products to their potential clients.
2. Company employees shop around for their required products, when found the following will happen:

a. employee is completing an order for
b. obtaining approval from a manager and possibly also at next-higher level following the "four-eyes" principle
c. sending the order form to the procurement department
d. getting signatures confirmed by the procurement department

e. having the procurement department produce an order to the supplier
f. entering the order into the company's accounts system (many companies now have an enterprise resource planning (ERP) system that automates much of this)
g. sending the order
3. Supplier and company exchange order information, so the customer can track the order's progress.

Electronic data communication is increasingly being used to improve the efficiency of the procurement process, resulting in the elimination of many manual operations. Many companies now have direct computer links with regular suppliers of primary products (raw materials), and a growing number of companies are also using data communication to procure support products and resources, such as stationary, computers, furniture, travel and temporary staff.

Data communication between companies and their suppliers can include:

– electronic data interchange (EDI)
– e-procurement

4.2.1 Electronic data interchange (EDI)

EDI is the format that companies and institutions use to exchange structured information by means of a direct computer connection (interface) with another company or institution. This exchange of information takes place on a one-to-one basis. An EDI document contains the same data normally found in a traditional paper document, but information is structured according to guidelines developed by national or international standards bodies. This enables it to be exchanged between different technology platforms with minimum human intervention. The information concerns:

– product information
– order placement
– dispatch of invoices

EDI offers opportunities for connecting the processes of different companies together like links in the supply chain. Ideally, the integrated business systems, also known as enterprise resource planning (ERP) systems, of the buyer and the supplier are linked. For example, a signal is triggered in the supplier's ERP system when the purchaser's stocks drop below a certain level, which automatically starts the entire delivery and invoicing process at the supplier – all without human intervention. The automotive industry and the retail food sector, with their 'just-in-time' (JIT) delivery practices, illustrate how suppliers and resellers can work together in an automated fashion.

A United Nations-endorsed standard, known as EDIFACT (EDI for Administration Commerce and Transport), has been developed to facilitate the efficient exchange of data between different companies. Other standards are also used for business-to-business messaging, and the applied messaging format depends upon, among other things, the compatibility of the ERP systems that the two trading partners use. SAP, Oracle and JD Edwards are a few of the better known suppliers of ERP systems. If both parties use an SAP system for example, they can also exchange electronic messages via the SAP format.

Companies use EDI for primary procurement of supplies that are necessary for their primary production processes, and later form part of the finished product. For example, supplies may include goods, such as raw materials and semi-finished products. Since the reliable delivery and consistent quality of these products is essential to the production process, most companies seek to establish long-standing relationships with a limited number of suppliers. Purchasing is often arranged through the company's own ERP system, which can be linked to the systems of the suppliers. The ERP system calculates the quantities of raw materials and semi-finished products needed, and then automatically orders the goods from suppliers.

A major advantage of EDI is that it makes stock management much more efficient. Average stock levels are reduced, shortening the cash conversion cycle. Another advantage is that the purchasing and accounts-payable administration is made much less cumbersome.

The disadvantage of EDI, however, is the cost involved. A common messaging standard must be set up with trading partners and an interface must be built between the various companies' ERP systems. Linking two systems together is generally a time-consuming and costly affair, so EDI is generally used only for communications with regular customers and suppliers.

Since EDI is expensive to set up and relatively inflexible, it is not normally used by smaller companies, nor is it used for handling large numbers of small-volume orders placed by many end users.

Alongside of EDI, companies are increasingly using the Internet to communicate with each other and their customers through a variety of e-commerce portals. An important difference between EDI and the Internet is that most companies can access the Internet with a PC, a personal digital assistant (PDA) or mobile phone. Additional advantages of the Internet are low cost and the use of a single uniform messaging standard (XML format).

It has been predicted that the EDI standard would be replaced by Internet protocols such as FTP, telnet and email. Although standards for these media are emerging, EDI is still the data format used for the vast majority of electronic commerce transactions.

4.2.2 E-procurement

E-procurement (electronic procurement) is the business-to-business purchase and sale of supplies and services through the Internet. In contrast with EDI, e-procurement is primarily aimed at secondary purchasing - products and services that do not form part of the end products sold to customers and do not directly support the production process. Typically, e-procurement websites allow registered users to identify buyers or sellers of goods and services, and they may also support transactions. Regular purchases may qualify customers for volume discounts or special offers, and some e-procurement software supports automated buying and selling. Participating companies expect to be able to control inventories more effectively, reduce purchasing-agent overhead and improve manufacturing cycles. E-procurement is increasingly being integrated with the trend toward computerised supply chain management.

With secondary purchasing, orders are not generated from the production process, but by the employee behind a desk. If this is done manually, order-handling costs for secondary products and services are generally high; typically varying from EUR 45 to EUR 145 per order. E-procurement systems have been developed to reduce these costs, and these systems are ideal for handling routine orders simply and effectively. This trend mirrors similar developments in personal expense management at many companies, in which employees submit expenses for reimbursement through an Internet application instead of paper forms. The whole flow and authorisation of expenses is automated, resulting in reduced handling time and cost.

The main advantage of e-procurement is increased efficiency for buyers and sellers alike. Buyers gain several benefits, such as Internet access to up-to-date product catalogues, including current prices and personalised promotions. Most systems also provide an automatic approval capability, which allows designated employees to make purchases up to predefined volumes and values. Internet systems generally provide up-to-date information and order status, and these systems can be easily adapted to reflect changing business needs. Finally, invoicing can be included through electronic channels and even the payment can be included within the process. It is clear that e-procurement and electronic invoicing reduce the administrative workload for both buyer and supplier.

4.3 Receipt of goods and checking packing slip and invoice

The placement of an order leads to the delivery of goods. A warehouse assistant checks goods against the packing slip to confirm they are indeed what was ordered, and that the quantity and quality are correct. Then the warehouse assistant passes the packing slip on to the financial department, where the packing slip is checked against the invoice. If the two documents match, the order is entered into the stock-administration system.

Until this checking procedure is completed, the received stocks cannot be used in the production process. Any delays or discrepancies lengthen the cash conversion cycle.

4.4 Payment and payment inquiry

The final steps in the purchase-to-pay process entails the actual payment and the processing of a supplier's enquiries on payment status. A company can shorten the cash-conversion cycle and improve the efficiency of the payment process by taking measures to enhance efficiency in these areas:

- payment type
- supplier's credit
- implementation or use of a payment factory

4.4.1 Payment type

A company can choose between a numbers of different methods to pay its accounts payable, including:

- electronic transfers
- cheque payments
- credit on purchasing-card payment
- payment through a letter of credit

ELECTRONIC TRANSFERS
The most efficient form of payment for a company is one that can be sent from its own electronic payment system, which is linked directly to its bank. These links are generally initiated through a traditional electronic banking system, Internet banking or even through a direct link with the bank's computer systems.

CHEQUE PAYMENTS

A company can also usually choose between cheque payments and electronic transfers. The commercial cheque is the most effective way of improving the cash conversion cycle for buyers, from a pure payment point of view. Although cheques are paper instruments, nowadays they are quickly converted into electronic form and included in electronic payment reconciliation and electronic process follow-up.

CREDIT ON PURCHASING-CARD

When companies purchase goods and services, they usually make payments with credit on purchasing cards. Commercial credit cards vary greatly in terms of purchasing plans and capabilities, depending on how companies intend to use them. For example, cards used for purchasing inventory, generally have large spending facilities as well as tracking and audit capabilities that facilitate procurement processing. Typically, only a limited number of employees are in charge of inventory purchasing. By contrast, many more people within the organisation use travel and entertainment cards. Popular in North America and increasingly so in Europe, this type of card has strict guidelines on its use, including welldefined spending limits.

LETTERS OF CREDIT

These are used mainly for large, international trade transactions, with a foreign supplier usually requesting their use. The benefit for the customer of this form of payment is that it receives documents proving that the goods have been shipped prior to making payment.

4.4.2 Supplier's credit

A second decision that a company must make about its accounts payable is whether it should make use of the supplier's credit by delaying payments until a later date. This sounds attractive, but the choice is complicated by the fact that suppliers usually offers customers discounts for making accelerated payments, such as within two weeks of delivery. By deferring payment until the payment deadline (the due date on the invoice), the customer loses the discount – so there is a price attached to using a supplier's credit.

The use of supplier's credit influences the duration of the cash conversion cycle. The company must work out what is more attractive: withdraw cash from a credit facility at the bank or take advantage of supplier's credit. The example below shows how the company can calculate which of the two is the better option.

A company buys its stock of raw materials from a regular supplier, with the following payment terms: 0.5% discount on payments made within 15 days, maximum payment term 50 days. The company can access credit from its bank at a rate of 1-month EURIBOR + 100 basis points (based on exact/ 365). The 1-month EURIBOR for this example is 3.00%.

The company must decide whether to make use of its supplier's credit or pay immediately (within 15 days) and take out bank credit.

The cost of the bank credit is: 3.00% + 1.00% = 4.00% on an annual basis.
If the company uses the supplier's credit, it loses the discount of 0.5%. In exchange for this, it receives 35 days 'credit' (50 days - 15 days), which effectively costs 0.5% per 35 days. Annualised this works out to: 365/35 x 0.5% = 5.21%.

Given the applicable current account rate, the company will not make use of the supplier's credit, but will pay the supplier after 15 days. After all, the bank's credit costs only 4.00% annualised, while supplier's credit costs 5.21%.

It should be noted, however, that the current account rate as well as the discount from suppliers can change at any time without any notice. If, for example, the 1-month EURIBOR were to rise in the interim to 4.50%, the cost of the bank's credit would increase to 5.50%, making supplier's credit more attractive. The company must, therefore, review the situation periodically.

Supplier's credit can be a welcome source of finance, particularly for companies with little or no access to bank credit, but accepting supplier's credit can also mean missing out on a discount for cash payment. As long as supplier's credit is cheaper than bank debt, it serves as an efficient funding source and has a positive effect on a company's cash conversion cycle.

4.4.3 *The payment factory*

A final point of consideration in the payment process is how to organise a company's outgoing payments. Some companies arrange all of their outgoing payments centrally through a bespoke business unit known as a 'payment factory'. This can improve the efficiency of the company's payment process considerably, but its impact on the duration of the cash conversion cycle is limited. Instead, payment factories improve operations related to payment execution and reduce associated costs. As we have seen, cost reduction is one of the main factors in achieving higher profits.

A payment factory also permits more efficient handling of payment enquiries from suppliers, a process that some banks support with customised information services. For example, some banks provide customers with a special web page that shows the status of payments they have made to suppliers. A payment factory often forms part of a shared service centre (SSC), which is set up to provide the company with a range of services relating to the 'purchase-to-pay' and 'order-to-collect' cycles (dealt with below). The shared service centre is discussed later in this chapter.

5
The order-to-collect cycle

The second part of the cash conversion cycle is the order-to-collect cycle, also known as 'accounts receivable management'. It comprises all the steps that the company takes from the moment it receives an order until payment is settled.

With the order-to-collect cycle, the company aims to:

- collect receivables as fast as possible
- collect the highest possible percentage of receivables as soon as possible
- maximise the efficiency of the accounts receivable process

To most companies, accounts receivable represent the most important investment in working capital, so they require careful management. The size of the accounts receivable portfolio is determined by:

- the volume of sales on credit and associated payment terms and conditions
- the payment behaviour of its current and future clients

Let's take a look at the measures a company can take in each step of the order-to-collect cycle to achieve the objectives listed above.

- credit standards
- payment conditions
- invoice production
- collection

5.1 Credit standards

Most companies sell on credit, which means that the customer is only required to make payment some time after receiving the goods. Exceptions to this include the retail sector, in which customers typically pay at the moment they buy the goods. In this sector, then, we can expect negative net working capital, because retailers have a minimum of account receivables and they normally make purchases using their suppliers' credit.

When a sale is made on credit, the supplier grants its customer credit, but before doing so the company will normally evaluate the customer's financial strength. When granting supplier credit, the company takes on the risk of delivering goods to a customer who may subsequently become insolvent. This makes the credit evaluation a critical part of the decision to grant credit, so it is usually carried out on the basis of documented credit standards.

A credit standard contains guidelines for assessing the customer's creditworthiness and evaluating whether it's safe to grant supplier's credit. With the aid of credit standards, the company determines who is eligible for credit and to what limit.

A company uses the following types of information to assess the creditworthiness of its customers:

- information from internal sources
    - historical data on payment behaviour
    - application form for new customers
    - information from account and sales managers
- information from external sources
    - annual reports
    - credit ratings from agencies like Moody's, Standard & Poor's
    - specialised agencies such as Dun & Bradstreet

If the above sources fail to provide sufficient certainty concerning the customer's repayment capacity, the company can opt to insure its supplier's credit, and special insurance policies are available for this purpose. Or a letter of credit is used to minimize the risk of non-payment.

Credit facilities help to oil the wheels of commerce to allow customers to buy on credit. They are often a necessary requirement for doing business, but they also have disadvantages, which include:

- an increased risk of non-payment (doubtful debtors), with negative financial and administrative consequences
- an increased amount of capital tied up in accounts receivable, leading to reduced liquidity and increased overdraft

– the need for more accounts payable and receivable administration to deal with the larger volume of sales on credit – especially for companies with administrative systems that are largely manual and lacking in standardised processes

Companies normally follow the generally accepted credit standards for their industry segments, but exceptions are sometimes made by the sales department in consultation with management.

The extension of supplier's credit naturally has consequences for the duration of the cash conversion cycle: it lengthens the cycle.

258

5.2 Payment conditions

After deciding to grant a customer credit, a second question immediately presents itself: how long is the customer permitted to postpone payment and should fast payment be rewarded? In the previous section on cash payments, we looked at this from the buyer's perspective, so now we will examine it from the seller's point of view.

When formulating payment conditions for its customers, a company must take into account multiple interests within the company. The cash manager obviously would like customers to pay as quickly as possible, but salespeople are often inclined to offer attractive payment conditions in order to close a deal. In weighing up these different interests, it is helpful to bear in mind that the customer will go through exactly the same evaluation process.

The company can make its payment conditions commercially attractive in two ways:

– extending the payment term
– granting (higher) discounts for payment in cash

5.2.1 Extending the payment term

One way of increasing sales is by extending the payment term, but as we've already seen, this comes at the cost of a longer cash conversion cycle, which means a higher requirement for working capital.

Disadvantages of relaxing payment conditions are:

- more trapped working capital – less liquidity
- a larger accounts receivable portfolio with an increased risk of non-payment
- difficulties with reducing payment terms in the future as customers come to expect extended terms

5.2.2 Extending a (higher) discount for cash payment

Extending a (higher) discount for cash payment is another method for boosting sales, and it has these advantages:

- the cash conversion cycle is speeded up
- sales increase (but margins per unit sold are reduced)

In the example below, a company is considering relaxing its payment conditions or granting a discount for faster payment.

EXAMPLE

If a company lengthens its credit term from 30 to 60 days, it predicts the average accounts receivable balance will increase from EUR 100,000 to EUR 250,000.

Part of this increase is attributable to the longer payment term because most existing customers are expected to opt for later payment. Since the payment term has doubled, it is assumed that the average number of days that accounts receivable remain outstanding will also double. The remainder of the increase in the accounts receivable balance (EUR 50,000) is attributed to increased sales.

The overall result of the extended payment term is a considerable increase in the amount of capital tied up in accounts receivable. However, this increase can be eliminated if, assuming all other factors remain the same, the company delays paying its suppliers by the same amount of time. This would result in a zero-sum game.
If stocks remain level and the company continues paying it's suppliers as before, it will need to use more of its liquid funds or obtain credit from the bank.

Every year (360 days) the company sells goods worth EUR 600,000, with a payment term of 60 days without any discount. Accounts receivable average EUR 100,000 (calculated as follows: 600,000 x 60 /360).

Suppose the company decides to change its credit policy to '1/10 net 60', which means that the customer receives a 1% discount if payment is made within 10 days of invoice, but must pay by no later than 60 days after invoice. The company expects 60% of its customers to make use of the discount and pay exactly after 10 days, so EUR 360,000 (60% of EUR 600,000) are to be paid at the discounted price.

Let's calculate the consequences of the new policy.

The cost of the discount is 1% of EUR 360,000, or EUR 3,600 per year.

Against this, the reduction in the accounts receivable balance leads to additional interest income.

The average outstanding debt term is now 30 days (0.6 x 10 + 0.4 x 60) instead of 60 days. 60% of the customers pay within 10 days and 40% still pay after 60 days, so the average accounts receivable balance drops to EUR 50,000 (As we already saw, an accelerated accounts receivable turnover leads to a proportionate decrease in the accounts receivable balance. The turnover rate is two times faster, and as a result, the accounts receivable balance is cut in half.)

Assuming 8% interest on bank credit to finance the accounts receivable balance, the reduction in the accounts receivable balance leads to a saving of EUR 4,000 (50.000 x 8%). In this case, the net effect of the new credit policy is positive (EUR 4,000 – EUR 3,600 = EUR 400), assuming the higher level of sales is achieved!

In this instance the decision to grant a discount appears to have limited success, but if the new policy generates more additional turnover than estimated, it may have been worthwhile.

5.3 Invoice production

Once an order is received and the goods are sent, the company must prepare an invoice. Speed is critical here because the sooner the customer receives the invoice, the more likely it is to pay within the coming 60 days for example.

Many companies send out invoices once a week, but savings can be realised by issuing invoices as soon as goods are delivered. For example, given an average accounts receivable portfolio of EUR 20,000,000 and an interest rate of 5%, the savings to be made by switching from weekly to daily invoicing results in 3.5/365 x 5% x EUR 20,000,000 = EUR 9,588.

A company can easily save EUR 9,588, by moving to a daily invoicing procedure. It can do so by using an EDI or ERP system, and with the latter, invoices can be prepared and sent automatically.

The company can also prepare a bill of exchange, or the documents required for documentary credit or collection, and enclose them with the invoice. Nowadays these documents can be transmitted to the bank electronically, with new technology making the process much more efficient.

5.4 Collections

After sending the invoice, companies want to collect payment as quickly and efficiently as possible, and to do this choices must be made about the:

- type of collection product and routing of the collection
- possibility of a collection factory
- collection policy to be pursued
- possibility of outsourcing accounts receivable management

5.4.1 Type of collection product and routing of the collection

By choosing the most appropriate collection product and routing for incoming payments, the company can try to shorten the cash conversion cycle and improve the efficiency of its account receivable collection process.

In the case of deliveries to new customers, companies can usually specify or even dictate how the customer must meet payment obligations. The company can, for instance, oblige a foreign customer to open a documentary credit in its favour. Another alternative is to receive the payment by means of documentary collection.

In addition, the company can request that customers sign direct-debit mandates, so that receivables can be collected automatically from the customers' accounts. This provides greater payment certainty and also allows the company to determine exactly when the invoiced amounts are to be collected, resulting in a shorter cash conversion cycle. The company will also seek to discourage payment by cheque, because cheques take much longer to process, and take much more accounting resources than electronic receivables.

Customers, of course, will consider the terms of payment when deciding whether to make purchases from a company, and overly restrictive terms can be damaging to sales.

Finally, companies with high volumes of sales outside their home country will want to replace incoming cross-border payments as far as possible with local payments. To this end, they can open a collection account in each country where they have a high value of receivables.

5.4.2 Collection factory

A final consideration in the payment process is how a company organises its incoming payments. As we saw above, a company can set up a payment factory for its outgoing payments, and, similarly, it can set up a collection factory for its incoming payments. A collection factory can significantly improve the collection of accounts receivable, and like the payment factory, it often forms part of a shared service centre (SSC). A collection factory makes sense only if it is connected to the company's accounting and reconciliation department, and relevant accounts and reconciliation data is automatically forwarded to the factory. A high volume of collections is generally necessary to make this economically justifiable.

5.4.3 Collection policy

Unfortunately for a company, not all customers pay their bills promptly, so it must chase late payers. They are not necessarily bad customers: often major clients pay later than agreed because they understand how dependent the supplier is on their business.

The collection policy outlines the company's procedures for collecting its accounts receivable. The aim of the collection policy is to encourage good payment behaviour among customers.

The company can reduce the costs of late payments and non-payment through the following measures:

– sending a reminder if the payment has not been made with, say, 10 days after the due date of the invoice
– sending a follow-up letter if the receivable is overdue
– telephoning the customer after, say, 30 days
– visiting the customer in person, say, after 60 days
– stopping deliveries on credit and delivering on a COD (cash-on-delivery) basis only
– engaging a collection agency

In addition to these steps, the company can also enlist the sales staff to help with securing timely payment by the client, but it must be handled carefully to avoid jeopardising ongoing sales. Most sales organisations are assessed and rewarded based on deals only, so they have little incentive to assist with the collection process. If, however, they are assessed on paid invoices as well, they have an interest in accelerating collection, and unpaid invoices rapidly decline. This works most effectively in industries in which salespeople have close relationships with clients.

Before adopting any of these measures, the company must always take the following considerations into account its commercial interests and the increased collection costs.

Despite all these measures, some receivables will inevitably never be paid; for example, the customer may go bankrupt. If the company has taken out credit insurance, it will seek payment from the insurance company. The collection policy also spells out how the company insures against unpaid receivables. This type of insurance can be expensive and is generally used only for less creditworthy clients, or for very large deals in which non-payment could jeopardise the company.

5.4.4 Outsourcing of the accounts receivable management

Some of a company's potential liquid funds are tied up in the accounts receivable portfolio, which means that the company has allowed its customers to postpone payment for a certain period of time. Consequently, in addition to exposing itself to the risk of late payment, the company must wait before receiving its money. This problem can be overcome by transferring the receivables to a third party, which is known as 'off-balance sheet' financing. This type of financing offers the company three advantages:

- it gains immediate access to liquid funds upon transfer of the accounts receivable portfolio
- it is no longer required to undertake collection activities
- the company eliminates in some cases the administration of accounts receivable collection

There are two methods for outsourcing receivables:

- factoring
- asset securitisation

FACTORING
With factoring, a company outsources the administration of accounts receivable to a specialised factoring firm by transferring its receivables portfolio to the firm. In such an arrangement, the factoring firm buys the receivables portfolio from the company at a discount and takes on the risk of collecting payment from all customers in the portfolio. The discount applied depends on the quality of the underlying receivables, with steeper discounts applied to receivables that have a higher risk of non-payment. The factoring company absorbs any losses resulting from uncollected receivables.

ASSET SECURITISATION
With securitisation, a company finances accounts receivable on an off-balance sheet basis by transferring some of its assets to a firm set up specifically for gener-

ating immediate liquidity from receivables. The newly formed company is a separate legal entity, known as a 'special purpose vehicle' (SPV).

The SPV places the company's accounts receivable on its own balance sheet and issues debt certificates, called 'asset-backed securities', to finance the accounts receivable portfolio. These securities can include instruments like bonds, medium-term notes or commercial paper. They are secured by the accounts-receivable portfolio of the SPV.

The return received by the holders of the debt certificates is paid from the income that is generated by the assets transferred to the SPV. The coupon received on the notes depends on the credit rating of the underlying assets, in this case the receivables. In many securitisation programmes each tranche of receivables is given its own credit rating by the credit rating agencies. If the SPV defaults on its obligations, the accounts receivable portfolio is transferred to the investors.

The big advantage of securitisation for a company is that it can cash all its accounts receivable by transferring them to the SPV and gain instant access to liquidity. In this way, outsourcing shortens the cash conversion cycle, but it does so at a cost. SPVs can be expensive and time consuming to set up, and the funding discount may be steep if the credit quality of the receivables portfolio is low.

Although factoring and securitisation are both forms of financing based on the sale of receivables, they are not interchangeable alternatives. In the case of securitisation, for example, the seller of the receivables continues to manage them, whereas in the case of factoring they are usually assigned to the factoring company. In addition, securitisation programmes differ from factoring in the following points:

- Assignment of accounts receivable – undisclosed (factoring: usually disclosed)
- Credit-risk analysis – at portfolio level (factoring: individual customer/ individual receivable)
- Volume – unlimited (factoring: limited)
- Funding costs – these depend on the programme's rating (in the case of factoring these depend on the rating of the debtor).

5.5 Evaluation of accounts receivable management

A company needs to monitor its debtors' payment behaviour on a regular basis, and it can do this by analysing both individual receivables and the entire portfolio.

Analysis of individual accounts normally focuses on outstanding receivables for which the payment deadlines have expired. The fact that payments may be overdue can be caused by customers, by the bank or by the company itself.

As previously mentioned, sometimes late payment is intentional: customers may postpone payment until they receive the first reminder. In such cases, a change in the credit terms may prompt the customer to improve their payment behaviour. In other instances, a customer may not pay because they are unhappy with the products delivered, and they may have even communicated this to sales team, who have not shared this information with the accounting department. Analysis of individual receivables should include all departments involved – including accounting, sales and customer service – so that the company can react in an appropriate and timely manner.

The company also needs to monitor the performance of the entire accounts receivable portfolio, which is important because:

- the portfolio can tie up a large portion of the company's liquidity
- accounts receivable patterns are useful for forecasting future receivables cash flows
- changes in the size of the total accounts receivable portfolio can point to a significant development in or outside the company, such as changes in:
  - sales
  - delivery conditions
  - the economic environment
  - actions of competitors

The company can analyse its debtors' payment behaviour at the portfolio level in two ways:

- calculate the receivables turnover rate
- make up a maturity calendar

5.5.1 Receivables turnover rate

Accounts-receivable turnover is defined as the average period from the moment an invoice is generated to collection of receivables. We show how to make this calculation in a later section, which deals with Days Sales Outstanding.

The receivables turnover rate can, for example, be compared with the credit term stipulated by the company. If the receivables turnover rate is considerably longer than the credit term, the company should take this as a warning signal.

A company can also look at how accounts receivable turnover has performed over time. An increase in the receivables turnover rate can indicate worsening payment behaviour by debtors, which suggests the need to tighten payment terms.

Finally, a company can compare its receivables turnover with that of its competitors or published industry average. The best performing company will have turnover below the relevant industry average.

5.5.2 Maturity calendar

A second instrument for analysing payment behaviour within the portfolio is the maturity calendar, which categorises receivables according to time elapsed since invoice. Maturity calendars give companies a clear picture of overdue payments. Generally, the older the receivable the less likely it is to be collected. An example of a maturity calendar is shown below.

EXAMPLE

Category	Accounts due (euro)	%
0-30 days	1,750,000	70%
30-60 days	375,000	15%
60-90 days	250,000	10%
>91 days	125,000	5%
	2,500,000	100%

With a credit term of 30 days, 30% of the outstanding invoices in the above example are overdue. The maturity calendar gives more specific information than the receivables turnover rate. The latter only indicates the average payment term of the entire portfolio, but the maturity calendar shows the extent to which receivables are overdue.

The information from the maturity calendar can also be used to predict the collection of receivables for liquidity forecasting purposes. The table displays the following payment pattern:

- 70% of sales are collected within one month
- 15% of sales are collected in the following month
- 10% of sales are collected two months after sale
- 5% of sales are collected after three months

(We assume that 1% of receivables are paid in each of months three to six and that 2% is finally written down.)

In the example below we use these data to forecast the collection of receivables in a given month.

EXAMPLE

Sales in the first half year are as follows:

January	EUR	250,000
February	EUR	200,000
March	EUR	300,000
April	EUR	250,000
May	EUR	400,000
June	EUR	350,000

The company can make the following receivables collection forecast for June:

$0.01 \times 250{,}000 + 0.01 \times 200{,}000 + 0.01 \times 300{,}000 + 0.10 \times 250{,}000 + 0.15 \times 400{,}000 + 0.70 \times 350{,}000 =$ EUR 337,500

In addition to analysing its debtors' payment behaviour, a company may also want to evaluate the entire accounts receivable policy. Each step of the cash conversion cycle must be checked, so the cash manager will look at:

- the sale of goods and the terms and conditions
- how goods are dispatched
- how and when invoices are sent
- the quality of information on the invoice
- how late payments are monitored
- how and when payment reminders are sent
- the use of collection agencies
- how payments are reconciled when administering accounts receivable
- contacts with any provider of accounts-receivable administration services

From time to time, the company may want to find out whether the credit standard, the payment conditions and the collection policy are optimised to create value for the company. In addition, the cash manager may also consider outsourcing accounts receivable management.

There are numerous sources of delay in the order-to-collect cycle, all of which can result in late collection of accounts receivable. These delays are known as 'float', and they come in many forms:

- production float: the time that elapses between receiving an order and dispatching the goods
- system float: the time that elapses between preparing and sending the invoice
- accounts receivable float: occurs when the debtor pays after the payment deadline
- bank float: the time that a payment is 'in transit' at the bank
- 'cheque float' (mail float): delay due to the time that the cheque is in the mail, the time that elapses until the cheque is offered to a bank and the time that elapses until the cheque is paid out
- information float: the time that elapses between the arrival of the money in the account and notification of the cash manager
- concentration float: delay due to the need to concentrate the balances of various accounts in a single position.

The last three types of float – cheque, information and concentration – can be decreased by setting up a collection factory, and all types of float can potentially be reduced by setting up a shared service centre.

6
Stock (inventory) management

The final part of the cash conversion cycle consists of stock management. Stocks tie up part of the company's liquid funds, and the longer they remain within the company, the longer they require working capital, which lengthens the cash conversion cycle.

Almost all companies need to maintain stocks for production and sales activities. The production department normally manages stocks, but decisions on stock levels need be taken in consultation with purchasing, sales and treasury. However, in most firms the treasury department has less or even no influence on this, although it is important for treasury to be involved in these decisions.

Stocks come in three forms:

- raw materials and supplies
- semi-finished products or goods in process
- goods in process and finished product

The cash manager is interested in the company's stock policy because:

- maintaining stocks leads to interest costs
- ordering stocks generates a negative cash flow
- paying for stocks requires a forecast of future liquidity demands

INTEREST COSTS OF STOCKS

As mentioned above, stocks generally account for a sizeable share of a company's total assets, so they tie up a considerable part of its liquid funds. They are also a non-earning asset, so stocks that are financed by outside sources, such as bank or supplier's credit, also incur debit interest. Since one of the cash manager's principal tasks is to optimise the company's interest result, he or she must closely monitor the size of stocks and try to exert influence to minimise stocks on hand.

NEGATIVE CASH FLOW FROM ORDERS

Another reason for the cash manager to be interested in the company's stock policy is that the periodic purchase of raw materials and supplies results in a cash outflow. The cash manager must bear this in mind when drawing up cash forecasts. His or her goal is to optimise timing of the orders by using the least amount of liquid funds.

The cash manager is also interested in the company's stock policy because it will affect the company's investment behaviour. By knowing and understanding this policy, the cash manager can also take cash outflows into consideration when making investment decisions.

6.1 Reasons for maintaining stocks

The three key motives for remaining stocks are:

- transaction motive
- precautionary motive
- speculative motive

TRANSACTION MOTIVE

A company normally keeps stocks to absorb the effects of non-synchronous incoming and outgoing product flows. Stocks of raw materials, supplies and semi-finished products make the production process smoother by allowing the company to respond to sales peaks and special customer orders.

PRECAUTIONARY MOTIVE

A company may want to maintain a buffer of stocks against unforeseen circumstances, such as strikes at suppliers or disruptions in successive stages of the production process. This is critical for securing its ability to always deliver goods to its customers within the required and pre-agreed response time.

SPECULATIVE OR HEDGE MOTIVE

If the prices of raw materials are expected to rise sharply, the company can decide to maintain larger stocks to cover itself against price increases. The reverse also occurs: if prices look likely to fall sharply, the company can temporarily maintain lower stock levels. This is a form of financial speculation, and many companies use specific financial instruments to hedge against price fluctuations in their raw materials. Examples include options and futures, which are traded on commodity exchanges.

The most important disadvantages of keeping stocks are:

- interest costs – investment of capital ties up liquid funds, leading to higher interest costs or lower interest income
- stocking costs – such as transport, storage, administration, security, preservation insurance and decay
- the risk of redundant or unmarketable stocks due to changes in demand or production methods

The cash manager is primarily focused on interest costs.

6.2 The required size of stocks

The size and composition of stocks differ between companies. This is influenced by three main factors:

- financial factors
- commercial factors
- operational factors

FINANCIAL FACTORS

Stocks absorb capital and can create an interest cost, and the amount of interest incurred varies from company to company. Some firms find it easier than others to gain access to the necessary sources to finance its stock.

COMMERCIAL FACTORS

From a commercial point of view, it is important to know how customers will react if a company is unexpectedly unable to deliver. If the company sells tailor-made products, the discontinuity risk may not be significant; but if, for example, a supermarket cannot keep popular items in stock, it will rapidly lose its customer base. Moreover, companies active in markets with irregular sales patterns are likely to maintain higher stock levels.

Customer service is also an important commercial consideration. For example, a company may be committed to delivering a certain minimum percentage of goods on time, and the higher the target, the greater the need for ample stocks.

OPERATIONAL ASPECTS

The size of stocks is also determined by operational factors, and managing these operational factors is known as 'production operational management' (POM). Operational factors can include:

1. the nature of the production process
2. product storage life
3. nature of the purchasing market
4. logistics of the purchasing processes

The nature of the production process includes: methods, throughput time and reliability of the production process. A reliable production process allows the company to maintain fewer stocks of semi-finished or finished products, which are used as buffer against production disruption.

The second operational factor that determines the size of stocks is the product's storage life and susceptibility to obsolescence (colour, style, taste). The greater the risk of obsolescence, the lower the stocks must be.

The third operational factor is the nature of the purchasing market. If purchases are made seasonally, the company needs to obtain large stocks when they are available, and these supplies will dwindle until fresh stocks become available again.

A final factor that determines stock levels is the logistics of the purchasing processes. Many companies use Electronic Data Interchange (EDI) (see previous section), which enables companies to interface directly with the supplier's computer system, giving the supplier real-time and exact information on the company's forthcoming purchasing demands. This enables just-in-time delivery.

The company with an integrated purchasing plan can afford to maintain lower levels of stock, providing it can rely on suppliers to deliver products quickly and in accordance with specifications. Companies generally only make use of EDI to communicate with favoured suppliers, with whom they have good and long-standing relationships.

On the basis of the financial, commercial and operational factors, the company will set a certain minimum stock level. This creates a tension between financial and commercial interests. The cash manager wants to keep stocks as low as possible in order to minimise interest costs, while the sales team presses for the highest possible stocks to avoid disappointing customers. This balancing act between two opposing objectives has to be carefully managed and controlled by the organisation.

7
Shared service centres

Many companies, particularly multinational corporations (MNCs), can achieve efficiency gains through the introduction of a shared service centre (SSC). An SSC has a material impact on the company's core processes. An SSC combines multiple tasks, processes, general ledgers and IT infrastructures in one central location, and reduces them to one procedure and process per task. Harmonising procedures by introducing uniform enterprise resource planning (ERP) systems can produce measurable financial gains. Another common benefit is more accurate financial reporting. Introducing an SSC can lead to considerable efficiencies if it is done well. At a minimum, an SSC can provide insights into a company's end-to-end receivables and payables process.

For some companies, setting up an SSC may require more investment than they'll ever get back in cost savings, so instead they may look at centralising payment execution through a payment factory. With this arrangement, local subsidiaries retain their own accounts payable and accounts receivable management, but the payment factory provides a single interface to the company's various banks. While a payment factory does not provide all the benefits of an SSC, it can lead to a reduction in transaction costs. Furthermore, centralising payments provides a better understanding of cash flows, which helps to improve liquidity management.

The tasks that an SSC often fulfils are:

- payments and collections
- accounts payable management
    - receiving invoices
    - checking invoice and packing slip
    - reconciliation
    - making lists of payable invoices for liquidity forecasting purposes
- accounts receivable management
    - sending invoices
    - reconciliation
    - making maturity calendars
    - making list of late payers
- purchasing
    - centralised purchasing
    - management of strategic reserves
    - tactical purchasing

Furthermore, the SSC can also be entrusted with the centralised execution of tasks that are not related to working capital management. These include:

- personnel affairs
    - employee benefits
    - recruitment
    - salary and wage administration
    - training
    - career planning
- real estate
    - lease administration
    - real estate management
    - maintenance
- information technology
    - data centre management
    - computer network management
    - network support
- finance and accounting
    - group bookkeeping
    - preparing fiscal balance sheets
    - administration of expenses and business travel
- compliance activities
- internal accountancy services

Finally an SSC can carry out some or even all of a company's treasury management tasks.

The creation of an SSC can take place in various stages. For example, the SSC can initially operate as a payment and collection factory, and subsequently, it can assume responsibility for the entire accounts receivable and payable management. Later, additional responsibilities can be added to the SSC's range of tasks.

The advantages of the central execution of tasks are:

- economies of scale
- greater scope for automating services
- the opportunity to engage better-qualified staff
- more uniform service
- better opportunities for liquidity management
- enables companies to focus on their core businesses

One key challenge of SSCs, to MNCs in particular, is that they require individual operating companies to hand over key functions to the parent company, which they may be resistant to doing. Another challenge is that the lines of communication between operating companies and their suppliers and customers may be unclear and indirect. If any problems occur with invoices or payments, suppliers and customers have to turn to unfamiliar SSC staff for help, rather than their local contact, who is more familiar with local circumstances.

Despite these disadvantages, more and more international companies have found that the SSC's financial and control benefits justify its establishment. As with many business trends, SSCs first began appearing in the United States, but they are becoming increasingly widespread among European and Asian companies.

8
Calculating the duration of the cash conversion cycle

In the previous paragraphs we have demonstrated the importance of keeping the cash conversion cycle as short as possible. We have also looked at measures a company can take to shorten the duration of the cash conversion cycle, but how can the company measure the duration of the cash conversion cycle?

We have seen that the following balance sheet items have an impact on the cash conversion cycle:

- accounts payable
- accounts receivable
- stocks

The duration of the cash conversion cycle can be worked out by computing the turnover ratios of accounts payable, accounts receivable and stocks. The ratios reveal how long each of the three items remains on the balance sheet. In the case of accounts payable (days payable outstanding or DPO), the ratios show the average time that the company makes use of supplier's credit, thereby improving its working capital position. With accounts receivable (days sales outstanding or DSO) and Inventory Turnover (IT), the ratios show how long these items take up the company's liquid funds.

In the following subsections we show how the DPO, DSO and IT ratios are calculated. We then use these turnover rates to calculate the duration of the cash conversion cycle. Finally, we show how to measure the potential savings to be had from shortening the cash conversion cycle.

The balance sheet and turnover data given below are used for this example.

Figure 7 *Balance sheet and turnover figures*

(x EUR 1,000,000)			
buildings	100	equity	170
machinery	50	long term debt	150
stock	150	accounts payable	100
accounts receivable	130	short term debt	50
cash	40		
total	470	total	470

(x EUR 1,000,000)		
sales on account	EUR	1.000
cost price of sales	EUR	700
procurement on account	EUR	500

8.1 Days payables outstanding (DPO)

Days payable outstanding, or (average) turnover rate of the accounts payable, shows how quickly the company pays its suppliers, and is calculated as follows:

$$\text{days payables} = \frac{\text{accounts payable}}{\text{procurement on account}} \times 365$$

in our example:

$$\text{days payables} = \frac{100{,}000{,}000}{500{,}000{,}000} \times 365 = 73 \text{ days}$$

In this example, the company pays invoices, on average, after 73 days. If the industry average were 50 days, the company should consider why it pays later than the industry average, as well as reviewing the effect of this policy. It may be the case, for example, that paying later gives the company a competitive advantages over its peers. The firm is using supplier's credit to fund its own operations for 23 days longer than its peers, and for this period is not relying on other sources of funding.

An extension of the accounts payable ratio leads to a proportionate increase in the accounts payable item and has a positive effect on the company's liquidity.

A company can increase its accounts payable turnover rate by:

- negotiating more favourable delivery conditions
- making more use of supplier's credit
- always paying on the payment deadline

8.2 Days sales outstanding (DSO)

The days sales outstanding (DSO), or average turnover rate of the accounts receivable, can be defined as the average time that elapses between invoice and collection of receivables from customers. This collection process is also known as the 'order-to-cash conversion cycle'.

We calculate the accounts receivable turnover rate as follows:

$$\text{days sales outstanding} = \frac{\text{accounts receivable}}{\text{sales on account}} \times 365$$

in our example:

$$\text{days sales outstanding} = \frac{130{,}000{,}000}{1{,}000{,}000{,}000} \times 365 = 47 \text{ days}$$

In this case, the company receives payment, on average, 47 days after sending out an invoice. If the industry average were 40 days, the company should consider why it collects seven days later than the industry average. The difference may put the company at competitive disadvantage to its peers, because it is effectively providing credit to its customers seven days longer than the industry average, which it must fund either internally or through bank credit.

An acceleration of the accounts receivable turnover rate, in this example, would reduce the average to 30 days. This would lead to a proportionate decrease in the accounts-receivable balance, and a proportionate reduction in the liquidity cost because fewer funds are trapped in receivables.

A company can reduce its DSO by:

- renegotiating the payment term
- granting discounts for early payment
- making adjustments to the invoicing system to enable faster invoicing or to state payment instructions more clearly on the invoice
- reorganising the accounts receivable administration into a smoother process
- tightening the collection policy, by selecting a more efficient method of payment, such as a direct debit mandate
- discouraging use of cheques

When calculating the accounts-receivable turnover rate, only the outstanding items are included. Un-invoiced sales (system float) are not included. As a result, the turnover rate of accounts receivable is structurally understated.

8.3 Inventory days outstanding (IDO)

The inventory days outstanding (IDO) shows how long, on average, the total inventory remains within the company.

IDO is calculated as follows:

$$\text{stock turnover rate} = \frac{\text{stock}}{\text{cost price of sales}} \times 365$$

in our example:

$$\text{stock turnover rate} = \frac{150{,}000{,}000}{500{,}000{,}000} \times 365 = 78 \text{ days}$$

Inventory with a slow turnover remains on the balance sheet longer and occupies more capital than inventory with a fast turnover, so a company should try to keep inventory as low as possible. That said, however, keeping inventory too low can result in additional ordering costs. In this example, the inventory remains within the company, on average, for 78 days, but it doesn't say anything about individual items in the stock. For example, this figure may be partly the result of obsolete stock that is unsellable.

An acceleration of the inventory turnover rate leads to a proportionate decrease in the inventory item on the balance sheet, and a proportionate increase in available liquidity.

Companies can reduce IDO by:

- better managing stock
- ordering of stocks 'just in time'

8.4 Duration of the cash conversion cycle

The cash conversion cycle is the result of the turnover rates of stocks, accounts receivable and accounts payable. If we know the turnover rates, we can calculate the total duration of the cash conversion cycle as follows:

duration of the cash conversion cycle
=
days sales outstanding
+
stock turnover rate
-/-
days payables

Assuming the turnover rates presented above, the duration of the cash conversion cycle can be calculated as follows:

Duration of cash conversion cycle = 47 days + 78 days - 73 days = 52 days.

This means that every euro put into the company is locked in the company's operational processes for 52 days.

8.5 Savings by shortening the cash conversion cycle

In this final section we indicate how much the company can save by changing the various turnover rates. The balance sheet and turnover data are the same as in the earlier example, and an interest rate of 5% is assumed.

The net working capital of the company amounts to (150 + 130 + 40 - 100 - 50) million euros = EUR 170,000,000. The annualised interest costs of maintaining working capital for this company are: EUR 170,000,000 x 5% = EUR 8,500,000.

Let's look at the interest that the company can save by getting its customers to pay faster by means of a more efficient order-to-collect cycle.

The days sales outstanding ratio is 47 days. If the company manages to reduce this by seven days to 40 days, the accounts-receivable balance will decrease. We begin by calculating the amount of this decrease:

$$\text{days sales outstanding} = \frac{\text{accounts receivable}}{\text{sales on account}} \times 365$$

is rewritten as follows:

$$\text{accounts receivable} = \frac{\text{sales on account x days sales outstanding}}{365}$$

The new value for the accounts receivable item thus becomes:

$$\text{accounts receivable} = \frac{1{,}000{,}000{,}000 \times 40}{365} = 109{,}589{,}040$$

This shows a reduction in the accounts-receivable balance of EUR 20,410,960, which means an identical amount of liquid funds have been released. The company realises an annualised interest gain of:

EUR 20,410,960 x 0,05 = EUR 1,020,548

This is a considerable gain, more than 1% of total sales, and making similar changes to other ratios would produce even higher gains. It clearly shows the impact of strong working capital management. The company can make similar improvements to shortening the inventory days oustanding rate and lengthening the days payables outstanding.

Chapter 13
Foreign Exchange Risk Management

Introduction

As companies are increasingly international in nature, treasurers frequently have to contend with incoming or outgoing foreign currency cash flows. Apart from the challenges that accompany international payments, a treasurer is also faced with foreign exchange risks. This is because foreign exchange rates tend to be in constant flux. The introduction of the euro may have eliminated foreign exchange risks within the European Monetary Union, but they continue to apply outside the euro zone.

1
What is foreign exchange risk?

Foreign exchange risk, also known as currency risk, is the risk that fluctuations of foreign exchange rates may have a negative impact on the earnings of a company or its value. A corporate treasurer may be faced with three different types of foreign exchange risks:

- transaction-related risks
- currency translation risks
- economic risks

1.1 Transaction-related risks

Transaction-related foreign exchange risk is the risk that company profits will be reduced if purchasing or selling prices are negatively affected by exchange rate fluctuations. This risk occurs when goods or services are imported or exported and payment is made in a foreign currency. Every company with international dealings in other currencies other than the home currency runs transaction-related foreign exchange risks.

Transaction-related foreign exchange risk impacts the profitability and, therefore, the Income Statement of a company.

EXAMPLE

A German luxury car dealer has sold ten Jaguars on order. The selling price is EUR 250,000. The dealer orders the cars from the British factory, which will deliver them in ten months' time. The invoice price is GBP 125,000. The factory requires the dealer to pay for the Jaguars when they are delivered. The dealer will then need to buy sterling in order to pay the factory.

The current GBP rate is GBP 0.7000 per EUR 1.00. This means that the purchase price will amount to EUR 171,428.57 (125,000 / 0.700).

The dealer runs the risk that the GBP rate will rise during the coming months. For example, if the GBP rate after ten months amounts to EUR 0.5000, he will have to pay EUR 250,000 to buy GBP 125,000. The purchase price will then equal the selling price and he will not make a profit at all!

Transaction-related risks are the most common types of foreign exchange risk. Covering such risks is part of the daily activities of a treasury department. In this chapter, therefore, we will restrict our attention to transaction-related risks and to the financial products that can be used for hedging.

1.2 Currency translation risk

Currency translation risk is the risk that foreign exchange rate fluctuations will directly affect a company's value. A business is prone to currency translation risks if it possesses assets in a specific currency but does not have matching liabilities in the same currency.

EXAMPLE

A company takes over another company in the United States and needs to pay the acquisition price in US dollars. In order to finance this takeover, the company obtains a euro denominated bank loan.

Once the company has transferred the acquisition sum, it lists the new US subsidiary as an asset on its balance sheet. This balance sheet item is stated in euros. If the US dollar exchange rate falls, the company will express this decline in its balance sheet – the value of its subsidiary will be reduced. The company lists the loan used to fund the acquisition as a balance sheet liability in euro. The fall of the dollar exchange rate does not affect the reported loan.

The drop in the dollar exchange rate leads to a decline in the value of the asset in question, while the value of the relevant liability remains the same. As a result, the company's equity is reduced.

Covering currency translation risks is an ad-hoc activity of a treasury department. This type of risk can be covered by obtaining a loan in a foreign currency or by converting a loan in one's own legal tender to another currency.

1.3 Economic risk

Economic risk is the risk that a company runs if the country in which its production occurs becomes 'expensive' in comparison with other countries. This would undermine the business's competitive position. The may occur because labour costs have risen, but it could also be due to a structurally higher exchange rate for the local currency.

The treasury department, however, is only indirectly involved in covering economic risks. Typically, it is the duty of the executive management of the company to determine how economic risk is hedged or managed. This is because often the only solution is to transfer production to a cheaper country. A treasurer may influence production strategy by expressing his view of future changes in foreign exchange rates.

2
Objectives, tasks and instruments of foreign exchange risk management

The objective of foreign exchange risk management is to shield a company's earnings and/or value from fluctuations in foreign exchange rates. Foreign exchange risk management involves the following tasks:

- determination of policy in relation to foreign exchange risks
- identification of foreign exchange risks
- development of a foreign exchange rate forecast
- closing hedging transactions

2.1 Determining policy in relation to foreign exchange risks

As a first step, a company needs to create a policy for dealing with foreign exchange risks. Some companies decide to eliminate all foreign exchange risks (defensive strategy). As soon as they detect a foreign exchange risk, they immediately take action to eliminate this risk. Other companies prefer not to react, but to leave these implicit foreign exchange positions entirely open. Many US companies follow this policy. Between these two poles of opinion, there are companies which partially cover their foreign exchange risks (offensive strategy).

These companies need to choose which foreign exchange risks they wish to cover and what part of them. Additionally, they have to decide for how long they plan to cover their risks.

To make these decisions companies first need to gain insight into the level of the currency risks they face. This is determined by two components: the actual exposure and the predicted future currency movements. The level of the currency risk can be calculated by the following equation:

Currency risk = exposure x currency movement

The treasurer first has to identify the company's exposures and then must estimate the possible movements in the relevant currencies.

2.1.1 Identifying foreign exchange exposures

Transaction risks may arise from export contracts, import contracts, tenders or from ongoing cash flows. Exposures related to transaction risk are sometimes divided into two separate types, each requiring a different approach in order to identify and hedge the related currency risk. We can distinguish between:

- contract exposures
- cash flow exposures

2.1.2 Contract exposures

Contract exposures are exposures related to single material individual contracts where prices are negotiated individually. The amount of these exposures can generally be predicted rather accurately. Figure 1 shows the different stages of either a 'purchase-to-pay' cycle or an 'order–to-collect' cycle and the related contract exposure.

Figure 1   *Contract exposure*

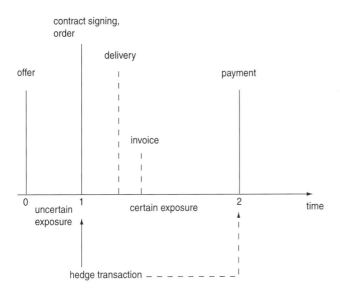

Between the moment that the company has either made an offer to its client or has received an offer from its supplier in period 0, and the moment the contract is signed in period 1, the company does not know whether it will actually run a currency risk. The risk will only occur if the contract is signed. If indeed the contract is signed, the company runs a transaction risk until the invoice has been paid. The risk lasts from period 1 to period 2.

Once an uncertain contract exposure has become a certain contract exposure, it can be hedged on a contract-by-contract basis. The hedge transaction should be executed immediately after the signing of a contract in period 1 in the diagram. The hedge transaction should cover the future cash income in period 2 in the diagram. Sometimes a company may want to hedge an uncertain exposure as well. The company then executes a hedge transaction as early as period 0. To take into account the uncertainty of the exposure, companies then often use currency options.

2.1.3 Cash flow exposures

Some companies are faced with a large number of small deliveries and/or collections, resulting in a large number of small but steady and predictable cash flows. The customers of those companies may order goods on an ongoing basis. Often, the prices are listed in a price list which is valid for a certain period (normally 3 to

12 months). Usually, the prices in the price lists are stated in the local currency. Some companies, however, allow their customers to pay in their home currency. The company than has a cash flow currency exposure.

In this case, it is not sensible to hedge the currency exposure on an order-to-order basis. The treasurer would have to execute many small hedge transactions.

Instead, the treasurer would use a cash flow forecast to identify the currency risk. If the company, for instance, forecasts sales revenues amounting to USD 15 million in one year, it may want to hedge the total exposure at the beginning of the period. Alternatively, the company may choose to divide the total hedge transaction into portions of 1/12 of the total amount, covering each month separately.

Figure 2 shows the continuous flow of funds related to small deliveries from the moment a price list has been issued until the moment the next price list is issued.

Figure 2   *Cash flow exposure*

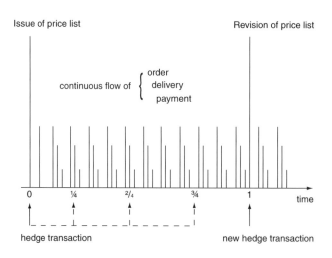

In figure 2 the company issues a price list in period 0 and in period 1. The company executes its hedge transactions when it issues the price list. Hedge transactions should cover the entire period for which the price list is valid, so the first hedge transaction should cover the interval between period 0 and period 1. The company may choose to spread the hedge transaction over four specific intervals: period 0, 1/4, 2/4 and 3/4.

The advantage of cash flow hedging versus contract hedging is that the treasurer has to execute fewer hedging transactions. The disadvantage is that the cash flow forecast might prove inaccurate. The uncertainty may apply to the volumes of the predicted cash flows or to the timing of the cash flows. In these cases, the hedge transactions might not fit with the actual exposures, leaving the company with a residual currency risk.

2.2 Developing a foreign exchange rate forecast

If a treasurer has identified an exposure but has decided to allow a specific foreign exchange risk to continue to exist or to wait before covering the position, he will need to estimate the implications of this decision.

To do so he will have to predict future changes in foreign exchange rates, or make a foreign exchange forecast. Such a forecast is made periodically prior to a treasury meeting, which is attended by the director of finance in addition to the treasurer and cash manager. Treasurers produce foreign exchange forecasts on the basis of their personal assessments, ideas presented by the banks and information sourced from newspapers and other media. However, foreign exchange markets are very difficult to predict, especially beyond the very near term.

2.3 Entering into transactions

Entering into foreign currency transactions with banks represents the final duty to be performed as part of foreign exchange risk management. A treasurer can use a broad range of financial products to cover his foreign exchange risks.

3
The currency market

The currency market is the place where various types of currencies are traded. In the currency market, there are specific rules and procedures regarding:

- exchange rate notation
- settlement date
- execution of a foreign exchange transaction

3.1 Exchange rate notation

Foreign exchange rates are stated in a standardised manner referred to as foreign exchange notation. In most cases the rate is quoted by expressing a single unit of one currency in terms of another. The first currency is the trade currency (the 'merchandise'), also called base currency, while the second is the price currency (the one in which the price of the merchandise is quoted):

EUR/USD = 1.2000.

In the notation, the euro is the trade currency and the US dollar is the price currency. A rate of 1.2000 means that the value of 1 euro is equal to 1.20 US dollars.

If the foreign exchange rate of the euro against the US dollar is EUR/USD = 1.2000, and a treasurer wishes to buy EUR 1,000,000 against US dollars, the treasurer will have to pay 1,000,000 x 1.2000 = USD 1,200,000.

If, on the other hand, the treasurer wishes to buy USD 1,000,000 with euros, the approach is simply invented. Now the dollar amount is the stated merchandise but the exchange rate reflects the opposite. In order to establish how many euros we need to pay for the dollar amount, we will need to use the reverse rate. Now the treasurer needs to pay 1,000,000 x 1/1.2000 = EUR 833,333.33.

What would it mean if the EUR/USD rate were to fall? Expressed in terms of dollars, the value of the euro would drop. In other words, the euro exchange rate would decline in relation to the US dollar and this naturally means that the USD dollar exchange rate would simultaneously rise.

3.2 Settlement date

Settlement is the actual delivery of the values that are traded in a financial contract. The day on which a financial transaction is settled is called the settlement date. In this connection, we can draw a distinction between the following two alternatives:

- delivery on the spot
- delivery in the future

Usually settlement of a foreign exchange transaction takes place on the second working day following the transaction's conclusion. If this is the case, the foreign exchange transaction is referred to as a spot transaction.

Where two parties enter into a foreign exchange transaction under the terms of which delivery is to be completed in the future, we call this a forward exchange contract. It is also called an outright transaction. In the case of a forward exchange contract (delivery in the future), the parties can choose to have delivery occur on any date they prefer (but not during a weekend or on a bank holiday).

Following is an example of a spot transaction.

EXAMPLE

Detex Gmbh. is notified by its bank on 2 April that the sum of USD 2,000,000 is to be deposited on its account with a value date of 4 April. The treasurer of Detex Inc. calls the bank on the same day and requests the US dollar exchange rate in euros.

A specialised salesperson in the dealing room, the corporate dealer, quotes him an exchange rate. Detex Inc. sells the amount at the stated rate. Settlement is effected two working days later, in this case on 4 April.

4
Foreign exchange risk management in practice

Companies generally prefer to avoid exchange risks. However, in many cases this is not possible. Companies then have to search for ways of managing them. We refer to this as covering a foreign exchange risk.

4.1 Avoiding foreign exchange risks

In theory any company can eliminate exchange risks by entering into import and export contracts in their home currency. This shifts the problem to its trading partner. Whether a company can do so depends on the strength of its bargaining position.

For example, a company based in the euro zone could eliminate all transaction related foreign exchange risk by entering into all contracts in euros. As it happens, the company treasurer will need to ensure that the relevant agreement does not contain a currency clause. Such a clause could stipulate that a price stated in euros will be modified if the EUR/USD exchange rate falls below a certain percentage, for example 5%. If such a clause is included in the contract, the euro zone company still faces exchange risk.

Another way to avoid exchange rate risks is to ensure that costs and revenues are denominated in the same currency. If, for instance, the customers of a euro-based company demanded that invoices should be stated in US dollars, the euro-based company could try to source its raw materials as far as possible in US dollars. The company might even consider locating production, as far as possible, in a US dollar denominated country.

A European treasurer who regularly receives and pays amounts in US dollars in order to avoid unnecessary foreign exchange risk would be well advised to open a foreign exchange account. Such an account is a current account held in a currency other than that of the company's home country – in this case a US dollar account. Without a US dollar account, the company would first have to buy foreign currency in order to pay for its operational costs and then sell the same currency at a later stage once it received customers' payments. But the exchange rate may have dropped by then, causing a loss.

With a US dollar account, the company could temporarily hold incoming US dollars in its US dollar account. The treasurer could then debit this account to cover any future outgoing US dollar payments. The treasurer could open the US dollar bank account in the country where the company is based or with a US bank. Many companies hold a variety of currency accounts in currency centres such as Amsterdam or London.

4.2 Covering foreign exchange risks

In many cases, companies will make offers stated in a foreign currency and/or will be invoiced in a foreign currency. These companies, as a result, have to face foreign exchange risks. They can use several financial instruments to cover these risks:

- forward exchange contracts
- currency futures
- currency options

5
Forward exchange contracts

A forward exchange contract – also referred to as an 'outright transaction' – is a currency transaction which provides for delivery on a future date. The parties involved respectively contract to buy and sell a foreign currency amount at an agreed rate – the forward exchange rate – on a date in the future, the delivery date.

The maturity date of a forward exchange contract is always two days before the delivery date (settlement date). For example, the maturity date of a forward exchange contract which provides that JPY 3 million will be sold for euros on 10 November is 8 November (assuming both dates are not business holidays). On the maturity date, the bank will contact its customer with a reminder that the forward exchange contract is due to be settled in two days.

A forward exchange contract is an over-the-counter (OTC) product. Every forward exchange contract is a transaction in its own right, concluded between two market players. Dates and rates are solely determined by the two parties entering into the trade.

5.1 Differences between spot and forward exchange rates, and swap points

The exchange rate of a forward exchange contract is determined at the time when the agreement is concluded. It represents the exchange rate to be used when the currencies are exchanged on the settlement date. The forward exchange rate is calculated as follows:

Forward exchange rate = spot rate + premium or discount.

There are three possible ways in which the spot rate can differ from a forward exchange rate:

- forward exchange rate exceeds the spot rate, in which case we refer to a 'premium'
- forward exchange rate is less than the spot rate, in which case we refer to a 'discount'
- forward exchange rate is identical to the spot rate, in which case they are 'at par'

The following rules apply in this respect:

- the currency of the country with a higher interest rate trades at a discount
- the currency of the country with a lower interest rate commands a premium

---

EXAMPLE

Since euro interest rates are higher than those in Japan, the euro is discounted against the Japanese yen. The forward exchange rate for EUR/JPY is lower than its spot rate.

We calculate the forward exchange rate of a currency by adding the relevant premium to the spot rate of the currency or by deducting the discount from it. Here is an example of the six-month forward exchange rate for the euro, expressed in terms of sterling (spot rate EUR/GBP = 0.7000), and the three-month forward exchange rate for the euro, expressed in terms of Japanese yen (spot rate EUR/JPY = 140.00).

	EUR/GBP	EUR/JPY
Spot rate	0,7000	140,00
premium (+) or discount-)	+ 0,0071	– 105
Forward rate	0,7071	138,95

The premium or discount is stated as swap points. The swap points can be roughly indicated by using the following formula:

$$\text{premium / discount} = \text{exchange rate} \times \text{difference in annual interest rate}^* \times \frac{\text{days}}{360}$$

* as a percentage, for example, 0.01.

EXAMPLE

The six-month euro money market rate amounts to 2.75% and the six-month GBP money market rate amounts to 4.75%. The EUR/GBP exchange rate is 0.7000. The actual number of days is 182.

We can see that the GBP interest rate exceeds the EUR one. This means that the EUR commands a premium over the GBP. The EUR/GBP forward exchange rate therefore exceeds the spot rate.

This premium can be calculated as follows:
Premium = 0.7000 x 0.02 x 182/365 = 0.0071.
The premium therefore amounts to 71 points.

According to this calculation, the EUR/GBP forward exchange rate will amount to 0.7071.

The precise formula for calculating swap points is as follows:

$$\text{swap points} = \frac{\text{interest rate differential}^*}{(\text{m/n x 1/spot rate}) + i^*/\text{spot rate}}$$

Where:

m = the basis for calculating interest (year = 360 or 365)
n = the term of the swap contract (the time between the spot and the forward dates)
i = the interest rate of the currency that is mentioned first in the exchange rate notation

* The interest rate differential and i are stated as a percentage, for example, 0.01 and 0.0575.

EXAMPLE

On 8 February a French exporting company enters into a contract of sale with a British customer for the supply of parts priced at GBP 2,000,000. The scheduled delivery date is 10 October and payment is expected on 10 November.

In order to cover its foreign exchange risks, the French company enters into a 9-month forward exchange contract, under the terms of which it will sell GBP 2 million with euros on 10 November. On 8 February the EUR/GBP spot rate is 0.6255 (the spot date is 10 February) and the 9-month premium amounts to 0.0045.
In this case, the EUR/GBP forward exchange rate will amount to 0.6255 + 0.0045 = 0.6300.

On behalf of the forward exchange contract, on the settlement date (10 November) the customer's GBP account will be debited for GBP 2 million and its EUR account will be credited for 2,000,000 / 0.6300 = EUR 3,174,603.17.

5.2 Offsetting a forward exchange contract

If an import or export transaction is not executed for one reason or another, payment will not be made either. Suppose that a treasurer has entered into a forward exchange contract to buy a foreign currency with an import transaction in mind. If the transaction does not proceed, he will have no need for the bank to effect actual delivery of the currency. The opposite is true in the case of an export transaction. If it does not proceed and the treasurer therefore does not receive any payment in a foreign currency, he will not be able to deliver the relevant foreign currency under the terms of any forward exchange contract that may have been concluded.

In either case the treasurer can conclude an offsetting forward exchange contract to negate the initial contract.

On 8 August the company referred to in the previous example receives notice from the United Kingdom that his customer is bankrupt and that delivery will not proceed. The company will, therefore, not receive GBP 2 million on 10 November. However, this amount has already been sold to the bank under the terms of the forward exchange contract. Now the company finds that it has a short position in GBP starting 10 November. It has a contractual duty to deliver currency it does not have. It will want to remedy its short position by entering into an offsetting forward exchange contract: a purchase of GBP 2 million with euros on the settlement date of 10 November.

However, foreign exchange markets are volatile. Let us assume that the EUR/GBP exchange rate has fallen to 0.6200 (sterling has thus become more expensive) in the meantime. Since the term from 8 August to 8 November is only three months, we need the 3-month premium. This amounts to 0.0015. On 10 November the forward exchange rate for the off-setting contract will amount to 0.6215.

Consequently, on 10 November the company will need to pay the sum of EUR 3,218,020.92 (2,000,000 / 0.6215) for the GBP 2,000,000. On 8 November the corporate dealer will be notified by his back office that two forward exchange contracts concluded with this customer will mature on 8 November. Although the dealer knows that the second forward exchange contract was concluded to cover the first, she will nevertheless call her customer to notify him to this effect.

On 10 November the following sums will pass through the customer's accounts.

GBP account: GBP 2,000,000 debited;
GBP 2,000,000 credited.

and

EUR account: EUR 3,174,603.17 credited;
EUR 3,218,020.92 debited.

We can see that these two contracts have resulted in a loss of EUR 43,417.75. On the one hand, this is due to the fact that on 8 August the sterling exchange rate was higher than it was on 8 February. In addition, the 3-month premium commanded over the euro used for the forward exchange contract of 8 August amounted to less than the 9-month premium used for the original forward exchange contract.

6
Currency futures

A future is an exchange-traded financial contract which stipulates that its buyer will do the following:

- either purchase a specific financial sum from the seller of the future at a predetermined time in the future and at a rate which the parties agree on when they enter into the contract, or
- settle the difference between the market rate of the underlying product and the contract price with the seller

Unlike forward exchange contracts, currency futures are always traded on an exchange. Because futures are traded on an exchange, their terms and conditions are standardised. The following aspects have been standardised:

- the value of the contract – the number of units of value covered by the contract
- its term – the contract's maturity or expiry date

The Chicago Mercantile Exchange is the most important international market for trade in currency futures. This exchange lists futures in many currencies, such as the euro, sterling, the Australian dollar, the Brazilian real and the Swiss franc. At the Chicago Mercantile Exchange, the various currencies are actually delivered on their respective settlement dates.

The rate the parties agree to when they enter into a currency futures contract is the forward exchange rate of the two currencies involved. It is always determined on the basis of the spot rate on the day in question, and the premium or discount applicable over the remainder of the term. At the end of every day, the rate is compared with that of the previous day and the difference is settled between the futures exchange and the other party. We refer to this as a variation call. Any party wishing to enter into a futures contract must deposit an amount into an account held with the exchange by way of security. This is known as the margin call.

Currency futures are mainly used in Anglo-Saxon countries, in addition to forward exchange contracts, to cover a future currency position.

On 8 February an American company enters into an agreement of sale with a German customer for the supply of computer equipment for the sum of EUR 2,500,000. The delivery date is 8 June and payment is expected on 8 July.

The American supplier wishes to cover itself against a drop in the EUR exchange rate by selling EUR/USD futures contracts on the Chicago Mercantile Exchange. The standard contract value of EUR/USD futures is EUR 125,000. The supplier will, therefore, sell 20 contracts (EUR 2,500,000 / EUR 125,000). The EUR/USD series expires on Fridays. In October this is 6, 13, 20 and 27 July. The supplier opts for the series which is closest to the probable date of payment, 11 July.

296 | The current EUR/USD exchange rate is 1.1900 and the contract rate for the EUR/USD series which expires on 13 July, is 1.1847.

The table below lists the changes in the rate of each futures contract during its term and shows how the profit or loss made on it is settled every day.

Period	Spot rate EUR/USD	Swap points until 6/7	Contract rate	Daily profit and loss
day 0	1.1900	0.0053	1.1847	n.a.
day 1	1.1902	0.0052	1.1850	2,500,000 x - 0.0003 = – USD 750 *
day 2	1.1890	0.0051	1.1839	2,500,000 x 0.0011 = USD 2750
day 3	1.185	0.0050	1.1845	2,500,000 x - 0.0005 = – USD 1250
				p.m.
4 May	1.1925	0.0020	1.1925	p.m.
5 May	1.1938	0.0020	1.1918	2,500,000 x 0.0007 = USD 1750
				p.m.
5 July	1.8715	0.0001	1.1714	p.m
6 July	1.8708	0	1.1708	2,500,000 x 0.0006 = USD 1500

Cash managers use currency futures in the same way as they use forward exchange contracts. Actually, the main difference between the two is that forward exchange contracts are traded over-the-counter and are, therefore, more flexible than futures contracts. Another advantage of forward exchange contracts is that a treasurer will not have to contend with daily transfers based on the settlement of exchange rate variations.

A benefit of futures is that their prices are published every day and pricing is, therefore, completely transparent. Thus it is not necessary to shop around for the best price. Additionally, the other party to a futures contract is always an official exchange. With futures contracts, the risk of default is smaller than where one enters into an over-the-counter transaction with a bank as one's contracting party.

7
Currency options

A currency option is a financial product which entitles the person who purchases it to buy (in the case of a call option) or sell (a put option) foreign currency at an agreed rate (the strike price) during the term of the option up to the date it matures (the expiry date). This right may be valid for a pre-arranged term (an American option) or only at the expiry date (a European option). To obtain this right, the buyer of the option has to pay a premium.

The person who sells an option is called the writer. He receives the option premium. In exchange for the latter, he undertakes to sell (in the case of a call option) or buy (a put option) a sum in a specific currency.

The right to buy euros is called a EUR call. Since the right to buy euros is equivalent to the right to sell US dollars, this currency option is also referred to as a US put. The following notation is broadly used: EUR call / USD put.

7.1 Listed options and over-the-counter options

Some options are traded on an exchange. We refer to them as listed options. Listed options are standardised options. The following three aspects of a currency option contract are standardised:

- the value of the contract
- the term
- the strike price

OTC currency options are tailor-made options covering virtually all convertible currencies. (These currencies can be freely exchanged for others.) In principle, any amount or term is possible.

OTC currency options are mostly settled by means of actual delivery. When a currency option is exercised, a currency transaction is actually executed at the strike price. If they wish, the parties can then offset their resultant positions in the market.

7.2 The value of an option

The option premium is made up of the following two parts:

-   intrinsic value
-   time and expected value

7.2.1 Intrinsic value

The intrinsic value is the difference between the market rate of the underlying instrument and the strike price.

A call option has intrinsic value if the market rate of the underlying instrument is higher than its exercise rate. If the market rate of the underlying instrument rises further, the intrinsic value will increase in direct proportion. A put option has intrinsic value if the rate of the underlying instrument is less than its strike price. The intrinsic value of an option can never be negative but is always equal to or greater than nil.

We can use the terms below to specify whether or not an option has intrinsic value.

IN THE MONEY (ITM)
If an option has intrinsic value, we can also say that it is 'in the money'. The greater the intrinsic value of an option, the deeper it is in the money.

AT THE MONEY (ATM)
If the market rate of the underlying instrument is equal to its strike price or almost so, the intrinsic value of the option in question will be nil, or close to it, and we refer to it as 'at the money'.

OUT OF THE MONEY (OTM)
If the rate of the underlying instrument exceeds the strike price of a put option, or is less than that of a call option (in either case the intrinsic value is nil), we say that the option is 'out of the money'.

The intrinsic value of a EUR call /USD put and EUR put/US call option with a strike price of EUR/USD 1.2000 changes as follows in accordance with the following varying market exchange rates.

EUR/USD spot rate	Intrinsic value Call EUR/USD 1.2000	Intrinsic value Put EUR/USD 1.2000
1.1900	0 (otm)	0,0100 (itm)
1.1950	0 (otm)	0,0050 (itm)
1.2000	0 (atm)	0 (atm)
1.2050	0,0050 (itm)	0 (otm)
1.2100	0,0100 (itm)	0 (otm)

7.2.2 Time value

In the case of both a call and a put option, we can consider the intrinsic value to be the minimum value of the option in question. The option premium generally exceeds the intrinsic value. That part of it which exceeds the intrinsic value is referred to as the time value. If an option has an intrinsic value equal to zero (an out-of-the-money option), its premium will only comprise its time value.

Several months prior to its expiry date, the EUR call /USD put option with a strike price of 1.2000 of the previous example is listed at USD 0.0075. At the same point in time, the EUR/USD exchange rate amounts to 1.2040. We can now calculate the time value of this call option as follows.

The intrinsic value of the call option is the difference between its market and strike price: 1.2040 – 1.2000 = 0.0040.

The time value is the difference between the option premium and the intrinsic value: 0.0075 – 0.0040 = 0.0035.

7.3 Currency options in practice

Options provide a company with a way of limiting potential losses on a currency position, while allowing it to benefit from favourable changes in exchange rates. However, the company will pay a price for this: the option premium.

Both importers and exporters can use options. This is typically true for companies wishing to tender for a foreign project. These companies can use options as an instrument to cover potential foreign exchange risks without committing to an unwanted currency position if the bid is unsuccessful.

An importer in the euro zone who must make foreign currency payments over a certain period of time, and who anticipates an increase in the exchange rate of the currency in question, may wish to eliminate the foreign exchange risks to a large extent by buying a call option in the relevant currency (FC). This option is also a put option on the euro: (EUR put / 'FC' call).

If the exchange rate of the relevant foreign currency in relation to the euro is higher (and the EUR/FC rate is thus lower) than the strike price of the option on the expiry date, he will exercise his option. If the exchange rate of the relevant foreign currency in relation to the euro is lower (and the EUR/Foreign Currency is thus higher) than the exercise rate, he will not exercise his option but will buy the relevant currency on the spot market.

On the other hand, an exporter can cover the exchange risks attaching to future receipts by buying a put option on the foreign currency (EUR call / FC put).

EXAMPLE

A US importer is required to pay an Austrian supplier EUR 100,000 for a consignment of skis in two months' time. In order to cover his foreign exchange risks, he buys a EUR call / USD put option with a principal value of EUR 100,000, and a term of two months. The strike price of the option is EUR/USD 1.2000 and the option premium is USD 4.45 per EUR 100. In total, the option premium therefore amounts to USD 4,450. The current EUR/USD spot rate is 1.1800.

If, on the expiry date after two months, the EUR/USD rate is 1.2700, the treasurer of the US company will exercise the option. That is to say he will purchase euros at a EUR/USD exchange rate of 1.2000 in accordance with the options contract. The call option premium amounted to USD 0.0445 per euro. On balance, he buys these euros at a EUR/USD exchange rate of 1.2445 (strike price of 1.2000 + option premium of 0.0445).

While it is true that this is more expensive compared to the original spot rate (EUR/USD 1.1800), if he had not covered himself, he would have had to purchase the euros at a EUR/USD exchange rate of 1.2700 (the exchange rate on the expiry date).

If, on the expiry date after two months, the EUR/USD rate is less than 1.2000, the importer will not exercise his option and will let it expire. Instead, he will buy euros at their lower current market rate. However, he has already paid for the option premium of USD 0.0445 per euro. On balance, he will then have paid the market exchange rate plus the option premium.

An Italian exporter has a GBP claim based on exports to the United Kingdom. The due date for payment is in two months' time. The sterling exchange rate is EUR/GBP 0.6667. The Italian company wishes to cover itself against a drop in the value of the British pound (this is the same as a rise in the value of the euro) while simultaneously keeping the opportunity to profit from any increase in its exchange rate. In this case he would therefore want to buy a EUR call / GBP put option.

The strike price of the option is EUR/GBP 0.7000. The principal value of this option is EUR 1,000,000. The option premium amounts to GBP 0.0120 per euro.

We can now distinguish between the following two alternatives on the expiry date:

1. The option is in the money – the EUR/GBP exchange rate is 0.7200, for example.
    The treasurer will exercise his option. He will sell GBP (buy EUR) at the strike price of 0.7000. However, he has also paid the option premium. The effective rate of exchange for the sale of his British pounds, once the option premium cost is incorporated, will therefore be EUR/GBP 0.7120.

2. The option is out of the money – the EUR/GBP exchange rate is 0.6800, for example.

The option expires without any value. The treasurer sells sterling for euros in the marketplace at the prevailing exchange rate of 0.6800. His effective EUR/GBP exchange rate amounts to 0.6920 (the market rate of 0.6800 + option premium of 0.0120).

7.4 Zero-cost options

Companies are often reluctant to pay option premiums and, therefore, are inclined to refrain from purchasing options. With this in mind, banks have developed various constructions which provide the benefits of options but require treasurers to pay a smaller premium or none at all. In this section we will consider two options constructions for which no option premium is payable. We refer to them as zero-cost options:

- cylinder options
- profit-sharing options

7.4.1 Cylinder options

A zero-cost cylinder is an option where a company either:

- simultaneously buys a call option and sells a put option for the same principal amount and for an identical premium; or
- simultaneously buys a put option and sells a call option for the same principal amount and for an identical premium.

Suppose that a treasurer has the following requirements:

- he wishes to cover himself against an increase in the USD exchange rate
- he wants to benefit from a drop in the USD exchange rate, *up to a certain level*
- he does not wish to pay any option premium

In this case he can enter into a cylinder. He buys a EUR put/USD call option and instead of paying a premium, he writes a EUR call/USD put option with an identical principal sum for the same option premium. As a result of this transaction, the treasurer is protected against high USD exchange rates. He will also be able to profit from a decrease in the latter to a certain extent, that is to say, up to a specified level.

EXAMPLE

A European company needs to pay a supplier the sum of USD 1,000,000 in three months' time. The current EUR/USD exchange rate is 1.2000. The company treasurer wishes to cover the risk of an increase in the USD exchange rate (a fall in the EUR/USD rate) but wants to benefit from any decline in this rate and does not want to pay any option premium.

The 3-month EUR/USD forward exchange rate amounts to 1.2050. The option premium for a 3-month EUR put/USD call option with a strike price of 1.1850 is 0.1000. The option premium for a 3-month EUR call/USD put option with a strike price of 1.2250 is also 0.1000. The principal amount of both option contracts is the same: USD 1,000,000.

The treasurer buys a 3-month EUR put/USD call option with a strike of 1.1850 and writes a 3-month EUR call/ USD put option with a strike of 1.2250. This can be done free of charge. After all, the premiums for both options are identical.

What is the outcome of this strategy?

EUR/USD-spot rate after three months	EUR-put/ USD-call itm, atm, otm	EUR-call/ USD-put itm, atm, otm	Actions	effective EUR/USD-rate
1.1700	itm	otm	treasurer exercises	1.1850
1.1850	atm	otm	treasurer exercises	1.1850
1.1900	otm	otm	treasurer buys in the market	1.1900
1.2200	otm	otm	treasurer buys in the market	1.2200
1.2250	otm	atm	bank exercises	1.2250
1.2500	otm	itm	bank exercises	1.2250

The treasurer is protected against any increase in the value of the dollar below a EUR/USD exchange rate of 1.1850. In this case, the EUR put/USD call option is in the money and the treasurer will exercise his option. The bank has a duty to deliver USD at the rate of EUR/USD = 1.1850.

The treasurer is able to benefit from a minor increase in the value of the dollar. For example, if the USD exchange rate drops to EUR/USD 1.2200 neither option will be exercised and the treasurer will be able to buy USD on the market at EUR/USD = 1.2200.

We can also see, however, that the treasurer will not be able to benefit from any fall in the value of the USD exchange rate above EUR/USD 1.2250. In this case, the EUR call/USD put option will be in the money and the bank will exercise it. Because the treasurer is the writer of this option, he will have a duty to buy USD from the bank at the strike price of EUR/USD = 1.2250.

7.4.2 Profit-sharing options

A zero-cost profit-sharing option is a construction in which a company either:

- simultaneously buys a call option and sells a put option of a different value for an identical premium; or
- simultaneously buys a put option and sells a call option of a different value for an identical premium.

The treasurer now has the following requirements:

–   he wishes to cover himself against an increase in the USD exchange rate
–   he wants to benefit from *any* drop in the USD exchange rate
–   he does not wish to pay any option premium

In this case he again buys a EUR put/USD call option. Then he writes a EUR call/USD put option for a different premium but the same strike price. Unlike a cylinder, the value of options that he buys and writes are not identical. When he writes the option, he opts for a value which ensures that the total premium of this option is identical to that of the one he buys.

Again, as a result of this transaction the treasurer is protected against an increase in the exchange rate but now he will also be able to benefit from any rise in the value of USD.

EXAMPLE

A European company needs to pay a supplier the sum of USD 1,000,000 in three months' time. The 3-month EUR/USD forward exchange rate amounts to 0.9050. The premium for a 3-month EUR put/ USD call option with a strike price of 1.1850 is 0.0100. The premium for a 3-month EUR call/USD put option with a striking price of 1.1850 is 0.0200.

A treasurer wants to enter into a profit-sharing contract and buys a 3-month EUR put/USD call option at 1.1850 with a value of USD 1,000,000 and writes a 3-month EUR call/USD put option with the same strike price.

The question now arises as to the principal amount of the EUR call/USD put option which the treasurer will need to write in order to be able to pay the premium of the EUR put/USD call option with a principal value of USD 1,000,000.

Since the premium of the EUR call/USD put option is twice as high as that of the EUR put/USD call option, the treasurer only has to write a EUR call/USD put option for half the principal value of the EUR put / EUR call option contract, namely USD 500,000.

The result of these transactions is as follows:

For a principal of USD 500,000, the treasurer has fixed the foreign exchange rate. After all, if the exchange rate drops below 1.1850 in three months' time, the treasurer will exercise his option and buy USD 1,000,000 at 1.1850. If, on the other hand, the exchange rate exceeds 1.1850, the bank will exercise its option and the treasurer will be required to buy USD 500,000 at 1.1850. In either case the treasurer will buy USD 500,000 at a rate of 1.1850.

For the remainder of the principal, USD 500,000, the treasurer has also bought a EUR put/USD call option but this contract is not offset by another option. He is, therefore, protected against any increase in the value of the dollar to below EUR/USD 1.1850. In addition, he can also benefit in full from any drop in value. Because this applies to 50% of the total dollar amount, we refer to a '50% profit-sharing' option.

The following tabel shows this:

spot rate EUR/USD after three	EUR-put/ USD-call itm, atm, otm	EUR-call/ USD-put itm, atm, otm	Actions	effective EUR/ USD-rate (approximately)
1.1700	itm	otm	treasurer exercises, USD 1,000,000	1.1850
1.1850	atm	atm	neighter party exercises	1.1850
1.1900	otm	itm	bank exercises, USD 500,000 treasurer buys in the market at the market rate, USD 500,000	(1.1850 + 1.1900) / 2 = 1.1875
1.2200	otm	itm	bank exercises, USD 500,000 treasurer buys in the market at the market rate, USD 50,000	(1.1850 + 1.2200) / 2 = 1.2025
1.2500	otm	itm	bank exercises, USD 500,000 treasurer buys in the market at the market rate, USD 500,000	(1.1850 + 1.2500) / 2 = 1.2175

8
Forward exchange contracts versus currency options

Both instruments, forward exchange contracts and currency options, provide cover against unfavourable changes in foreign exchange rates. However, there are also differences between them. For instance, a forward exchange contract provides absolute certainty about future exchange rates and there are usually no costs involved in this product. On the other hand, currency options make it possible for one to benefit from favourable variations in exchange rates. However, apart from the fact that a company is required to pay the option premium, this is offset by the fact that the rate against which it is protected is often less favourable than the forward exchange rate. This is because a treasurer virtually always buys out-of-the-money options because they are more affordable. At-the-money options are logically very expensive.

Following is a list of the most important features of both products.

features	forward exchange contract	currency option
coverage of adverse movements in exchange rates	yes	yes
possibility of benefiting from favourable movements in exchange rates	no	yes
covered exchange rate level	forward rate	– call option: higher than forward rate – put option: lower than forward rate
premium	no	yes
currency vision	either – none or – extremely negative	favourable movements are regarded as possible

In general, one can say that conservative companies often prefer a forward exchange contract above a currency option. They are opting for certainty. The development of a foreign exchange forecast for the purposes of covering transaction risks is not very relevant to such companies. They eliminate all currency exposure risks. The cost of an option premium often sways the argument in favour of a forward exchange contract rather than a currency option.

However, a decision in favour of either product also depends on the company's foreign exchange forecast. If a business, for instance, is expecting a highly unfavourable exchange rate, it will not buy a currency option. The premium would amount to a waste of money because the company feels that it has no chance of 'success'. In addition, the exercise price is usually less favourable than the forward exchange rate.

9
Currency swaps

A currency swap is a transaction where one market player simultaneously enters into a contract with one and the same party for the purchase and sale of a specific foreign currency amount having the same value but different maturity dates.

A currency swap, thus, comprises two counter-balanced transactions involving the exchange of the relevant currencies. Once the currency swap expires, both parties will return to their original positions in respect of the various currencies. For this reason, a currency swap is not a product that can be used to cover foreign exchange risks.

By way of example, let us take a company which now sells the sum of USD 1 million to the bank in return for EUR 1 million and after a month buys back its USD 1 million at a forward exchange rate of EUR/USD 1.001 for EUR 999,900.

This currency swap is depicted in the following diagram.

Figure 3   *The cash flows of a currency swap*

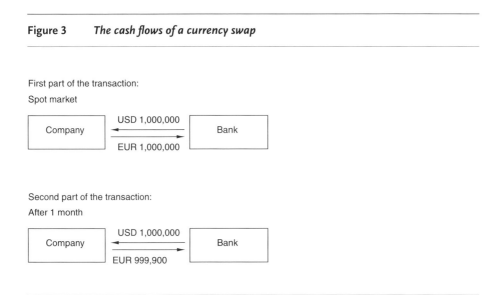

First part of the transaction:
Spot market

| Company | USD 1,000,000 ← / → EUR 1,000,000 | Bank |

Second part of the transaction:
After 1 month

| Company | USD 1,000,000 ← / → EUR 999,900 | Bank |

There are two practical ways in which a company can use a currency swap:

– to extend a forward exchange contract
– to offset opposite liquidity positions in various currencies

9.1 Extending forward exchange contracts

An import or export transaction may be delayed. If a forward exchange contract has been concluded in connection with such a transaction, the company in question will not yet require or be able to deliver the relevant currency. It is possible to extend the forward exchange contract with the aid of a currency swap.

An importer is expecting a delivery from a US supplier on 15 April. On 15 January he, therefore, enters into a forward exchange contract, in accordance with which he undertakes to buy USD 5 million with euros on 15 April. The forward exchange rate amounts to EUR/USD 1.2000 (spot rate of 1.1985 on 15 January).

On 13 April it appears that the delivery will be delayed by a month. The importer will, therefore, not require the US dollars on 15 April but on 15 May. However, based on the forward exchange contract, his euro account will be debited on 15 April and his USD account will be credited.

In order to ensure that he obtains the dollar amount on 15 May rather than 15 April, the importer calls his bank and asks for his forward exchange contract to be extended by means of a currency swap.

He agrees on the following transaction with his bank.
The customer will sell USD 5 million for euros on 15 April and, simultaneously, arrange for the purchase of USD 5 million on 15 May. A spot transaction and a forward exchange contract are, therefore, concluded at the same time; a currency swap.

On 13 April (delivery on 15 April), the spot EUR/USD rate amounts to 1.1050. The 1-month premium is 0.0005. The forward exchange rate for 15 May is thus 1.1055.

On 15 April the original forward exchange contract is settled, as is the spot transaction component of the currency swap. The sum of USD 5 million is credited and debited to the USD account, with the result that the two transactions offset each other. Based on the original forward exchange contract, the euro account is debited for EUR 4,545,454.50 (5,000,000 / 1.1000). However, based on the spot transaction, the euro account is credited for EUR 4,524,886.80 (5,000,000 / 1.1050). On balance, the euro account is thus debited for EUR 20,999.70 (EUR 4,545,454,50 – EUR 4,524,454.80).

On 15 May the USD account will then be credited for USD 5,000,000 and the EUR account will be debited for EUR 4,522,840.30 (5,000,000 / 1.1055). The dollar amount will therefore have a total cost of EUR 4,543,840 (EUR 20,999.70 + EUR 4,522,840.30).
(However, the company will have had an account deficit of EUR 20,999.70 from 15 April to 15 May. It will, therefore, have incurred interest charges in this respect.)

9.2 Offsetting liquidity positions in two currencies

Companies can also use currency swaps to offset a short-term liquidity shortfall in a specific currency with a surplus in another. We know that one of the objectives of cash management is to ensure that a company receives the maximum interest possible. The question now arises as to the extent to which currency swaps contribute to the achievement of this goal.

As we have seen, differences in interest rates are included in the forward exchange rate of two currencies in a currency swap. To a cash manager, a currency swap is beneficial. This is because interbank interest rates are used in the swap points. These are the rates which the banks charge each other when they hold each other's deposits. No spreads apply in the case of the surplus currency, nor is there a spread surcharge on the shortfall position.

EXAMPLE

A company has a temporary current account deficit of EUR 5 million and anticipates that this situation will prevail for three months. The company pays the equivalent of EURIBOR plus 2% on its current account deficit. The account manager at its bank knows that the company's cash manager has been extending a 3-month term deposit of USD 7.5 million at another bank for some time now. There he obtains exceptionally favourable rates equivalent to the 3-month LIBID (London Interbank Bid Rate, the bid rate equivalent of the LIBOR – London Interbank Offered Rate). When asked, the cash manager says that he could require the US dollar amount at any time to finance an acquisition in the United States, but that this transaction will not proceed within three months. Coincidentally, the term of the USD deposit expires today and the new current account monthly rate is determined on the following basis:

1-month EURIBOR	4.5%
3-month EURIBOR	4.5%
3-month LIBID	5.25%
EUR/USD spot rate	1.0000
3-month EUR/USD premium	0.0018

The account manager recommends that the cash manager uses his US dollars to cover his deficit in euros by arranging the following currency swap:

Spot transaction: sell USD 5,000,000 for euros at the spot rate of EUR/USD 1.000;

forward exchange contract: purchase USD 5,000,000 with euros in three months' time at the EUR/USD forward exchange rate of 1.0018.

The benefit to the company can be calculated as follows. First we will work out the costs involved in the event that the current situation remains unchanged (1). Following this, we will calculate the cost to the customer if he decides in favour of a currency swap (2). Then we will compare the two alternatives (3).

1.   Outcome if the current situation remains unchanged

The costs of maintaining the current situation can be calculated as follows:

a.	Interest paid on EUR deficit:	3/12 x 6.5%* x EUR 5,000,000	EUR 81,250
b.	Interest received on USD deposit	3/12 x 5.25% x USD5,000,000	
		= USD 65,626 at a rate of 1.0018**	EUR 65,507
c.	Interest paid on balance		EUR 15,743

*   4.50% + 2.00% = 6.5%
**   Assumed is that the euro rate will have remained unchanged.

2.   Outcome in the event of a currency swap

If the cash manager opts for a currency swap, he will temporarily use the dollars to eliminate his euro deficit. USD 5,000,000 is required to clear the shortfall of EUR 5,000,000. In this example, the EUR/USD exchange rate is 1.000. In the spot market the cash manager exchanges USD 5,000,000 for EUR 5,000,000.
After three months the cash manager will need to deliver euros to the bank again and he will receive USD 5,000,000 in return. The agreed price that will apply in three months' time is 1.0018. The customer will need to pay the bank EUR 4,991,016.10 (5,000,000 / 1.0018). In view of the fact that he had received EUR 5,000,000 when the currency swap commenced, the company has even managed to earn some-thing on the transaction.
The currency swap yields the company EUR 8,983.90, being the difference between the euros it receives (EUR 5,000,000) and those it had payed (EUR 4,991,016.10).

3.   The difference in outcome between the currency swap and maintaining the current situation

Costs involved in maintaining the current situation	EUR 15,743
Proceeds from arrangement of currency swap	EUR 8,984
Benefit to the company of entering into a currency swap	EUR 24,727

This benefit is largely due to the fact that the company has temporarily eliminated its short position in euros that was charged at a premium. As a result it is no longer required to pay the interest surcharge on its EUR current account deficit (2% * 3/12 * 5,000,000 = EUR 25,000). The explanation for the remainder is to be found in the margin on the swap rates.

10
Counterpart limits

When a bank agrees on a forward exchange contract or a currency swap with a company, both parties enter into a mutual obligation. For example, if a company enters into a forward exchange contract to purchase US dollars, the bank undertakes to supply the latter on the delivery date at the agreed rate of exchange and the company undertakes to buy the dollars at that rate. In this respect there is a risk that either party may fail to perform his duties. We refer to this as a counterparty risk.

EXAMPLE

A bank has entered into a 3-month EUR/USD forward exchange contract with Web4ever for USD 1 million, pursuant to which the bank undertakes to provide Web4ever with the dollar amount at an exchange rate of 1.2350. On the settlement date it appears that Web4ever is bankrupt and is no longer able to fulfil its obligations. The EUR/USD spot rate is 1.2450 at the time.

Because the Web4ever transaction will not be going ahead, the bank will now have to sell the US dollars (buy euros) on the market at the prevailing exchange rate of 1.2450. Under the terms of the contract the bank was to receive the sum of EUR 809.716,59 (1,000,000 / 1.2350) in return for the USD 1 million. However, a forced sale on the market only yields the bank EUR 803.212,85 (1,000,000 / 1.2450).

The bank therefore loses EUR 6.503,74.

However, if the prevailing EUR/USD exchange rate were 1.2100 on the settlement date, Web4ever wouldn't cancel the contract and settlement would simply proceed. The Web4ever treasurer (or receiver) would be able to take the US dollar amount which he receives in accordance with the forward exchange contract, and sell it in the market at a lower EUR/USD exchange rate (consequently, a higher USD value). The Web4ever treasurer would then be able to use the euros he receives, to fulfil his obligations to the bank under the terms of the forward exchange contract. The bank thus runs a one-sided risk: its risk of suffering a loss is not offset by a chance of earnings.

The bank manages counterparty risks by assessing the credit standing of the counterparty. Based on this assessment, it can decide whether or not to do business with the party in question and, if so, to what amount. In doing this, the bank uses much the same criteria as in its lending operations. The credit committee sets a so called counterparty limit. This limit indicates the maximum credit risk a bank will run with respect to one and the same counterpart. Such a limit covers the exposure related to loans but can also cover the exposures related to financial derivatives such as outright transactions, guarantees and documentary credits.

Some banks that enter into financial derivatives contracts with clients do not block the counterparty limit of that client, but instead block part of the balance on a specific account held by the customer in question. The disadvantage of the latter method is that it draws directly on the liquid assets of the company.

11
New guidelines for reporting financial derivatives

The growing use of financial derivatives, such as the forward exchange contracts and currency options dealt with in this chapter, and the incorrect or improper use of them in some cases, has led to a situation where the relevant supervisory authorities have developed guidelines for reporting and valuing these products in annual accounts.

Such guidelines have been in force in the United States since 2001. These guidelines are contained in FASB 133 of the US GAAP (Generally Accepted Accounting Principles). In the meantime, guidelines governing derivative reporting procedures have also been adopted as part of the International Accounting Standards (IAS) system in IAS 39. All European listed companies have to comply with the International Accounting Standards. Both sets of guidelines (FASB 133 and IAS 39) stipulate that companies must report the value of financial derivatives in their financial statements.

11.1 Distinguishing between hedging and non-hedging transactions

In both accounting regimes, FASB 133 and IAS 39, an essential distinction is drawn in accordance with the purpose for which derivatives are used. The following distinction is maintained:

- financial derivatives that cannot be considered to be a hedge
- financial derivatives that are used as a hedge.

A hedge is a protection against a foreign exchange and/or interest rate risk.

Derivatives are required to satisfy strict criteria in order to qualify as a hedge. First, a company needs to formulate risk management policy. Then, when it acquires a financial derivative, the company must clearly specify and document its relationship with a specific asset or liability (future or otherwise). In this respect, the company needs to demonstrate that it is reasonable to assume the hedge is effective. This is to say that no less than 80%, and no more than 125%, of any change in the value of the asset or liability to be covered, is offset by a change in the value of the financial derivative that it has obtained. Finally, the company will also need to be able to demonstrate on every reporting date that this level of effectiveness has been maintained.

11.2 Accounting for hedging and non-hedging transactions

Any change in the value of a financial derivative that cannot be held to be a hedge must be accounted for in the financial statements and in the profit and loss account.

Any change in the value of a financial derivative that qualifies as a hedge must also be accounted for in the balance sheet. Changes in the value, however, (on balance) don't have to be accounted for in the profit and loss account.

The change in value of a financial derivative that can be treated as a hedge is accounted for in the same way as that of the underlying asset or liability that is hedged (future or otherwise). In other words, if a variation in the value of the underlying asset or liability is expressed in a change in the balance sheet, that of the relevant financial derivative (which would offset it by definition) may also be reported as a change to the balance sheet. If the change in value of the underlying asset or liability is stated in the profit and loss account, the offsetting variation in the value of the derivative that is used as a hedge must also be reported in the profit and loss account. This is referred to as hedge accounting.

Chapter 14
Interest Risk Management

Introduction

Every company runs interest risks. There is virtually no company with an operating profit or net worth not affected in some manner by interest rate fluctuations. In this respect, a company treasurer 's duty is to achieve optimum interest income and to manage interest rate risks. For this purpose, he can use several financial products such as forward rate agreements, money market futures and interest rate swaps.

1
What are interest risks?

Interest rate risk is the risk that a change in interest rates may have a negative impact on the company's net profit or net worth.

In particular, for companies with high leverage ratios where much of the business is financed with loan capital, interest risks are major factor. In this case, it is urgent to manage these risks properly. Another key reason why companies need to devote attention to interest risk management is that lenders are increasingly alert to their interest coverage ratio. This ratio measures the relationship between the profit and interest charges of a company, expressed by the number of times the business earnings exceed its net interest paid. Many banks currently specify a minimum interest coverage ratio in their loan agreements. If the interest coverage ratio of a borrowing firm falls below this predetermined level, under the terms of the loan agreement the bank may be entitled to require the repayment of the loan or to raise the interest rate. As a result, a business can find itself faced with serious liquidity problems. Viewed in this light, it is important for any company with a low interest coverage ratio to exercise strict control over its interest risks.

Interest risks can be related to future liquidity positions or to existing medium or long term liquidity positions.

1.1 Future liquidity positions

Suppose that in December the treasurer prepares the following cash flow forecast for the coming year.

Figure 1 *Liquidity forecast*

	Jan	Feb	Mar	Apr	May	Jun	Jul	Aug	Sep	Oct	Nov	Dec
balance (mio)	2	1.5	2.3	0.7	1.2	0.4	23.7	22.9	21.5	4.2	1.6	0.8

In this example, the treasurer anticipates a major cash surplus in the period from July to September. This could be due to high seasonal income or a large one-off incoming payment, which will then be followed by a major investment at the beginning of October.

The treasurer, therefore, knows that he will have a material funds surplus for three months during a specific period in the coming year. He does not know, however, what interest he will receive on this surplus. If the controller asks the treasury department for an estimate of interest income in the year ahead, the treasurer will need to prepare a specific forecast. Supposing the 3-month money market rate is 6% at present, the treasurer could use this interest rate for his forecast. If, however, the 3-month money market rate at the beginning of July is 4%, the actual interest income will be well below his estimate. The company will, therefore, run an interest risk.

1.2 Existing long-term liquidity positions

When companies invest, they require funds for an extended period of time. This represents a lengthy liquidity shortfall. A company may arrange a long-term loan with a variable interest rate to cover this shortfall. With such a loan, the interest rate is readjusted at specific intervals, for example every three months. This interest rate is usually based on the related money market rate period such as the 3-month USD-LIBOR. Suppose that the loan has a remaining term of five years. In this case the interest charges payable on the loan would depend on changes in the 3-month USD-LIBOR for the coming period of five years. If the 3-month USD-LIBOR rises, the company's interest charges will also increase and the P&L account would be affected negatively. If the company were to agree on a loan with a fixed interest rate, the relevant interest charges payable over the next five years would be fixed and there would be no interest risk according to the above-mentioned definition.

On the other hand, according to the Generally Accepted Accounting Standards (GAAP) in the United States and the International Accounting Standards, some balance sheet items with a fixed interest rate must be accounted on a marked-to-market basis. With this approach, interest rate movements will be reflected in the value of all interest-bearing assets and liabilities, and in the value of all financial derivatives contracts and, subsequently, in the company's net worth. It is clear that the marked-to-market values of long-term assets and liabilities will fluctuate more than those of short-term items.

The treasurer is, thus, faced with a dilemma choosing the interest term for a fixed loan. If he chooses for a floating rate, the company's future net profit and its debt-service ratio will fluctuate with changes in interest rates. On the other hand, if he chooses for a fixed rate, a fall in interest rates may have an immediate and material impact on the company's net worth.

Most companies, however, are allowed to account their loans on a cost basis. This means that, during the term of the loan, it is accounted for at the nominal value. For these companies, the above dilemma does not exist and these companies can focus their attention to assessing the impact of a change in interest rates on their P&L account and to developping a strategy to cover this risk. This is also the focus of the remainder of this chapter.

2
Objective, tasks and instruments of interest risk management

The objective of interest risk management is to safeguard company earnings (as well as the company's net worth) against interest rate fluctuations. Like the management of foreign exchange risks, interest risk management involves the following tasks:

- determination of policy in relation to interest risks
- development of an interest rate forecast
- identification of interest risks
- entering into transactions

Because these tasks have been discussed in the previous chapter, we will not cover them here. We will confine ourselves to the description of the various instruments which are at the treasurer's disposal to cover interest risks:

- forward rate agreements (FRAs)
- money market futures
- interest rate swaps
- interest options: caps, floors, collars and swaptions

3
Instruments for hedging future short-term positions

To cover future short-term interest positions, a treasurer can use two products: future rate agreements and money market futures. Both products are, essentially, identical. The most important difference is that future rate agreements are over-the-counter products, while money market futures are traded on an exchange.

3.1 Forward rate agreements (FRAs)

Forward rate agreements (FRAs) are money market products which companies use to fix interest receipts or payments on future short-term liquidity shortfalls or surpluses.

In the money market, interest rates are established for various terms varying from one day to one year. All of these periods commence immediately. The relationship between the various terms and the attendant interest rates is depicted on the yield curve.

In addition to interest rates for terms that commence immediately, rates are also established in the money market for future periods. For example, a 3-month interest rate for a term that commences in six months' time and expires nine months from now; or a 12-month interest rate for a period that begins in a year's time and ends two years from now. Interest rates for future periods of time are called forward yields or forward rates. These forward rates are derived from ordinary interest rates. For example, the future interest applicable in the case of the 3-month rate for the period that begins in six months' time and ends nine months from now is calculated on the basis of the current ordinary 6-month rate on the one hand, and the current ordinary 9-month rate on the other.

Banks trade in a wide variety of interest rate instruments. Almost every bank has dealers who trade in these forward rates. For this purpose, the instrument used is a forward rate agreement or FRA.

By way of example, let us take the forward rate (also called FRA rate) for a 6-month period that commences in three months' time and ends nine months from now. Suppose that this rate is 3.00% (calculated on the basis of a current 3-month rate of 2.90% and present 9-month rate of 3.07%). Imagine that a FRA dealer at Bank A expects the 6-month rate to exceed 3.00% in three months' time, and that a FRA dealer at Bank B anticipates that the 6-month rate will be less than 3.00%. In this case the two dealers will be able to trade.

The dealers then agree on the following. In three months' time Dealer B will pay Dealer A a certain amount if the 6-month rate exceeds 3.00% at that point in time. For his part Dealer A will pay Dealer B a sum if this interest rate is then less than 3.00%. The level agreed upon is 3% and is referred to as the FRA contract rate. The amount that either dealer will have to pay the other, depends on the following two factors:

- the extent to which the actual interest rate deviates from the FRA contract rate;
- a principal sum over which the dealers agree to calculate this interest differential

The construction described above amounts to a 3 vs 9 FRA with a contract rate of 3.00%. The '3' refers to the time of fixing. The difference between the '3' and the '9' refers to the period for the interest rate in respect of which the trade occurs (also known as the underlying period, in this case 6 months). On the expiry date, the actual 6-months rate is compared with the contract rate (ie 3.00%).

As with most products, one can distinguish between buyers and sellers of FRAs. The buyer of a FRA will be paid by the other party if the actual market rate exceeds the contract rate; in this case if the 6-month EURIBOR exceeds 3.00% on the expiry date (hence after three months). In the above situation, dealer A is the buyer. Dealer B is the seller. The buyer pays the seller the difference between the actual interest and the contract rate on the expiry date if the former is less than the latter.

Companies with liquidity shortfalls in the future can purchase FRAs to cover themselves against interest rate rises. Where a company sells a FRA, it covers itself against a fall in the interest income related to a liquidity surplus in the future.

3.1.1 Dates and terminology

FRAs feature a number of important dates, namely:

- the contract date – the date on which the contract is concluded;
- the expiry date – the date on which the difference between the market rate and the contract rate will be determined;
- the settlement date – the day on which the interest differential will be paid (this is also the first date of the underlying period);
- the maturity date of the underlying period – the last day of the agreed or 'underlying' FRA period.

The term of the contract runs from the contract to the expiry date. The 'underlying period' runs from the settlement until the maturity date of this period.

EXAMPLE

The relevant dates of a 4 versus 7 FRA, which is concluded on 1 March are:

| 1 March (a) | 1 July (b) | 3 October (d) |
| | 3 July (c) | |

    Term of FRA contract   Underlying FRA period

a = the contract date
b = the contract expiry date
c = the settlement date
d = the maturity date of the underlying period

The term of this FRA is four months running from 1 March to 1 July (from a to b). The underlying period is three months from 3 July to 3 October (from c to d).

The first figure represents the term of the contract and the difference between the two figures stands for the duration of the underlying period. The reference rate may be the 3-month EURIBOR. In this case, after four months the contracted interest rate is compared with the then current 3-month EURIBOR.

A FRA is an over-the-counter (OTC) product. Any term or value is possible. The contract rates are always calculated on the basis of normal interest rates.

3.1.2 Settlement

Settlement refers to the payment of any amount due pursuant to a financial contract. The amount involved in the settlement of a FRA is calculated on the contract expiry date. The settlement amount of a FRA is calculated as follows:

- the published EURIBOR is compared to the contract rate on the latter's expiry date
- the difference in interest is then calculated in respect of the underlying period
- finally, this amount is discounted against the relevant EURIBOR-rate

The actual cash settlement occurs on the settlement date.

EXAMPLE

Two parties have entered into a 4 vs 7 FRA. This is to say that they have taken a view on the 3-month interest rate in four months' time. The 3-month EURIBOR is the reference rate. The contract rate is 3.75%. The principal sum of the contract is EUR 5,000,000. After four months, on the contract expiry date, it is determined that the 3-month EURIBOR is 3.95% on the contract expiry date. How will this FRA be settled? We will need to answer the following questions for this purpose:

Who has to pay whom?

What amount?

Because the reference rate exceeds the contract rate, the seller will have to pay the buyer.

The settlement amount is the cash value of the difference in interest rates in respect of the underlying period.

We will first calculate the difference between the contracted and the reference interest rates on an annual basis: 3.95% - 3.75% = 0.20%.

Then we will calculate the amount of interest in respect of the underlying period and the principal sum of EUR 5,000,000, i.e. 0.20% x EUR 5,000,000 x 91/360 = EUR 2,527.78.

Finally, we will determine the cash value if this amount is based on the 3-month EURIBOR and will use the following formula to do so:

$$\frac{\text{settlement amount}}{(1 + \text{days}/360 * \text{interest rate})}$$

$$\frac{2,5277.78}{(1 + 91/360 \times 0,0395)} = \text{EUR } 2,502,79$$

On the settlement date, the seller will therefore have to pay the buyer the sum of EUR 2,502.79.

3.1.3 FRAs in practice

Both companies with a defensive and with an offensive strategy can use FRA's.

DEFENSIVE STRATEGY
Some companies wish to preclude all risks and to cover every position. When the Treasurer of such a company notices a prospective liquidity surplus, he may want to fix the interest rate applicable to it. He can use FRAs for this purpose.

OFFENSIVE STRATEGY
In many companies, the treasury committee periodically compiles a forecast covering interest and foreign exchange rates. If this committee anticipates an increase in interest rates, for example, it may want to fix interest rates in the event that the company has a temporary short position in the future. When doing so, this committee will compare its interest forecast with the FRA contract rates for the period in question. If the FRA contract rates are lower than the committee's forecasts, the treasurer will choose to purchase FRAs for the periods in which there is a liquidity shortfall. Treasurers often use FRAs when the profitability of a large deal or transaction requires certainty of financing costs.

A FRA is a product in its own right. From a contractual perspective raising (or investing) funds is entirely separate from the FRA.

Following is a detailed example of a company faced with a short-term liquidity shortfall in the future which enters into a FRA based on its interest forecast.

EXAMPLE

The Treasurer of Artifor thinks that he will require EUR 20 million for a period of a year in 12 months' time. A year from now Artifor will need to borrow this amount from the bank at the applicable EURIBOR.

Artifor's treasury committee expects money market rates to rise. At present the 12-month rate is approximately 4.25%. The committee anticipates that the 12-month rate will amount to 5.5% in a year's time. Artifor's treasurer proposes to buy a 12 vs 24 FRA at 4.5%. This will fix future interest charges to 4.5%.

The settlement amount of the FRA will depend on the 12-month EURIBOR a year from now. On balance, however, the cost of financing the future liquidity shortfall will always be 4.5%.

If the 12-month rate rises to exactly 4.5% in a year's time, for example, there will be no settlement under the terms of the FRA. Artifor will then borrow the sum of EUR 20 million from the bank at the current market rate of 4.5%.

If the 12-month rate rises to 5.5% a year from now, for example, the bank will pay the difference between 5.5% and 4.5% in accordance with the FRA, which is 1%. Artifor, however, has to pay the market rate of 5.5% for the loan. On balance, the effective interest rate is 4.5%.

Should the 12-month rate falls to 3.5% in a year's time, however, the company will also obtain a loan at 4.5% net, being the agreed FRA rate. The effective rate is the combination of paying the market rate of 3.5% for the loan and paying the bank 1% based on the FRA purchased.

(This example ignores the credit margin which the bank would charge Artifor above the EURIBOR-rate.)

3.2 Money market futures

Like FRAs, money market futures are financial products traded in the money market used to fix future interest revenues or interest costs of short-term future cash surpluses or shortfalls.

The buyer of a money market future will receive a sum of money if the relevant interest rate falls. This is the opposite to a FRA. The seller of a money market future will be paid if the relevant interest rate rises.

All futures are traded on an exchange at standardised terms and conditions. In the case of money market futures, the following aspects have been standardised:

- the value of the contract
- the term – the end or expiry date of the contract
- the underlying instrument (a 1-month or 3-month deposit)

The underlying instrument of a euro money market future is a deposit stated in euros with a term of one or three months. In the euro-area, the reference rates that apply to these theoretical deposits are the 1-month and 3-month EURIBOR respectively. The price of a money market future is listed as follows: 100-/- forward rate for the underlying period.

As in the case with currency futures, throughout the term of a money market future its price is calculated and any profits and losses are settled immediately.

A treasurer wishes to sell a 3-month future with a contract term of nine months (for example, from mid-June 2002 to mid-September 2002). The current 3-month EURIBOR is 3.5% and the 9 vs 12 forward rate is 4.15%. The customer wishes to buy this future with a principal sum amounting to EUR 15,000,000. Since the value of a contract is EUR 1,000,000, he has to buy 15 contracts.

This future is now listed as 100 – 4.15 = 95.85. In the table below, we show how the 3-month FRA rate and the price of the future vary during the term of the latter.

period	forward-rate (June until Sept)	listing price 3-months EURIBOR future	daily profit/loss
day 1	4.13	95.87	EUR 15,000,000 x 0.0002 x 90/360 = EUR 750
day 2	4.10	95.90	EUR 5,000,000 x 0.003 x 90/360 = EUR 1125
day 3	4.11	95.89	EUR 15,000,000 x – 0.0001 x 90/360 = – EUR 375*
6 months	3.98 ('3 vs 6'- FRA)	96.02	
9 m - 1 day	3.94	96.06	
9 months	3.90 (3-month-EURIBOR)	96.10	EUR 15,000,000 x 0.0004 x 90/360 = EUR 1500

* If the price rises, the seller will have to pay the exchange.

The future expires after nine months. How much has it yielded or cost in total during its term?

The closing price of the future is higher than its opening price. The buyer of this future has, therefore, made a loss. The total profit on this future is as follows:

EUR 15,000,000 x (95.87 – 96.10) x 90/360 = minus EUR 8,625.

This profit is made up of the daily settlements: – EUR 750 – EUR 1,125 + EUR 375 +/– ...... -EUR 1,500.

The treasurer could also have bought a 9 vs 12 FRA. The contracted interest rate of the FRA would have been 4.15%. Instead of the daily settlement, this FRA would have been settled by one single settlement on the settlement date nine months after the contract had been concluded. The 3-month EURIBOR would have also been the reference rate. It amounted to 3.90% on the settlement date. This can be seen at the bottom of the Forward Rates column in the table.

In view of the fact that the treasurer has bought the FRA and the reference rate is lower than the contracted one, he will have to pay the difference.

Settlement amount: EUR 15,000,000 x (0.0390 - 0,0413) x 90/360 = minus EUR 8,625.

Cash managers use money market futures in the same manner as FRA's. The differences between FRAs and money market futures are similar to those between forward exchange contracts and currency futures and are listed below.

Figure 2 *Comparisons and differences between FRA's and money market futures*

FRA's	Money market futures
No exchange of principal	
Settlement only of interest differentials	
Over-the-counter	Traded on an exchange
One single bank acts as counterparty	The exchange acts as counterparty
No collateral demanded (instead, internal counterparty limits are used)	Collateral is obligatory (initial margin)
Non-standardised	Standardised
One single settlement at expiry date	Daily settlement of trade results
Buy with a liquidity shortfall; Sell with a liquidity surplus	Buy with a liquidity surplus; Sell with a liquidity shortfall

4
Instruments for existing long-term liquidity positions

While varying over economic cycles, most companies have to contend with long-term liquidity shortfalls and, generally, do not have long-term liquidity surpluses. The following sections assume that the relevant company has covered its long-term liquidity shortfall by concluding long-term loans with variable interest rates. In order to manage the interest risks involved with variable interest rates, the company treasurer can use the following products: interest rate swaps, caps and collars.

4.1 Interest rate swaps

An interest rate swap is a transaction entered into by parties who agree to exchange interest flows in the same currency during a specified period. An interest rate swap only involves the exchange of interest flows; principal sums are never exchanged. Just as in the case of FRAs, the parties agree on a notional principal in respect of which the exchanged interest payments are calculated. In the case of most interest rate swaps, one party pays the other variable interest for a specified period of time. The rate is revised at various intervals (the fixing dates). The other party pays a fixed interest coupon at a predetermined rate during the term of the contract.

Variable interest is based on a money market benchmark, such as LIBOR. The variable interest rate is paid whenever a new coupon is set. In the case of most interest rate swaps this commonly occurs either once a quarter or every six months. Fixed interest is usually paid at the end of every year. Incidentally, 6-month coupons can also be found. In rare cases, the fixed coupon is paid in advance. Where a company is party to a swap, a margin is added to the fixed interest if the company is paying it, and is deducted if it is receiving it.

Like FRAs, interest rate swaps are OTC products. The features of different interest rate swaps can vary greatly and the following matters need to be determined for each separate deal:

- principal sum
- short-term reference rate (EURIBOR, LIBOR, EONIA and so forth)
- level of the long-term interest rate
- term of the swap
- interest calculation method
- coupon frequency in the case of the long-term interest rate

The term of an interest rate swap is usually between one and ten years. The principals can vary greatly but the most common figures are between EUR 5 million and EUR 100 million. However, the minimum value of these swaps has been substantially reduced in recent years. Nowadays, it is possible to agree on interest rate swaps for amounts as low as EUR 125,000.

Below is a diagram depicting the interest flows in the case of an interest rate swap. A company has entered into a 2-year interest rate swap in accordance with which it will pay the bank the long-term interest rate of 6% and will receive the short-term rate in return (* 3-month EURIBOR).

Figure 3   *Interest flows of a swap*

For this example, the principal is EUR 10,000,000. The following interest payments are to be made based on the above example:

- Throughout the term of the swap (two years), the company pays the bank an annual coupon of 6% calculated on the agreed principal. The company, therefore, pays the bank an annual sum of EUR 600,000 (EUR 10,000,000 x 6%).
- For its part, the bank undertakes to pay variable interest on the agreed principal sum to the company periodically. The contract stipulates that the bank is to pay Artifor the 3-month EURIBOR.

We will now examine the variable interest of the above-mentioned interest rate swap in greater detail.

Suppose that the 3-month EURIBOR is 4.5% at the start of the swap. In this case, the bank will pay a coupon to the company after three months amounting to: 90/360 * 4.5% * EUR 10,000,000 = EUR 112,500.

Every three months, the 3-month EURIBOR is again set for the subsequent period. The bank pays the relevant coupon sum in arrears to the company based on this reset every three months. At the same time, a new rate will be set for the subsequent coupon period and this coupon will also be paid in arrears. Suppose that the 3-month EURIBOR amounts to 5% after three months. In this case, the bank will pay a coupon after six months amounting to 91/360 * 5% * EUR 10,000,000 = EUR 126,388. If the 3-month EURIBOR increases substantially to 7% after six months, the bank will pay a coupon after nine months amounting to 92/360 * 7% * EUR 10,000,000 = EUR 178,888 and so forth.

The end of the fourth coupon period for the short-term interest rate coincides with the annual coupon. At this point in time, we will see interest flowing in two opposite directions. The fixed and variable interest will cross paths. In some cases, the opposite interest cash flows are netted.

4.2 Interest rate swaps in practice

By entering into a swap agreement in relation to an existing loan, a company can change the effective interest profile of this loan. A company may convert a variable interest rate into a fixed one, or vice versa, without concluding a new loan agreement or amending an existing loan. Following is a practical situation in which a company could decide on an interest rate swap.

EXAMPLE

Artifor has a medium-term loan for EUR 10,000,000 with a remaining term of two years and an interest coupon which is based on 3-month EURIBOR plus a margin of 1.50%.

Artifor's treasury team anticipates that short-term interest rates will rise dramatically in the period ahead and would like greater certainty in respect of the company's future interest expenses. The terms and conditions of the loan do not make provision for the interest rate to be fixed.

For this reason, the treasury team decides to enter into an interest rate swap in accordance with which Artifor will start paying a fixed interest rate. When Artifor enters into the interest rate swap, its treasurer envisages the following flows of interest payments and of the principal sum.

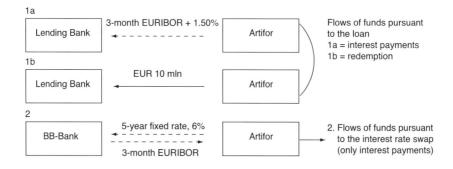

The loan simply remains in effect. In accordance with its terms, Artifor will be required to continue paying quarterly interest instalments and, after two years, will be required to repay the principal EUR 10,000,000 to the lending bank. However, as a result of its agreement to an interest rate swap, the net financial effect for Artifor will be as if it were paying a fixed interest rate for the next two years amounting to 6% + 1.50% = 7.5%.

N.B.1 The terms and conditions of the fixed interest are bond-based (30/360) while the margin is based on the money market usance (actual/360), with the result that one cannot simply add these rates but have to refine the actual calculations.

N.B. 2 In order to stress that an interest rate swap is a transaction entered into separately from the loan, we have assumed for the purposes of the above example that Artifor enters into an interest rate swap with a different bank (BB Bank) from the one from which it has obtained the loan (the lending bank).

It is important that the interest payments based on the swap keep close pace with those for the loan. If the Artifor treasurer wishes to preclude interest risks for the entire term and principal sum of the loan, he will need to ensure that the following aspects of the loan and interest rate swap coincide with each other:

- terms (the remaining term of the loan and the term of the interest rate swap)
- principal sums
- reference rates (both 3-month EURIBOR in this case)
- coupon dates for the short-term rates

It is obvious that the principal and term of the swap will need to be identical to that of the loan. However, one needs to be particularly careful in respect of the coupon dates. If a Treasurer decides to enter into an interest rate swap a month after the coupon date of a long-term loan with a variable interest rate, the first coupon date of this loan will already fall after two months. In this case we refer to a broken period. If the interest rate swap does not begin with an identical broken period, there will still be an interest risk. This is because the swap interest payments will not be based on EURIBOR of the same date as those of the loan.

In virtually all cases, at least one of these parties to an interest rate swap is a bank. This is a result of the fact that companies are often not prepared, or able, to take risks involving a financial contract with another business. Additionally, companies usually do not have enough opportunity to find a contracting party themselves.

4.3 Overnight index swap

An overnight index swap (OIS) is an interest rate swap that is traded in the money market. The term of the swap is usually shorter than one year. In an OIS, an overnight rate is exchanged against a fixed rate with a term up to one year.

One example of an OIS is the EONIA (Euro Overnight Index Average) swap. An EONIA swap involves the exchange of a fix euro rate (the EONIA swap index) for an

EONIA one for a specified term. EONIA is the official overnight interest rate in the euro money market. The EONIA level is the daily weighted average of all uncollateralised loans with a maturity of one day executed in the euro money market. It is comparable to the fed funds rate in the United States and to the SONIA-rate (Sterling Overnight Index Average) in Great Britain.

Figure 4 *EONIA swap*

An EONIA swap may be used by companies or organisations that place large sums in call deposits every day. The interest payable on these overnight or call deposits is based on the EONIA rate, for example EONIA -/- 3 basis points. Although these companies and organisations almost always have liquidity surpluses, they do not wish to place them in deposits with a longer term but prefer to have them in overnight deposits. They opt for an EONIA swap because they may wish to have the flexibility to fund unanticipated major cash outlays, for example, but still require certainty in respect of their interest income. They base the principal of the swap on the sum which they feel they can place in a call deposit in the period ahead based on their cash flow forecasts. They also base the term of the swap on these forecasts.

Following is a situation in which Artifor places a sum of EUR 50 million in a call deposit every day, and also enters into an EONIA swap for three months. The 3-month rate amounts to 4.75%.

Figure 5   *The use of a EONIA swap by a Artifor*

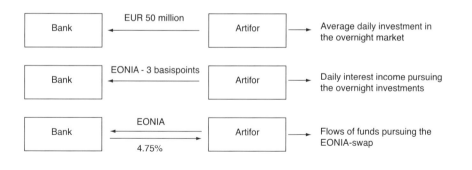

The picture shows that, on balance, Artifor will receive the following interest rate in the next three months: 4.75% - 0.03% - 4.72%. Incidentally, Artifor again has no obligation to arrange a call deposit with the same bank with which it enters into an EONIA interest rate swap. It can shop around every day in order to obtain the best return on its overnight money.

4.4 Interest rate options

Companies can use an interest rate swap in order to fix their interest expenditure in respect to a loan with a variable interest rate. A company would want to do this if it wished to protect itself against a rise in interest rates. The drawback of an interest rate swap is that the company is tied to the fixed rate. If the situation develops as the company expects and the interest rate does indeed rise, its treasurer will be pleased with this deal. If, however, short-term rates remain low, the company will suffer an opportunity loss. While it is true that in this case the treasurer will have security in respect of his interest charges during the term of the swap, he will not be able to benefit from the low short-term rates. The treasurer may want to use a different product to hedge his interest rate risk – an interest rate option contract.

4.4.1 Caps

A company with a long-term loan on a variable interest rate that wishes to secure its position against an increase in rates, and also wishes to benefit if short-term rates remain low, can agree on a cap. A cap is effectively a strip of options with consecutive expiry dates and the same strike price in all cases. The underlying value of a cap is the short-term interest rate, often the 3-month EURIBOR or LIBOR.

The buyer will be paid out on the basis of each separate option if the short-term interest rate exceeds the cap strike price on a single expiry date. If the short-term rate is less than the exercise price on an expiry date, the relevant option will expire without any value. Any options with a later expiry date will simply remain in effect.

The main features of a cap are the following:

- their principal sum is identical
- they have the same strike price
- their reference rate (for example, the 3-month EURIBOR) is the same
- their underlying periods are contiguous

A 12-month cap with the 3-month EURIBOR as its reference rate and a strike price of 5.25% consists of three options.

Figure 6   *The composing options of a 12-month cap*

Option	Expiry date	Underlying term	Strike level
1	t = 3 months	3 to 6 months	5.25%
2	t = 6 months	6 to 9 months	5.25%
3	t = 9 months	9 to 12 months	5.25%

N.B. One might expect an Option 0 to precede Option 1 and have an underlying period of zero to three months. However, such an option would expire as soon as it was agreed (after zero months). The reference interest rate (3-month EURIBOR) for the first period would already be known and, therefore, also the settlement amount. Consequently, it is not an option and for this reason it is omitted.

A 3-year cap with the 3-month EURIBOR as its reference rate would, therefore, consist of 11 individual call options (one for each quarter, less the first one). A 4-year cap with the 6-month EURIBOR as its reference rate would consist of seven call options (eight periods of six months each, less the first one).

The Artifor Treasurer has a medium-term loan with a variable interest rate (based on the 3-month EURIBOR) and a remaining term of two years. He is not entirely confident about short-term interest rates and would like to cover himself against any sudden surge in the 3-month EURIBOR. He therefore buys a 2-year cap with the 3-month EURIBOR as its reference rate. The cap's striking price is 4%. Its underlying principal is EUR 10,000.000.

The relevant expiry dates fall at the end of three, six, nine, 12, 15, 18 and 21 months.

Suppose that the 3-month EURIBOR changes as follows in the next two years.

period	3-months-EURIBOR	strike price	out of the money, in the money, at the money
3 months	3.45%	4.00%	otm
6 months	3.65%	4.00%	otm
9 months	3.95%	4.00%	otm
12 months	4.25%	4.00%	itm
15 months	4.40%	4.00%	itm
18 months	4.60%	4.00%	itm
21 months	4.75%	4.00%	itm

With hindsight it appears that the first three options were out of the money as their reference rate was lower than their strike price. These options had no value when they expired. The Artifor treasurer is not concerned about this. After all, if the 3-month EURIBOR remained low, then the interest charges for the loan were also low.

However, the last four options paid out the following amounts respectively.

pay-out rate	term	principal	calculation amount paid out	amount paid out
0.25% (4.25% – 4.00%)	12-15 months	EUR 10 mln	EUR 25,000/4*	EUR 6,250
0.40% (4.40% – 4.00%)	15-18 months	EUR 10 mln	EUR 40,000/4	EUR 10,000
0.60% (4.60% – 4.00%)	18-21 months	EUR 10 mln	EUR 60,000/4	EUR 15,000
0.75% (4.75% – 4.00%)	21-24 months	EUR 10 mln	EUR 75,000/4	EUR 18,750

* For convenience, we have set the number of days in all relevant quarters of a year at 90.

In the above example, the treasurer was indeed pleased that he had agreed on a cap. After all, it paid out in the second year. He would have preferred, however, to see the EURIBOR remain low. In this case, his interest charges would have been less in the second year than was actually the case.

The buyer will pay a price for the cap: the option premium. The cap premium consists of the sum of the premiums of the various options comprising the cap. There are two ways of paying this premium:

- up-front – the premium is paid when the cap is agreed
- amortisation – the premium is spread over the term of the cap

If the premium is amortised, it is usually expressed as an annual percentage of the underlying principal sum of the cap. In this way, the cap premium can be compared to an interest rate on a loan. The number of premium payments is identical to the number of constituent options plus one. A treasurer will opt in favour of having the amortised cap premium payments coincide with the dates on which the loan coupons are scheduled. This will ensure that the cap seamlessly complements the loan. This is also convenient to a treasurer for administrative purposes. After consultation with his accounting department, he can often use the same entry date to book the interest charges for the loan, the cap premium payments and any pay-out based on the cap under the item, 'interest paid'.

EXAMPLE

The up-front premium for a two year cap with a principal sum of EUR 10,000,000 and an underlying period of three months amounts to EUR 100,000.

The treasurer decides to amortise the premium. The treasurer pays the following amount every quarter: EUR 100,000 / 8 = EUR 12,500 (ignoring the impact of compound interest).

Expressed as interest charges, the premium amounts to an annual interest rate equivalent of 0.50% a year (EUR 50,000 / EUR 10,000,000).

4.4.2 Floors and collars

A floor is a number of consecutive put options on short-term interest rates, all of which have the same exercise price. Floors are used by investors with long-term investments on variable interest rates who wish to protect themselves against falling interest rates.

Since most companies normally do not have long-term liquidity surpluses, they usually do not buy floors. However, the reverse does occur. Sometimes a business will 'sell' a floor to a bank. It will do so in order to pay for a cap.

Many businesses prefer not to pay any premiums for options. They prefer a zero-cost construction. In such a case they will pay for a cap by selling a floor to the bank. By selling a floor a company becomes entitled to a premium. However, the latter is not paid to it directly, but is used to purchase a cap. The cap and the floor have an identical term, reference rate and exercise details.

We refer to the combination of a cap that is bought and a floor that is written, as a collar. A collar ensures that the company's interest charges will remain within a certain range. Today, banks offer many constructions and combinations of caps and floors via structured products.

A company has a medium-term loan with a remaining term of two years and a variable interest rate corresponding to the 3-month EURIBOR (no credit margin). The treasurer thinks that interest rates will remain virtually unchanged in the next two years (he expects there will be no major increase and interest rates will definitely not fall). However, company management wishes to limit interest risks as much as possible. The short-term rate is 5.3% at present and the two-year rate is 6%.

The treasurer could opt for an interest rate swap. By doing so he would fix the interest rate at 6% for two years and comply with management's wishes. However, we know that one of the treasurer's aims is to achieve the best possible interest levels for the company. We also know that the treasurer anticipates short-term rates will remain virtually the same. For this reason, he would find it sub-optimal to enter into an interest rate swap. This would immediately boost interest charges by 0.7%.

The treasurer may prefer the following alternative. He purchases a 7% cap and pays for it by writing a 5% floor. He, thus, enters into a collar agreement with his bank. Because he anticipates that short-term interest rates will not fall either, he is less concerned about writing a floor. He does not believe it likely to be in the money. As a result, the company's interest charges will fluctuate between 5% and 7%.

While it is true that the company will pay 7.5% on the loan if short-term interest rates exceed 7% (for example, 7.5%), it will receive 0.50% from the cap it buys. On balance, therefore, it will pay only 7%.

However, if short-term rates fall below 5%, to 4% for example, the company will indeed only pay 4% on the loan. But this will be offset by the fact that, based on the floor it sells, it will have to pay the bank 1%, being the difference between its strike price and the current short-term rate. The company will, therefore, effectively pay 5% on balance, despite a decline in market interest rates.

While short-term interest rates amount to between 5% and 7%, neither the cap nor the floor will be in the money. The result is that neither party will be required to pay on the option. In this case, the company's interest charges will remain the same as those it incurs based on the loan at the EURIBOR.

5
Counterparty limits

Most banks use counterparty limits for financial derivatives. Any customer (business or otherwise) may only assume liabilities vis-à-vis the bank based on financial derivatives up to a certain limit. By imposing such a limit, the bank maximises the risks it runs in respect of its contracting party. Every time the bank enters into a financial derivative transaction, it blocks part of this limit. This applies for the following products covered in this chapter:

- FRAs and money market futures
- swaps
- collars

What liabilities are involved with these products? In the case of FRAs and money market futures, both the bank and its contracting party give each other an undertaking to settle the difference in interest rates. Where a swap is involved, the company undertakes to fulfil certain interest-related duties throughout the term of the swap. In the case of a collar, there is always one option that has been bought and one that has been written. The bank's contracting party, therefore, always has a duty based on the option it has written.

E
Related Topics

Chapter 15
Cryptography

Introduction

Cryptography literally means 'secret writing' and is typically used for sending messages via a medium that is considered unsecure such as the Internet. With cryptography, a readable text can be made unreadable for outsiders. Cryptographic keys are used to encrypt and decrypt data. This data could be a payment order.

Figure 1 shows a cryptographic process. A payment order is first encrypted with the encryption key into a ciphertext, which is unreadable for outsiders. This ciphertext can be sent via an unsecure channel. The ciphertext is made readable again by decrypting it with the decryption key.

Figure 1   *Encryption and decryption of a payment order*

In general, there are two types of cryptographic systems:

- Symmetric systems = secret key cryptography
- A-symmetric systems = public key cryptography

In symmetric systems, the same key is used for encryption and decryption. Both the sender and the receiver have the same secret key. This key must be kept secret for all parties who are not allowed to read the messages. That's why symmetric systems are also called secret key systems.

In a-symmetric systems, a different key is used for encryption and decryption. In these systems, key-pairs are used. One key-pair consists of one private key and one public key. The private key is strictly bind to one party and must be kept secret. The public key is not secret and can be made known to all parties.

1
Symmetric systems = secret key cryptography

The most deployed symmetric system is DES (Data Encryption Standard). This standard was founded in the 70s at the request of the US National Institute for Standards Technology (NIST). DES is still used in many financial applications, albeit that the encryption process is now repeated a number of times in order to reach a sufficient security level. In Triple-DES the DES function is repeated three times. The successor of DES is called AES (Advanced Encryption Standard) or Rijndael, after the developers Rijmen and Daemen.

Symmetric systems can be used in two ways:

- generating a Message Authentication Code (MAC);
- generating a cypher text.

GENERATING A MESSAGE AUTHENTICATION CODE
Generating a MAC (Message Authentication Code), providing the services authentication and data-integrity. There are various ways of generating a MAC. We will now describe the different steps of the routing of a mesage that is secured with a MAC.

1. A MAC is generated by appyling a hash, or compression, function to the full payment order or only to several important fields (such as total amount, currency, processing date) of the payment order.
2. The hash result is encrypted with the secret key.
3. The bank can verify the MAC using the same secret key. If the MAC is correct, the bank knows that (1) the important fields are integer and that (2) the sender of the message is authentic, because the correct secret key was used.

Figure 2 gives a representation of a payment that is secured with a MAC.

Figure 2   *MAC generation and verification of a payment order using a symmetric system*

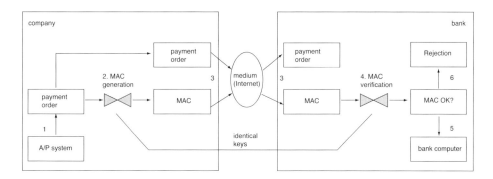

1. The company creates a payment order in its accounts payable system.
2. The company generates the MAC with the MAC key.
3. The payment order and the MAC are sent to the bank.
4. The bank verifies the MAC.
5. If the MAC is correct, the payment order is processed in the bank administration.
6. If the MAC is not correct, the payment order is rejected.

GENERATING A CIPHER TEXT

By generating a cipher text, only the owner of the secret key can read a cipher text. This provides the service confidentiality.

Remark: non-repudiation can not be guaranteed because both the company and the bank are able to produce the same MAC since they both possess the same secret key. Public key cryptography provides a solution for this.

2
A-symmetric systems = public key cryptography

Rivest, Shamir and Adleman were the founders of a new type of cryptography: public key cryptography. They found a system called RSA. RSA is the most deployed a-symmetric system.

In contrast with symmetric systems, a different key is used for encryption and decryption. In a-symmetric systems, key-pairs are used. One key-pair consists of a private key and a public key. A payment order, which is encrypted with a specific private key, can only be successfully decrypted with the corresponding public key. The other way around: A payment order, which is encrypted with a specific public key, can only be successful decrypted with the corresponding private key.

One key pair is bound to one party. For example: ABN AMRO has its own key pair, which means that ABN AMRO has an own private key and an own public key. The private key must be kept secret, for example by storing it on a smart card protected with a PIN. The public key is not secret and can be made known to all parties.

A-symmetric systems can be used in two ways:

- generating a digital signature;
- generating a cipher text.

GENERATING A DIGITAL SIGNATURE

This provides the services authentication, data-integrity and non-repudiation. Figures 3 and 4 show the procedures of a payment order which is secured by a digital signature created by a-symmetric keys.

Figure 3   *A digital signature is generated by the sender with his private key*

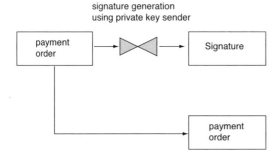

Figure 4   *The receiver verifies the digital signature with the sender's public key*

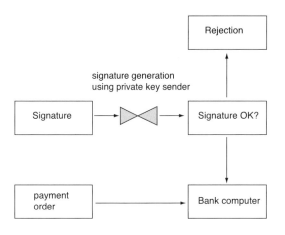

If the signature is correct, this means that:

- the sender is authenticated because the sender possesses the private key which belongs to the public key.
- the payment order is integer, because the signature would not match if the payment order would have been changed.
- the payment order can not be denied, because the sender is the only party who possesses the private key with which the signature was generated.

GENERATING A CIPHER TEXT

This provides the service confidentiality. Figure 5 shows the procedure of a payment order which is secured by creating cipher text using a-symmetric keys.

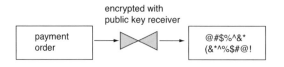

344

The payment order can only be read by the receiver because this is the only party who has the private key.

3
Certificates

When using public key cryptography, it is important to be sure that a particular public key belongs to a particular person or company (indicating that this person or company possesses the corresponding private key). To be able to verify this, a public key can be certified by a so-called 'Certification Authority (CA)'.

A CA generates digital certificates. A digital certificate contains (among other information): the public key plus the identity of the owner of the corresponding private key. A digital certificate also contains the CAs digital signature so that it can be verified whether a certificate authentic.

4
Overview of security services and cryptography

We will end this chapter by summarizing the security services that are offered by the various security systems.

Security service	Secret key cryptography	Public key cryptography
Authentication	MAC	digital signature
Integrity (with authentication)	MAC	digital signature
Non-repudiation	Not applicable	Yes, digital signature
Confidentiality	Encryption	Encryption

Chapter 16
Overview of clearing and settlement systems

Introduction

In this chapter we describe a number of clearing and settlement systems for electronic credit transfers and cheque payments. We portray the systems used in the United States, euro area, United Kingdom and Japan. At the end of the chapter, we will discuss CLS (Continuous Linked Settlement), a cross-currency settlement system.

1
Features of clearing and settlement systems

During the clearing process payments are sorted, claims for settlement are calculated and, finally, all relevant information regarding the transfers is exchanged between the bank of the payer, the bank of the beneficiary and the settlement institution. The calculation of the settlement claims may be on a gross or net basis (when for each bank outgoing and incoming payment are set off against each other).

During the settlement process, the valid claim of the beneficiary's bank is discharged by means of a credit transfer from the payer's bank to the beneficiary's bank. If payments are cleared through a clearing institution, settlement always takes place through accounts held by commercial banks at the central banks.

The main features of clearing and settlement systems are:

- types of participants
- types of transactions processed by the system
- operating procedure
- risk and risk management measures

1.1 Types of participants

Many clearing systems distinguish between direct and indirect participants (or direct and indirect members).

Direct participants of local clearing institutions are always local banks or local branches of foreign banks. Those banks have an account with the central bank. This is used for the settlement of credit transfers.

Indirect participants are mostly foreign banks with no account at the central bank. These banks can only take part in the local clearing system through remote access. The foreign banks use a local bank as a correspondent bank to pass on their payment instructions.

1.2 Types of transactions processed by the system

There are three different types of electronic credit transfers:

- high value payments
- specific interbank payments
- low value payments

HIGH VALUE PAYMENTS
High value payments (HVPs) are payments that have to be executed immediately. If originated by a multinational company, the majority of those payments are treasury payments. Most HVPs are processed through a gross settlement system.

SPECIFIC INTERBANK PAYMENTS
In the United States and Japan, a separate group of HVPs is identified. These are payments related to the settlement of foreign exchange or securities transactions, the adjustment of correspondent balances and the settlement of international commercial transactions. These specific transactions are cleared through specific clearing institutions like Clearing House Interbank Payment System (CHIPS) in the US and Foreign Exchange Yen Clearing System (FXYCS) in Japan.

LOW VALUE PAYMENTS
Low value payments (also called retail payments, bulk payments or customer payments) are mainly payments of small amounts that do not need immediate processing. Those payments, therefore, are usually settled in a net settlement system.

1.3 Operating procedures

There are two main types of calculation of settlement claim. If the calculation of settlement claims is on a gross basis, the settlement procedure is called gross settlement. If the calculation of the settlement claims is on a net basis, the settlement procedure is called net settlement.

1.4 Gross settlement

With gross settlement, the settlement institution checks the balance of the payer's bank account or its overdraft facility. If at least one of these is sufficient, the settlement institution will process the transfer by debiting the payer's bank account and crediting the beneficiary's bank account. The transfer is processed on the same day that the payer's bank sends the payment instruction to the clearing system – it is final and irrevocable. With most gross settlement systems, payment instructions are delivered and processed on an individual (case-by-case or order-by-order) basis.

The banks send payment instructions directly to the settlement institution. Every payment is settled individually and immediately. The payments involved are usually HVPs. The clearing systems which operate in this way are referred to as real time gross settlement systems (RTGS) systems.

1.4.1 Net settlement

With net settlement, the payer's banks always send their payment instructions to the clearing institution. All incoming and outgoing payment instructions from all the participating banks are sorted and matched by the clearing system. This means that for each separate bank all outgoing transfers are balanced against all incoming transfers, and a net amount to be paid or received is calculated. The clearing institution sends information about individual payments to the participating banks and information regarding the net transfers to the settlement institution. The participating banks are only liable for the resulting net amounts.

The settlement institution checks the balances of the net paying banks and, if these are sufficient, executes the settlement transfers. If not, all payments from the defaulting bank may not be transferred and all banks in this country may have serious problems.

Settlement information may be sent to the settlement institution following three different schedules:

- once a day, after the cut-off time of the settlement institution
- once a day, before the cut-off time of the settlement institution
- several times a day

ONCE A DAY, AFTER THE CUT-OFF TIME OF THE SETTLEMENT INSTITUTION. With most net settlement systems, settlement take place once a day after the cut-off time of the settlement institution. The beneficiary's account will be credited one working day after being cleared. This is the regular procedure with net settlement systems.

ONCE A DAY, BEFORE THE CUT-OFF TIME OF THE SETTLEMENT INSTITUTION
Some net settlement systems settle on the same working day. This is the case with the Euro1 system in the euro area.

SEVERAL TIMES A DAY
Some systems send settlement information to the settlement institution throughout the day. If the balances of the payers' banks' accounts with the central bank are sufficient, all payments are executed on a final and irrevocable basis on a same-day basis. The effect is similar to a gross settlement system, but this is still a net system with the specific risks of a net system.

The main advantage of net settlement systems which settle before cut-off time or several times a day is the fact that payments are executed the same day and then are final and irrevocable. In this respect these systems resemble a gross settlement system.

An important advantage of all mentioned net settlement systems over gross settlement systems is the fact that they demand far less liquidity. This is because the payers' banks only have to cover their net payment obligations instead of their gross payment obligations. Another important advantage is that it is much cheaper to process payments through a net settlement system. The disadvantage is that these systems entail more risk.

1.5 Risk Management

Today's payment systems create four important risks for banks:

- systemic risk
- credit risk
- operational risk
- fraud risk

1.5.1 Systemic risk

Systemic risk (Herstatt risk) is the risk that the failure of one bank to meet its payment obligation will cause other participants to be unable to meet their settlement obligations when due. Banks run a systemic risk when they participate in a net settlement system.

Settlement institutions may manage systemic risk in the following ways:

- credit limits
- net debit caps
- emergency pools
- financial ratios

CREDIT LIMITS

With some net settlement systems, participants are obliged to grant credit to all other participants in order for them to make payments to one another. Each participant limits the net amount of credit it will extend to other participants in the course of sending and receiving payments. This is known as bilateral credit.

NET DEBIT CAPS

In addition to the bilateral credit limits, some clearing institutions impose a binding net debit cap on each participant. This cap limits a participant's overall (multilateral) net debit position vis-á-vis all other participants. The net debit cap acts as a ceiling to limit overall systemic risk.

Clearing institutions use credit and debit caps continuously, and automatically monitor all payment messages. They will not permit the release of any attempted transfers that would cause a sending participant to violate any of these caps.

EMERGENCY POOLS

Some net settlement systems have set up emergency pools to cover possible settlement shortfalls at participating banks. There are two types of emergency pools:

The first type is a liquidity pool. This requires all participants to hold liquidity on accounts with the clearing institution at all times. Should a participant fail to meet its obligations, the liquidity pool is used to cover the defaulted payments.

The second type is a collateral pool. Under this alternative, each participating bank has to allocate collateral to the system. Participants are only asked to inject liquidity into the system if one of their number fails to settle. This is called an additional settlement obligation. If a participating bank cannot meet its additional settlement obligation, its collateral can used to obtain liquidity.

FINANCIAL RATIOS

Some clearing institutions set strong financial criteria or ratios for participants. By doing so, they ensure that participating banks will most probably not fail their settlement obligations.

Note:
Although systemic risk does not exist with gross settlement systems, a failed settlement would indirectly damage the trustworthiness of the financial system. Therefore, some gross settlement systems use the following safety measures:

- guarantees for all transferred funds to the receiver's banks
- intra-day overdraft facility

If the central bank guarantees all transfers, all payments sent to the settlement institution are final and irrevocable at the moment of sending. If the central bank grants the participant banks overdraft facilities, this will increase the banks' liquidity positions.

1.5.2 Credit risk, operational risk and fraud risk

Credit risk is the risk that the party originating a transaction (the ultimate payer) will default on his settlement obligation, causing a problem for the payer's bank. Settlement systems may manage credit risk by setting credit limits for all of the participant banks' clients.

Operational risk is the risk of processing mistakes or system disruptions.

Fraud risk is the risk that someone might alter a transaction or enter a false item, which could cause a loss for the payer's bank.

2
United States

Apart from cash payments, payment by cheque is the most widely used method of payment in the United States. The largest volume of dollars, however, is transferred through three electronic payment networks:

- Fedwire
- the Automated Clearing Houses (ACH) system
- CHIPS

Fedwire is the main processor of HVP transfers, while the ACH clearing system processes the vast majority of electronic low value payments. Some specific electronic transactions are processed through CHIPS.

2.1 Fedwire

The Federal Reserve operates the Fedwire funds transfer system, a real-time gross settlement system. Fedwire links the 12 Federal Reserve banks to participating institutions and several federal government agencies. Initiated funds transfers are immediate, final and irrevocable when processed.

2.1.1 Participants

All banks that maintain a reserve or clearing account with a Federal Reserve bank may use Fedwire to send payments to, or receive payments from, other account-holders directly. More than 9,500 banks participate in the system (including US branches and agencies of foreign banks).

2.1.2 Types of transactions

Banks use Fedwire to handle large-value, time-critical payments, such as:

- payments for settlement of interbank transactions
- purchase, sale, and financing of securities transactions
- disbursement or repayment of loans
- settlement of real estate transactions
- settlement of net settlement amounts calculated by clearing houses (NSS)

2.1.3 Operating procedure

The Fedwire funds transfer system operates from 9.00 p.m. the preceding calendar day to 6.30 p.m. eastern time. The deadline for initiating third-party transfers (i.e.

transfers initiated by a bank on behalf of its customers) is 6:00 p.m. eastern time. Participants can submit NSS files for processing between 8:30 a.m. and 5:00 p.m. ET files submitted earlier than 8:30 a.m. are queued for processing beginning at 8:30 a.m.

As a fully automated gross settlement system, Fedwire permits the electronic initiation, processing and completion of individual funds transfers in real time.

The Federal Reserve's real-time daylight accounting system, the Account Balance Monitoring System (ABMS), tracks changes in institutions' account balances resulting from Fedwire funds and securities transfers on a real-time basis. The ABMS also accounts for other transactions processed by the Federal Reserve, such as cheque settlements.

Fedwire payment messages are currently sent over an inter-district communications network that links the 12 Federal Reserve banks and their local communications networks. These also link financial institutions to the Reserve banks. Payment messages from financial institutions are routed to their local Reserve bank's host computer system for processing. If the payment message is destined for an institution in another Federal Reserve district, it is sent through the Fed's communication network to the other Reserve bank for processing on its host computer. The message is then communicated to the receiving institution.

Figure 1   *Procedure of an electronic transfer through Fedwire*

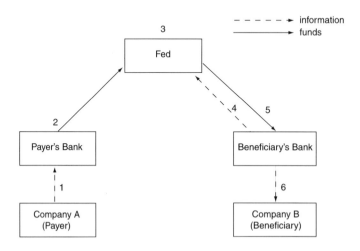

1. Company A, the payer, sends a payment instruction to its bank, the payer's bank, to transfer funds to company B;

2. The payer's bank uses Fedwire to transfer funds to Company B's bank, the beneficiary's bank, through the Federal Reserve System, the Fed;

3. The Fed debits the payer's bank reserve account and credits the beneficiary's bank's reserve account;

4. The Fed notifies the beneficiary's bank of the transfer including account information for Company B. If the beneficiary's bank is in a different Federal district from the payer's bank, the information is routed through the Fed 's communication network to the appropriate receiving Fed;

5. The beneficiary's bank credits Company B's account;

6. The beneficiary's bank notifies Company B of receipt of the transfer.

2.1.4 Risk management

In 1985, the Federal Reserve adopted a formal policy to reduce risk in the payment system, including the Fedwire funds transfer system. This policy ensures complete payment finality. It relies, in part, on:

- daylight overdrafts in Federal Reserve accounts
- a guarantee that funds will be transferred to the beneficiary's banks in the event the participating banks fails to settle
- in certain cases, collateral from participating banks to control intra-day credit risks

2.2 Automated Clearing Houses

The system of Automated Clearing Houses (ACH) is the net clearing system for electronic payments in the United States. In an ACH transaction, payment information is processed and settled electronically. The ACH is a network of regional associations, inter-bank associations and private sector processors. These ACH associations and processors are called ACH operators. The regional Federal Reserve banks operate many regional ACHs.

2.2.1 Participants

Almost all banks operating in the United States are members of the ACH.

2.2.2 Types of payments

The ACH is the clearing system for all low value electronic payments such as:
- direct deposit of payroll, social security and other government benefits, and tax refunds

- direct payment of consumer bills such as mortgages, loans, utility bills and insurance premiums
- business-to-business payments
- E-checks
- E-commerce payments
- Federal, state and local tax payments

Because ACH transactions are significantly less expensive than Fedwire payments, some companies have tended to migrate high value dollar transfers (HVPs) from the Fedwire system to the ACH system. The ACH has prevented this by limiting the maximum dollar amount of a single entry, or by increasing the price for the processing of large transactions.

2.2.3 Operating procedure

The ACH system currently is a batch-process, store and forward system. Payment instructions received by the bank from its clients during the day are stored and processed later in batches. They are then forwarded in batches to the bank's ACH operator. The cut-off time for ACH files varies with each bank.

Figure 2   ACH transaction participants; the process of information

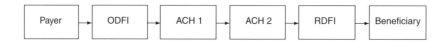

* ODFI = originating depository financial institution (the payer's bank);
* ACH 1 = originating ACH operator;
* ACH 2 = receiving ACH operator;
* RDFI = receiving depository financial institution (the beneficiary's bank).

We will now show the steps of a typical ACH credit transaction in which a company initiates salary payments to its employees. The following graph shows the clearing process and the settlement of the salary payments through the Federal Reserve System.

Figure 3   *Salary payments through automated clearing houses*

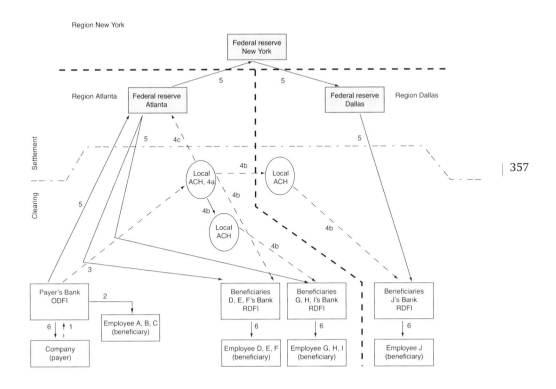

1.   A company (the originator of the payments) sends an ACH batch file that may contain hundreds of salaries transactions to its bank (the ODFI). This file contains:
     – each employee's account number
     – the transit routing number of the beneficiary's bank
     – the amount of the transfer
     – the transit routing number of the payer's bank
     – the company's account number
     – other information
2.   The payer's bank strips off so-called on-us transactions for employees who have accounts with itself and settles these directly via book transfer;
3.   The payer's bank merges the remaining company's payment instructions involving other banks with transactions from other firms and sends them to its local ACH operator;
4.   a. The local ACH operator sorts out those transactions which involve banks in its area and calculates the resulting net settlement claims for each participating bank;
     b. The local ACH operator sends the remaining transactions in batches to other ACH operators containing all transactions pertaining to each particular beneficiaries' bank. The other ACH operators present these files to the beneficiaries' banks.

c. The local ACH operator sends a message to the regional Federal reserve bank with the settlement information of the regional and interregional transfers.

5. Settlement, or transfer of value, occurs when specified in the file. For salaries, this is normally after two days. Payments between members of one and the same ACH operator are settled on a net basis. Payments between members of different ACH operators are settled on a gross basis.

6. The payer's bank (ODFI) debits the company's accounts and the beneficiaries' banks (RDFIs) credit the accounts of the employees holding accounts with them.

2.2.4 Risk management

The ACH system has no formal risk management measures for managing systemic and credit risk.

To prevent settlement risk, the ACH system requires Originating Depositary Financial Institutions (ODFIs – processing institutions) to establish and monitor exposure limits for all ACH originating operators. An ODFI has a credit exposure (an amount of credit risk it is exposed to) to the payer / originator of an ACH transaction. To prevent credit risk the Federal Reserve Payments Risk Policy recommends that an ODFI:

-   performs credit assessments on payers generating large volume ACH files
-   establishes inter-day credit limits for payers
-   reacts to minimise risk if a payer's financial condition is deteriorating

2.3 CHIPS

CHIPS (Clearing House Interbank Payment System) is a real-time net settlement system for the New York area, owned and operated by the New York Clearing House Association.

2.3.1 Participants

CHIPS participants include commercial banks, investment companies as defined by New York State banking law, or banking affiliates of a commercial banking institution with an office in New York City. A non-participant wishing to send payments over CHIPS must employ a CHIPS participant to act as its correspondent or agent. In April 2006, the CHIPS network had 46 participants. Most of these were US banks or agencies of foreign banks.

2.3.2 Types of transactions

The payments transferred over CHIPS are primarily related to international inter-bank transactions, including the dollar payments resulting from foreign currency transactions and eurodollar placements and returns.

Payment instructions are also sent over CHIPS for the following purposes:

- large and small payment transactions
- US dollar foreign exchange settlements
- financial settlements (ex. loan and interest payments)
- commercial payments
- offshore investments

2.3.3 Operating procedure

CHIPS operates from 9.00 a.m. to 5.00 p.m. (Eastern Time), with settlement usually completed before 5.15 p.m (Eastern Time).

Payment instructions are processed immediately upon release by the sender, unless they would cause the sender to exceed his bilateral credit limits or net debit limit. A payment message is final and irrevocable once it has been released to the receiver. Participants can use the payment-on-demand capability. This allows them to add funds intra-day in order to guarantee the immediate release of a payment.

Figure 4   *Routing of electronic payments through CHIPS*

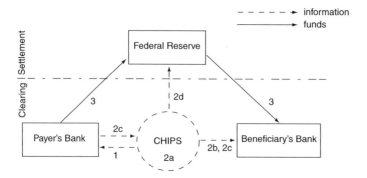

1. The payer's bank sends a payment message to CHIPS;
2   a. CHIPS checks the bilateral credit limit and the net debit cap;
    b. If there is no violation, CHIPS releases the payment message to the receiver's bank. The payment then is irrevocable;
    c. Soon after 4.30 p.m., CHIPS informs the participants of their net positions;
    d. By 5.15 p.m., CHIPS sends net settlement information to the Fed;
3. Just after 5.15 p.m., settlement takes place by debiting and crediting bank accounts at the Fed.

2.3.4 Risk management

The receiver's bank, which credits a customer and allows use of these funds, bears the risk that the sending bank will not settle. Liquidity risk among CHIPS participants is managed by the following means:

- credit limits
- net debit caps
- an emergency pool – a collateral pool designed to cover default by the largest system net debtor

Apart from these limits, the CHIPS operating system continuously and automatically monitors all payment messages. The system refuses all transfers which exceed a credit limit or a net debit cap.

2.4 Cheque clearing in the United States

In the United States, many millions of cheques are still issued each day. Some are deposited in the same institution on which they are drawn ('on-us cheques'). The remaining cheques are cleared through interbank mechanisms. About half of these cheques are cleared through local and national cheque clearing houses and correspondent bank networks. The other half is cleared through the Federal Reserve Banks.

In the next paragraph, we will first describe the routing of an on-us cheque. Then we will discuss the various ways of interbank cheque clearing.

2.4.1 On-us cheques

Approximately 30% of all cheques are on-us cheques. With these cheques, the issuing bank (this is the bank on which the payer has issued the cheque) and the bank of the beneficiary are one and the same. On-us cheques, therefore, are settled via accounting entries on the books of the payer's bank. The bank credits the beneficiary's account and, at the same time, debits the payer's account with itself.

2.4.2 Interbank cheque clearing

When two different banks are involved, there are a number of different ways the cheques may be cleared:

- direct bilateral settlement
- bilateral settlement making use of a correspondent bank
- settlement through a cheque clearing house

DIRECT BILATERAL SETTLEMENT
In this case, the beneficiary's bank sends the cheque directly to the issuing bank. The issuing bank debits the accounts of the payer and sends a payment transfer to an ACH. Figure 5 shows the process of cheque settlement if cheques are directly exchanged. Once the cheque has been received by the issuing bank, the clearing and settlement are processed in the same way as electronic transfers.

Figure 5 *Traditional cheque processing through an ACH*

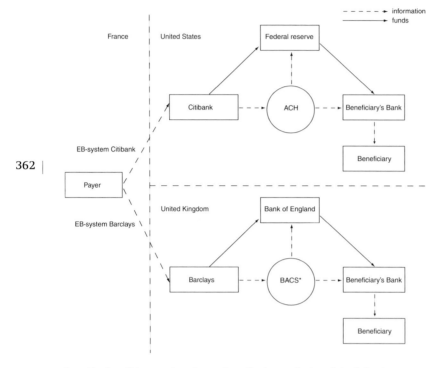

1. The beneficiary sends a cheque for collection to the beneficiary's bank.
2. The beneficiary's bank sends the cheque to the issuing bank.
3. The issuing bank checks the balance of the payer's account and debits his account.
4. The issuing bank sends a transfer instruction to the ACH.
5. a. The ACH sends a settlement instruction to the Fed.
    b. The ACH advices the payment to the beneficiary's bank.
6. The fed debits the issuing bank account with itself and credits the beneficiary's bank account with itself.
7. The beneficiary's bank credits the beneficiary's bank account. (If the beneficiary's bank collects the cheque under usual reserve, the beneficiary's account will be credited directly after step 1).

BILATERAL SETTLEMENT MAKING USE OF A CORRESPONDENT BANK

Cheques on banks located outside the geographic area in which the collecting banks are located may be deposited with correspondent banks by the collecting institution. Correspondent banks present cheques drawn on each other directly. Correspondent banks settle the cheques they collect for other banks through accounts on their books.

Cheques are most commonly cleared through a cheque clearing house. This may be an independent clearing house or a Federal Reserve bank. In both cases, settlement takes place at a Federal Reserve bank. Figure 6 shows the clearing and settlement of cheques through a cheque clearing house.

Figure 6   *Cheque processing through a cheque clearing house*

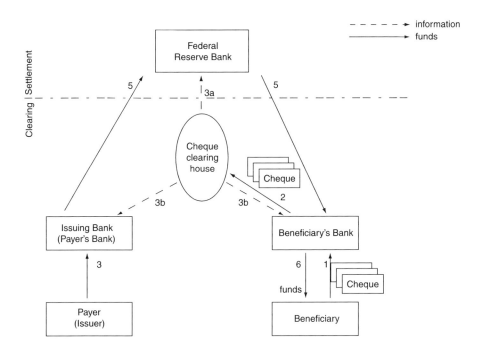

| 363

1.   The beneficiary sends a cheque for collection to the beneficiary's bank.
2.   The beneficiary's bank sends the cheque to the cheque clearing house.
3.   a. The cheque clearing house sorts all payment instructions and sends a settlement instruction to the Fed.
      b. The cheque clearing house advices the payment to the issuing bank and to the beneficiary's bank.
4.   The issuing bank checks the balance of the payer's account and debits his account.
5.   The Fed debits the issuing bank account with itself and credits the beneficiary's bank account with itself.
6.   The beneficiary's bank credits the beneficiary's bank account. (If the beneficiary's bank collects the cheque under usual reserve, the beneficiary's account will be credited directly after step 1).

Today, cheques cleared by the Federal Reserve System are processed on high-speed equipment that itemises, records and sorts cheques based on information contained in the magnetic ink character recognition (MICR) line printed along the bottom of cheques. The Federal Reserve System settles the cheques it collects through the reserve, or clearing, accounts it maintains for banks.

Cheques cleared locally are usually transported by ground couriers. Cheques drawn in regions distant from the banks are generally delivered via air transportation. The Federal Reserve System manages an extensive air transportation network to exchange cheques among its 47 cheque-processing facilities, and uses local courier networks to deliver cheques to the issuing banks.

2.4.3 Check 21

In October 2004, the Check Clearing for the 21st Century Act, also known as Check 21, became effective. Check 21 facilitates check truncation – the process of imaging a cheque by the beneficiary's bank. The bank sends the image electronically to an electronic clearing house, where it is processed as if it were a normal electronic transfer. This process is known as electronic cheque presentment (ECP). Truncation has the benefit of processing electronic images far more quickly and efficiently than the exchange of paper documents.

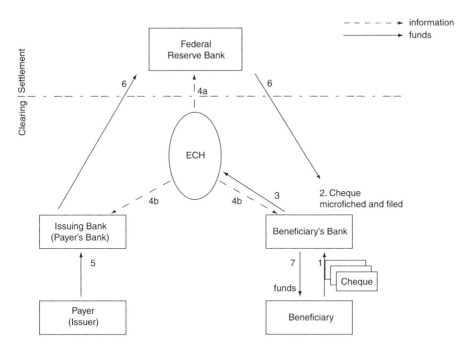

| 365

1. The beneficiary sends the cheque to its bank.
2. The beneficiary's bank images the cheque and stores the cheque.
3. The beneficiary's bank sends the electronic image to the electronic clearing house (ECH).
4. a. The electronic clearing house (ECH) clears all cheque-transfers on a net basis and sends net settlement information to the Fed.

    b. The ECH advices the payment to the issuing bank and to the beneficiary's bank.
5. The issuing bank checks the balance of the payer's account and debits his account.
6. The Fed debits the issuing bank account with itself and credits the beneficiary's bank account with itself.
7. The beneficiary's bank credits the beneficiary's bank account. (If the beneficiary's bank collects the cheque under usual reserve, the beneficiary's account will be credited directly after step 1).

Much of the innovation in cheque processing has been pioneered by the Federal Reserve System, which collects about 25% of cheques. Approximately 20% of the cheques collected by the Federal Reserve are electronically presented.

3
The euro area

Payment systems in the European Union (EU) were originally created with the aim of meeting domestic requirements. They were rather diverse in nature and, therefore, not suited to the needs of the single currency area. Against this background, the EU financial infrastructure has undergone rapid changes both in the run-up to and following the introduction of the euro in 1999. These changes have been reflected in the development of pan-European payments systems such as:

-   TARGET
-   Euro1
-   STEP1 and STEP2

3.1 TARGET

Within the EU, the Trans-European Automated Real-Time Gross Settlement Express Transfer (TARGET) system is the real-time gross settlement system for the euro. At present, TARGET is a decentralised system consisting of 15 national RTGS systems, the European payments mechanism (EPM) of the European Central Bank (ECB) and the Interlinking system. The latter is a telecommunications network linking the national RTGS systems and the ECB. The Interlinking system is provided by SWIFT. As a result TARGET offers a uniform platform for processing cross-border euro payments.

In 2007, the current TARGET system will be replaced by TARGET2. The new system will have a single technical platform, the Single Shared Platform, with a common standard. As TARGET2 has also been developed to process domestic high value payments, participating countries will no longer need their domestic RTGS systems. TARGET transfers are processed by SWIFT. TARGET2 system will be comparable to the US Fedwire system.

TARGET2 will be introduced over three years. In 2007, Austria, Cyprus, Germany, Latvia, Lithuania, Luxembourg, Malta and Slovenia will adopt the new system. They will be followed in 2008 by Belgium, Finland, France, Ireland, The Netherlands, Portugal and Spain. Finally, in 2009, Denmark, Estonia, Greece, Italy, Poland and the United Kingdom, as well as the ECB itself, will be migrated.

3.1.1 Participants

Approximately 10,000 financial institutions participate in TARGET, directly or indirectly, across the European Union. There are some 1,000 direct participants, including the ECB and the national central banks (NCBs) of all EU member states. This includes states that have not yet adopted the euro. Commercial banks operating in the EU participate through national RTGS systems. Additionally, as an exception, the following entities may be admitted as participants in national RTGS systems, subject to the approval of the relevant national central banks:

- treasury departments of central or regional governments of member states
- public sector bodies of member states authorised to hold customer accounts
- investment firms authorised and supervised by recognised competent authorities
- organisations providing clearing or settlement services subject to oversight by competent authorities

In addition to the direct participants, there are approximately 9,000 indirect participants. In total, approximately 51,000 banks are accessible through the system.

3.1.2 Types of transaction

Banks use TARGET for real-time credit transfers in euro. It processes both interbank and customer payments, and there is no upper or lower limit placed on the value of payments. All payments are treated equally, irrespective of their value. All payments through TARGET are final and irrevocable.

Transfers through TARGET, however, are rather expensive. Therefore, the system is usually only used for high value payments. The charge for TARGET cross-border payments between direct participants is based on the number of transactions sent by a participant within a single RTGS system according to a regressive scale. For two types of payments, settlement through TARGET is mandatory:

- payments directly connected with central bank operations in which the Eurosystem, comprising the ECB and the 12 central banks of the euro countries, is involved on either the recipient or sender side
- the settlement operations of large-value net settlement systems operating in euro

3.1.3 Operating procedure

As TARGET is an RTGS system, payment transactions are settled individually on a continuous basis in central bank money. Cross-border TARGET payments are processed via the national RTGS systems and exchanged directly, on a bilateral basis, between NCBs. Payments through TARGET are comparable with traditional correspondent banking payments. The following example concerns a payment order by a Dutch bank to a French bank. Both banks hold accounts with their respective central bank, de Nederlandsche Bank and the Banque de France. These central banks, in turn, hold accounts with each other.

Figure 8   *TARGET*

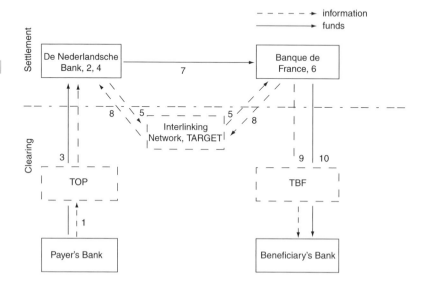

1. The Dutch bank sends a SWIFT message with the payment instructions to De Nederlandsche Bank (DNB), the Dutch central bank, through DNB's RTGS system (TOP).
2. DNB checks whether the payment order meets the required standards and contains the necessary information. DNB also checks whether the amount of the payment does not exceed the balance of the account of the sending Dutch bank or the amount of credit lines available to it. Finally, DNB checks if the receiving RTGS system is operational.
3. Once DNB has declared the payment valid, it debits the account of the sending bank immediately and irrevocably.
4. DNB converts the payment order to the message standards of the Interlinking network, if necessary, and see to it that the security requirements are met.
5. DNB sends the payment order through the Interlinking network to Banque the France (BDF) , the French central bank.
6. BDF checks if the incoming message meets the security requirements and verifies if the beneficiary's bank, as specified in the payment order, is a participant in the national RTGS system. If this is the case, BDF converts, if necessary, the message from Interlinking standards into French message standards.
7. BDF debits the account of DNB with herself.

8. BDF sends a settlement acknowledgement to DNB through the Interlinking network. If DNB does not receive the expected acknowledgement within 30 minutes, it must investigate the status of the payment, i.e. start an error detection procedure.

9. BDF sends the payment message through the French RTGS system (TBF) to the French beneficiary's bank.

10. Banque de France credits the account of the beneficiary's bank.

The Interlinking system provides end-of-day procedures, ensuring there is a final and irrevocable position at the end of each business day. These procedures include a check that all bilateral messages sent between NCBs have been received, and that the total values of cross-border payments sent and received by the NCBs during the day match. No Interlinking component may close before it has finalised its position with all bilateral partners.

| 369

TARGET is operational on weekdays from 7 a.m. to 6 p.m. (CET), with a cut-off time for customer payments at 5 p.m (CET). TARGET is closed on Saturdays and Sundays and on the six public holidays common to nearly all EU countries:

- New Year's Day (1 January)
- Good Friday
- Easter Monday
- Labour Day (1 May)
- Christmas Day (25 December)
- 26 December

3.1.4 Risk management

TARGET settles payments in central bank money with immediate finality. In TARGET, the account of the receiver's bank is never credited before the account of the payer's bank has been debited. As a result, there is always the certainty for the receiver's bank that funds received through TARGET are unconditional and irrevocable. The receiver's bank is, therefore, neither exposed to credit nor liquidity risk from these payments.

3.2 Euro1

Euro1 is a clearing system on a same-date net settlement basis run by the Euro Banking Association (EBA). The EBA is a co-operative organisation set up by EU-based commercial banks and several EU branches of non-EU banks. The EBA's mission is to act as the initiator, and assist in the development, of Europe-wide payment infrastructures. Like TARGET, Euro1 uses SWIFT message standards.

3.2.1 Participants

In January 2006, there were 70 banks (direct participants) and 55 bank subsidiaries (sub-participants). The direct participants, which are also known as clearing banks, must fulfil the following criteria:
- having its registered address in an OECD country (the OECD is the organisation of 30 well-developed industrialised countries)
- having a registered address or branch in the EU from which it participates in the system
- having direct access to TARGET via a domestic RTGS system
- conducting settlement transactions in one of its home countries' clearing systems
- being a member of EBA

3.2.2 Types of transactions

Euro1 processes credit transfers only. Although there are no restrictions regarding the value or originator of the transactions processed, the EBA intended Euro1 primarily as a high value payments processing system. Payment instructions are processed on an individual basis.

3.2.3 Operating procedure

Like the Interlinking system, the Euro1 system is operated by SWIFT. The processing of payments starts at 7:30 a.m. (CET) and ends at the cut-off time of 4:00 p.m. (CET). Settlement takes place at the end of the same day through the settlement accounts with the ECB. After the cut-off time, clearing banks with debit positions pay their single obligations into the EBA settlement account at the ECB through TARGET. After all amounts due have been received, and upon instruction from the EBA Clearing Company, the ECB pays the clearing banks with credit positions, also through TARGET. This takes place before TARGET's cut-off time, which means that all Euro1 payments are settled on a same-day basis.

All information related to payments via EBA is processed through SWIFT. All Euro1 payments must carry the three -letter tag – 'EBA' – within the SWIFT message. Participants can use one of the following SWIFT messages: MT 102, MT 103, MT 104, MT 202, MT 204, MT 400.

The following is an example of a Euro1 payment where the payer's bank is a Dutch bank and the beneficiary's bank is a French bank. Both banks are clearing members of EBA. For the sake of simplicity, the payer's and the beneficiary's banks undertake no other Euro1 transactions on that day.

Figure 9   *Electronic transfer cleared by Euro1*

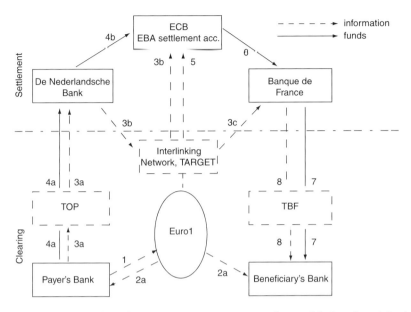

371

1. The payer's bank sends a Euro1 payment instruction in favour of the beneficiary's bank to the Euro1 system.

2. a. The Euro1 system calculates the net positions of the payer's bank.
    At 4.05 p.m. CET, the EURO1 system informs the payer's bank that it has a (net) debit position.
    b. At the same time, the EURO1 system informs the beneficiary's bank that it has a (net) credit position. Also, information about all individual incoming payments are sent to the beneficiary's bank (here there is only one single payment).

3. a. Before 4.15 p.m. the payer's bank sends a payment instruction to the Dutch Central Bank (d e Nederlandsche Bank).
    b. De Nederlandsche Bank passes the payment instruction via the Interlinking System to the European Central Bank.
    c. The Interlinking System advices the payment to the Banque de France.

4. a. De Nederlandsche Bank debits the payer's bank's account with DNB.
    b. The ECB debits the account of the Dutch Central Bank and credits the settlement account of EBA. Also, the ECB advises the transfer to the EBA.

5. Upon receipt of all payments due by short participants, the EBA sends instructions to the ECB to transfer the credit balance of the benefeciary's bank to the Banque de France in favour of the beneficiary's bank.

6. The ECB debits the settlement account of EBA and credits the account of BDF in favour of the beneficiary's bank.

7. Before 4.35 p.m. the Banque de France credits the account of the beneficiary's bank with the BdF.

8. The French domestic RTGS system, TBF, advices the payment of the beneficiary's bank.

Not shown in this diagram:
After crediting the account of the beneficiary's bank, BDF informs the ECB about this transfer. The ECB, in turn, informs EBA. Upon receipt of all confirmations, EBA notifies all participants that the settlement operations are complete.

3.2.4 Risk management

Certainty of settlement is provided through the following main features:

- financial criteria for the participating banks:
  - having own funds of at least EUR 1.25 billion
  - having a short-term credit rating of at least P2 (Moody's) or A2 (S&P) or equivalent
- a maximum debit and credit cap of EUR 1 billion has been imposed on all clearing banks (the clearing banks may determine their individual caps themselves below these thresholds)
- to ensure that settlement takes place in case one or more participants fail to cover their short positions in the system, a collateral pool of EUR 1 billion has been set up at the ECB.

3.3 STEP1 and STEP2

In order to enable shortening of the execution time of low value cross-border euro payment instructions, EBA has developed two systems that support straight-through-processing of those payments: STEP1 and STEP2. STEP stands for Straight-Through Euro Payment. Both systems use the existing infrastructure of Euro1. STEP1 has been developed to process single payment instructions. STEP2 has been developed to process bulk payments.

In 2003, the European Cross-border Credit Transfer Directive of the EU Commission came into effect. According to this Directive, banks in the euro area must charge the same fee, and offer the same float and value-dating conditions, for cross-border payments as they do for domestic payments. As of January 2006, the directive applies to all euro payments up to EUR 50,000.

The Directive drove banks to form a council in order to arrange a new payment environment, the European Payment Council (EPC). This council seeks to build a uniform platform for payments in euros for domestic and cross-border credit transfers, direct debits and card payments – the Single Euro Payments Area (SEPA).

One of the recommendations of the EPC is the development of Pan-European Automated Clearing Houses (PE-ACH). Payments that will be processed through a PE-ACH must use the BIC (Bank Identification Code) of the beneficiary bank. To apply as a PE-ACH, domestic clearing houses face large investments in their technical infrastructure. The first PE-ACH that came into operation was the STEP2 system.

3.3.1 Participants

All Euro1 clearing banks are members of the STEP systems. Further, any other bank with a system office located in an EU member state can join the STEP1 by using a Euro1 clearing bank as 'settlement bank' for its low value payments. The former banks are called STEP1 banks. Only Euro1 banks or STEP1 banks are allowed to join the STEP2 system.

3.3.2 Types of transactions

STEP1 is developed to process single credit transfers with the following characteristics:

–   non-urgent
–   low value (the amount of the payment should not exceed the level defined in the Code of Conduct of the system)

STEP2 has been developed to process bulk credit transfers and direct debits. STEP2 processes not only pan-European payments, but also domestic payments. The major Italian banks have agreed to use the STEP2 platform for the processing of their bulk payments. Also Luxembourg banks use STEP2 to process their national retail transfers.

3.3.3 Operating procedure

STEP payments are processed by the same system as Euro1 payments. In order to distinguish STEP payments from Euro1 payments, the former carry a specific three-letter tag – 'ERP' for Euro Retail Payment – within the SWIFT message. The STEP1 system processes the following SWIFT messages: MT102, MT 103, MT 104, MT202, MT 204 and MT400.

To comply with the EC Regulation 2560/2001, each STEP2 payment instruction also has to contain the IBAN number of the beneficiary and the BIC-code of the receiving bank.

As long as STEP1 banks meet the cut-off time of 14.00 (CET), like Euro1, STEP1 transactions are processed on a same-day basis.

The cut-off time for transmitting the payment files for STEP2 banks is 22.00 (CET) on day D-1. For all STEP2 banks, STEP2 generates separate bilateral payments instructions vis-á-vis all other STEP2 banks. STEP2 banks have to transfer the total gross settlement amounts before 8.00 on day D to their settlement banks. If a STEP2 bank fulfils its settlement obligation, all settlement files will ultimately be settled on day D within the Euro1 system. If a STEP2 banks fails to transfer all or a part of the settlement amount due, all or some of their bilateral payment files will not be settled on day D, but are queued for settlement on day D+1.

3.3.4 Risk management

STEP1 and STEP2 payment instructions are settled through the Euro1 system. The STEP1 and STEP2 systems, however, do not involve additional risks for the Euro1 system. The reason for this is that all STEP1 and STEP2 balances are included in the settlement balances of the EURO1 settlement banks. And these balances are capped. To limit the use of their limits with EBA, the EURO1 settlement banks in turn set settlement limits for the STEP1 banks they facilitate.

Normally, a EURO1 settlement bank demands that the STEP1 banks it facilitates transfer their settlement amount before 14.30 (CET). But even if a STEP1 bank fails to transfer the settlement amount, the EURO1 settlement bank has a duty to fulfil the settlement transfer of the STEP1 bank in the Euro1 settlement process. In contrast with STEP1 payments, EURO1 banks are allowed to hold the STEP2 settlement files if the STEP2 banks fail to transfer the gross settlement amounts.

3.4 Cheque processing in Europe

There are no specific systems for clearing cross-border cheques in the EU. Cheques are mainly cleared through local clearing via the correspondent banking system.

4
United Kingdom

The UK RTGS system, CHAPS, has a processing unit for sterling as well as for the euro. Bulk payments are processed through the Bankers Automated Clearing Services (BACS) system. All clearing systems in the UK are managed by individual companies which, in turn, belong to an umbrella body, the Association for Payment Clearing Services (APACS).

4.1 Gross settlement – CHAPS

The UK RTGS system is called CHAPS (Clearing House Automated Payment System). CHAPS is one of the largest RTGS systems in the world, second only to Fedwire in the United States. It provides members and their participants with a same-day payment mechanism. It is run by the CHAPS Clearing Company.

4.1.1 Participants

The participants for the CHAPS system are divided into direct members and indirect members. There are 16 direct member banks, called settlement banks, currently participating. These include British banks, non-British Banks e.g. ABN AMRO Bank and Bank of America, and the British central bank, the BoE. Direct members of the clearing systems are institutions with responsibility for settling all transfers, and consequently all interbank obligations arising from these systems.

For CHAPS sterling, there are also approximately 425 indirect members (also known as participants), which use their accounts with the direct members to send and receive CHAPS payments. The settlement members are responsible for indirect members' activities and settle on their behalves.

4.1.2 Types of transactions

There is no restriction on the type or value of transactions handled, provided they are unconditional sterling payments. A significant proportion of CHAPS payments originate in the foreign exchange market and other wholesale markets, owing to their requirement for a prompt settlement service.

CHAPS is, however, also used to facilitate same-day transfers arising from a range of other activities e.g. general commercial transactions. Some transfers can even be quite small. In fact, 40% of all transactions are under GBP 10,000.

4.1.3 Operating procedure

The CHAPS system currently opens for normal service at 6 a.m. (UK time). CHAPS banks can initiate transfers for their own account, or for the account of their customers, until 4.00 p.m (UK time).

Most settlement members will, however, negotiate cut-off points with their customers. Any requests to make CHAPS transfers received after a set deadline will be handled on a 'best efforts' basis. (After the 4.00 p.m. cut-off, settlement members can make transfers on their own behalf, or on behalf of other credit institutions or other money market participants, for the purpose of settling their end-of-day positions; they cannot process normal customer payments after this time.) The CHAPS sterling day ends at 4:20 p.m. After this time, CHAPS sterling settlement banks can use the Enquiry Link to make transfers under the Late Transfer Scheme (until 5 p.m.) and the sterling end-of-day transfer scheme (until 5:25 p.m.).

Each CHAPS payment is settled through accounts that direct members hold with the BoE before details are sent to the receiver's bank. A payment is processed as follows:

Figure 10 *Procedure of an electronic transfer through CHAPS*

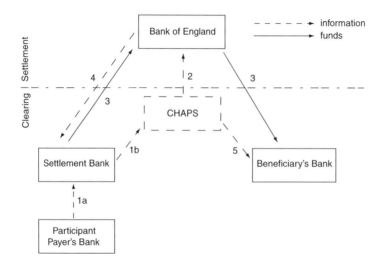

1. a. A participant (indirect member) sends a payment instruction to a CHAPS direct member or Settlement Bank.
    b. The direct member passes the payment instruction on to CHAPS.
2. The CHAPS system sends a settlement request in SWIFT format to the Bank of England, while the main message is retained in the payer's bank's gateway.
3. If the settlement bank has sufficient funds on its account, the Bank of England settles the transaction by debiting the account and crediting the beneficiary's bank's account.
4. The Bank of England returns a confirmation message to the settlement bank;
5. When this confirmation is received, the main message containing the full payment details is released automatically to the beneficiary's bank, which has the assurance that it has received final and irrevocable funds on its account at the Bank of England.

4.1.4 Risk management

As a rule, banks should only forward settlement requests to the BoE when they have sufficient funds on their settlement account to allow the transaction to be processed immediately.

The BoE provides intraday funds to the members of CHAPS through an intraday sale and repurchase (repo) facility. Only settlement members of the CHAPS system can obtain liquidity from the BoE through intraday repos.

4.2 BACS

BACS (Bankers' Automated Clearing Services) is the UK's ACH responsible for clearing bulk electronic transfers, both debit or credit transactions. BACS operates the clearing. It processes the great majority of electronic interbank funds in the UK on a net settlement basis.

4.2.1 Participants

The membership of BACS consists of only 12 UK banks, including the BoE and one building society. These credit institutions are responsible for settling all settlement obligations arising from the BACS clearing process. Settlement members of BACS are able to sponsor other organisations as users of the BACS service. Users are allocated a BACS user number by their sponsor and are able to submit payment instructions directly to BACS. There are about 35,000 users, including a wide range of commercial and public sector bodies.

4.2.2 Types of transfers

BACS provides electronic bulk clearing for:

- credit transfers
- direct debits
- standing orders
- other non-urgent automated credit transfers

There are no general restrictions on the purpose of the underlying transactions. Similarly, there are no restrictions on the size of the transactions handled. However, most transfers are retail payments and average per item values tend to be small compared with the CHAPs clearing.

4.2.3 Operating procedures

Users submit payment data to the BACS clearing house through BACSTEL, a tele-communications service which offers direct connection to the BACS computer centre. Users may submit payment instructions to BACS from between two days and two years ahead of the date for payment.

Payments submitted to BACS are subject to a three-day clearing and settlement cycle. The deadline for receipt of payment information from users is 9.00 p.m. (UK time) on day 1 of the cycle. These data are then sorted into bank order at BACS and transmitted onward to destination credit institutions. A destination bank may be either a receiver's bank or a payer's bank, depending on whether the account in question is credited or debited. This process should be completed by 6 a.m. the following day (i.e. day 2). The payer's bank receives a report confirming each submission on day 2. On day 3, transfers are debited/credited to respective payer/beneficiary accounts, usually at the beginning of the day.

The interbank settlements take place at the BoE on a net basis on day 3 of the clearing process. This settlement occurs at 9.30 a.m. The BoE transfers the multilateral net amounts directly to the settlement accounts using the RTGS processing system.

Figure 11   Procedure of an electronic transfer through BACS

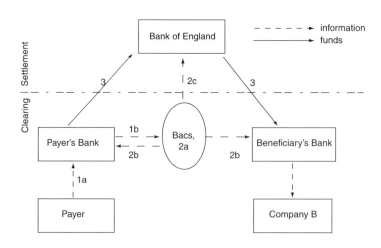

1.   a. On day 1, a payer sends a payment instruction to his bank.
     b. The payer's bank passes the payment on to BACS;

2. a. During day 2, BACS sorts all payments instructions.

b. Also during the day, BACS sends information to the payer's bank and the beneficiary's bank.

c. On day 3, BACS sends settlement information to the Bank of England.

3. On day 3, at 9:30 a.m., the settlement takes place at the Bank of England.

4.2.4 Risk management

Each settlement member is responsible for settling payments on behalf of its clients. To manage credit risk, there is a system of credit limits per client, and all violations on these limits need authorisation by the settlement bank.

379

4.3 Cheque processing in the UK

Like in the United States, in the United Kingdom cheques are a commonly used payment instrument. But unlike the United States, UK laws prohibit some new techniques in cheque processing. Together with the geographical position, close to the euro area, this is a reason for the development of many new initiatives on the processing of electronic payments, even for euro transfers. The Cheque and Credit Clearing Company is responsible for the bulk paper clearing of cheques and credits in England, Wales and Scotland.

In the United Kingdom, it has been legally possible since 1996 to permit presentment to the beneficiary's bank at a location other than the beneficiary's branch and to allow electronic presentment. Currently, cheques are generally truncated at a central point of the beneficiary's bank and electronic methods are used for presentment. Digital imaging of cheques, however, is employed typically only for internal processing and storage.

Member banks do not send all cheques to the cheque clearing houses. The bulk of cheques are issued for small payments. Banks send payment information for low value cheques to the cheque clearing house electronically and store the physical cheques themselves. All high value cheques are physically sent to the cheque clearing house for settlement.

OVERVIEW OF CLEARING AND SETTLEMENT SYSTEMS

Figure 12 *Cheque processing through a cheque clearing house in the UK*

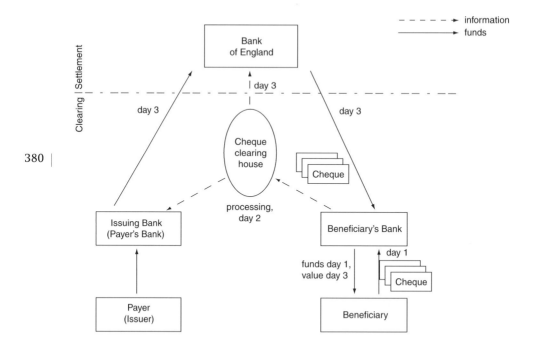

Note: the differents steps of this cheque clearing process are already described in figure 6.

5
Japan

In Japan, there is no specific segregation between high or low value clearing. Most payments are processed by four interbank clearing systems:

- BOJ-NET, a RTGS system for the settlement of bank-to-bank transactions
- FXYCS, a net clearing system for high value payments
- Zengin, for all domestic funds transfers
- Electronic Cheque Clearing System, for clearing of bills, cheques, promissory notes and other interbank receipts among the banks

5.1 BOJ-NET

BOJ-NET (Bank of Japan Financial Network System) is an on-line system for electronic fund transfers among financial institutions that hold accounts with the central bank of Japan, the Bank of Japan (BOJ). The system completes, on an on-line basis, fund transfers between current deposit accounts that financial institutions maintain with the BOJ. Since January 2001, the BOJ-NET system is a real-time gross settlement system.

The central bank manages the system and writes rules governing the use of BOJ-NET. To be eligible for BOJ-NET services directly, members must hold an account with the central bank.

The language used in the BOJ-NET system is Japanese. This is the reason why BOJ-NET is not a member of the SWIFT network.

Apart from the direct funds transfers between the different members, BOJ-NET also completes settlements of the positions resulting from operations by the two Japanese clearing houses:
- the Foreign Exchange (Gaitame) Yen Clearing System (FXYCS)
- the Zengin Data Telecommunications System (Zengin System), an electronic domestic funds transfer system, which is managed by the Tokyo Bankers Association (TBA)

5.1.1 Participants of BOJ-NET

There are about 260 participants, including local banks, foreign banks, securities companies and other financial institutions.

5.1.2 Types of transaction

The payment services provided by BOJ-NET include:

- fund transfers associated with interbank money market and securities transactions
- in-house funds transfers
- final settlements resulting from privately-managed clearing systems, (such as FXYCS, Zengin and check clearing system)
- funds transfers between financial institutions and the central bank, including treasury funds transfers. (Most of ABN AMRO Tokyo's BOJ-NET payments are JPY clearing for network and correspondent banks, cross-border commercial, treasury interbank and government bond transactions)

- as of 2008: indivual FXYCS payments and high value Zengin payments

5.1.3 Operating procedure

Participants make funds transfers from one BOJ account to another by sending payment instructions from BOJ-NET terminals within the individual participant's installations.

Funds transfers handled by BOJ-NET are settled on either:

- a real-time gross basis from 9:00 a.m. to 5:00 p.m. (both Japanese time), or
- a designated-time net basis. There are four designated settlement times (all Japanese time):

1. 9:00 a.m. (calls)
2. 1:00 p.m. (cheque clearing, calls, futures)
3. 2:30 p.m. (FXYCS), 3:00PM (Government bond DVP)
4. 5:00 p.m. (clearing handled by Zengin).

5.1.4 Risk management

The BOJ does not extend daylight overdrafts. If a participant does not have sufficient funds in its account for a real-time funds transfer, the payment instruction is automatically rejected. In the case of designated-time fund transfers, the BOJ monitors the position of the participants beforehand, so that they will not have negative balances in their BOJ accounts, and that designated time settlement can therefore be executed.

5.2 The FXYCS system

The Foreign Exchange Yen Clearing System (FXYCS) is a net settlement clearing system for international and/or foreign exchange related JPY transactions. It is sometimes called the Japanese version of the New York CHIPS system. The system was originally introduced in October 1980 and is managed by the Tokyo Bankers' Association (TBA). Since the beginning of March 1989, the system has been operated as an electronic settlement system by the BOJ as a part of the BOJ-NET system.

5.3 Participants

FXYCS has approximately 250 members. There are 50 direct members, including several foreign banks. Apart from the direct members, there are some 200 outsourced banks.

5.3.1 Types of transfers

The following high value payments are processed:

– International commercial transactions
– foreign exchange-related JPY transactions

5.3.2 Operating procedure

Banks can deliver their payments instructions to FXYCS until 1.45 p.m. (Japanese time). The system runs the netting procedure and sends the net settlement instructions to BOJ-NET. The settlement is undertaken by the BOJ as part of BOJ-NET, at 2.30 p.m. (Japanese time). The payments are thus settled on a same-day basis. The language used with FXYCS is English. In fact, FXYCS is a SWIFT member. Note that the settlement via BOJ-NET is still in Japanese.

Figure 13   *Electronic transfer, cleared by FXYCS*

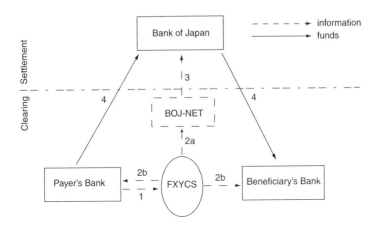

1. A payer's bank sends a payment instruction to the FXYCS system.
2. a. The FXYCS system sorts all payments and sends information the netted settlement obligations to BOJ-NET.
   b. The FXYCS system sends information on all individual transactions to the participating banks.
3. BOJ-NET passes the settlement instruction through to the Bank of Japan.
4. The Bank of Japan debits the payer's bank account in favour of the beneficiary's bank account. This settlement takes place the same day at 3:00 p.m. Japanese time.

5.3.3 Risk management

Like most net settlement systems, FXYCS has taken several measures to manage systemic risk. Since December 1998, several requirements and features have been introduced in FXYCS clearing rules by the Bankers Association, including:
- net credit limit
- debit caps
- collateral requirement
- loss sharing rule
- liquidity – providing scheme

With these new rules, the number of FXYCS direct participants has gone down from 263 to 42 members due to higher operating costs and more sophisticated risk management controls under the new regime. (ABN AMRO Tokyo remains a direct member but many smaller financial institutions are now outsourcing payment operations to larger member banks.)

5.4 Clearing of domestic transfers – Zengin

The Zengin Data Telecommunication System is a countrywide electronic system for clearing domestic transfers. All transfers are cleared on a net settlement basis. Zengin is operated by the TBA and has centres in Tokyo and Osaka. Zengin has an online link to the BOJ.

5.4.1 Participants

All domestic banks are members of Zengin together with only three foreign banks. Other foreign banks may participate in the system via a link with a member bank.

5.4.2 Types of transactions

The Zengin system is designed to handle domestic fund transfers for third parties. Transactions include all domestic payments. The bulk of these payments are low value payments.

5.4.3 Operating procedure

Payment instructions are transferred to the Zengin centre on a transaction-by-transaction basis between 8.30 a.m. and 3.30 p.m. (Japanese time). Participants' debit and credit positions are calculated within the system. The net obligations of each bank are discharged by debiting or crediting the bank's account at the BOJ at 5.00 p.m. (Japanese time) on the same day.

Figure 14   *Electronic transfer, cleared by Zengin*

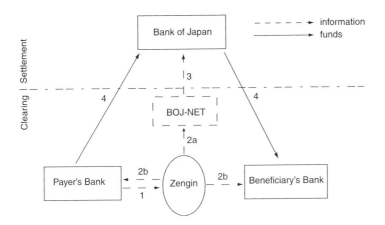

1. A payer's bank sends a payment instruction to the Zengin system.
2. a.The Zengin system sorts all payments and sends information the netted settlement obligations to BOJ-NET.

   b. The Zengin system sends information on all individual transactions to the participating banks.
3. BOJ-NET passes the settlement instruction through to the Bank of Japan.
4. The Bank of Japan debits the payer's bank account in favour of the beneficiary's bank account. This settlement takes place the same day at 5:00 p.m. Japanese time.

5.5 Cheque processing in Japan

There are still approximately 185 cheque-clearing houses throughout Japan. The clearing houses are managed by their respective local bankers' associations. More than 80% of the total clearing value is concentrated at the Tokyo Clearing House (TCH), with 525 participating financial institutions.

Each cheque-clearing house sets its own rules however.To enhance the efficiency in cash management of financial institutions, the harmonisation of these rules has been promoted among the clearing houses. For example, the settlement time has been standardised at 1.00 p.m. (Japanese time) since the introduction of BOJ-NET. Any revisions to the roles of clearing houses which make final settlement in the BOJ accounts require BOJ approval.

5.5.1 Participants

Major banks participate directly as associated members of the TCH. Small financial institutions participate through direct participants.

The cheque-clearing systems mainly handle fund transfers resulting from exchange of cheques associated with commercial trades between firms. They also deal with bills of exchange and cheques resulting from asset transactions of bonds and equities, negotiable certificates of deposit, and foreign exchange.

5.5.2 Operating procedure

Bills of exchange and cheques collected at the TCH are cleared and settled in the following manner:

- cheques are presented by the payees at the beneficiaries' banks
- these items are passed on to the TCH, where the net credit or debit position of each participant is calculated
- the net positions are settled at 1.00 p.m. (Japanese time) on the settlement day through the individual banks' BOJ accounts

The TCH began automation of the clearing process with the 1971 incorporation of computers and facilities which read and sort out cheques. The cheques are read for processing through Magnetic Ink Character Recognition (MICR) technique.

In general, proceeds can be withdrawn by the beneficiary on the day after the settlement day because interbank settlement in these systems is not finalised until 11.00 a.m. on the day after the settlement day, when it has been confirmed that cheques have not been dishonoured. Cheques which can be cleared through the TCH will be value-dated next day upon presentation.

Foreign currency cheques or JPY cheques which are payable outside the jurisdiction of the TCH are credited only upon collection of funds, unless the customer is accommodated with a cheque discount facility.

6
The CLS (Continuous Linked Settlement) system

It is estimated that payments totalling some EUR 4,000 billion are made in all the payment systems of the world every day. On an annual basis, this amounts to almost 40 times the value of the gross domestic product of all the countries of the world, and 300 times global export turnover. Foreign exchange transactions account for as much as 80% of the turnover of our national systems of payment. With all foreign exchange transactions, banks run settlement risk.

In order to avoid the settlement risk, 60 international banks developed a method of settlement in which payments in different relevant currencies are processed simultaneously. This means that a payment in one currency is only effected once it is certain that it will be counterbalanced by a receipt in the other currency. This method is called the payment-versus-payment (pvp) method. With pvp, the principal of each foreign exchange transaction is guaranteed. On order to operate this kind of settlement, the CLS Bank was founded as a division of CLS Services Ltd.

The various currencies in which transactions can be settled, are as follows:

-   US dollar
-   Canadian dollar
-   Australian dollar
-   New Zealand dollar
-   Euros
-   Sterling
-   Swiss francs
-   Korean Won
-   Swedish crown
-   Danish crown
-   Norwegian crown
-   Japanese yen
-   Singapore dollar
-   Hong Kong dollar
-   South African Rand

6.1 Settlement risk

A foreign exchange transaction is the sale of one currency for the purchase of another. Settlement usually takes place through accounts in the correspondent banks in the country in which the relevant currency is issued.

A Dutch bank (A) purchases dollars from a Japanese bank (B) and pays for them in euros. In the current international payment infrastructure, the payment of euros and the receipt of dollars occur separately from each other. The euros are transferred through accounts held at the ECB, the dollars are settled at the Federal Reserve Bank in New York.

An important aspect of settling currency transactions concerns the time differences between the national payment systems. Yen payments are processed earlier in the day than euro payments, which in turn precede those in dollars. Therefore, when Bank A buys dollars and makes its payment in yen before the cut-off time of the FXYCS-system in Japan (i.e. 2.30 p.m. Japanese time - which is 11.30 p.m. New York time, prior day), Bank A still has to wait and see if it will receive the dollars it is buying. In fact, Bank B could be in default Bank A runs this risk from the cut-off time of the FXYCS-system in Japan until the cut-off time of the Federal Reserve in New York, i.e from 11.30 p.m. on day 1 until 8.00 p.m. on day 2. The described risk is called settlement risk. The following picture shows the two separate settlement flows of a USD/JPY foreign exchange transaction.

Figure 15 *Settlement of a USD/JPY foreign exchange transaction*

cut-off time: 11.30 p.m. New York time, day 1

| Bank A | → JPY → | Bank of Japan | → JPY → | Bank B |

8.00 p.m. New York time, day 2

| Bank A | ← USD ← | Federal Reserve | ← USD ← | Bank B |

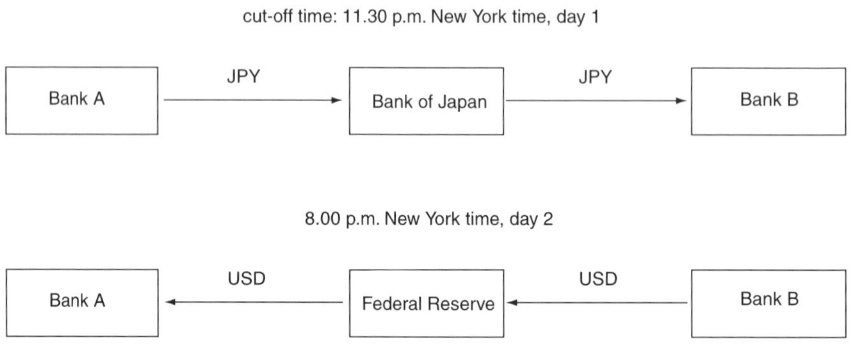

6.2 Members

The CLS bank has three types of members:
- settlement members
- user members
- third parties

Both settlement and user members are shareholders of the CLS Bank. For each currency, the CLS Bank holds an account with the central bank. The settlement members have their own account with CLS Bank, broken down into sub accounts for each currency. User members are required to make use of an account held by a settlement member for the financial settlement of their own transactions. Both types of members can submit transactions to CLS Bank directly. They are, therefore, also subject to certain operational terms and conditions. Other banks outside the system are referred to as third parties and are required to use a settlement member to have their transactions processed.

6.3 Operating procedure

The CLS Bank processes all foreign exchange transactions separately using a gross settlement system. The bank makes use of a payment-versus-payment procedure. This implies that the CLS Bank establishes a direct link between two opposite payments based on one single foreign exchange transaction. The CLS Bank debits the account of a participant only when it is certain that this is offset by a credit entry to an account of the same participant in a different currency.

With other gross settlement systems, the parties must always ensure, in the event of outgoing payments, that there is a sufficient balance on the account in the currency concerned. With the CLS system, the participants can have a debit position in a certain currency during the day. One condition is that participants must have sufficient balances on their accounts in other currencies at the CLS Bank. These balances are then used as collateral for the transactions in the deficit currencies. As a result, the CLS system is liquidity efficient for the participants.

The CLS Bank does not take the whole balance on the accounts in other currencies into consideration when computing the collateral. The bank subtracts a certain security margin from the balance, the so-called haircut. The bank does this in order to take possible fluctuations in the exchange rates during the day into consideration. In the event of a haircut of, for example, 15%, the collateral value of a balance in a different currency is equal to 85% of the balance concerned. A bank may, for example, use 85% of its balance in Japanese yen as collateral for a transaction where it has to deliver dollars.

The ING Bank enters into a foreign exchange transaction with the Royal Bank of Scotland. It sells EUR 120 million in exchange for GBP 80 million. The balance on ING Bank's euro account with the CLS Bank amounts to EUR 60 million. The CLS Bank would not carry out the transaction based on the euro balance.

However, ING has a credit balance of USD 100 million on its USD account. At a EUR/USD exchange rate of 1.25 this amounts to a euro amount of EUR 80 million. The CLS Bank applies a haircut of 10%. This means that the collateral value of the USD credit balance is equal to 90% x EUR 80 million = EUR 72 million.

390 | The CLS Bank will carry out the foreign exchange transaction because the ING Bank has sufficient collateral.

The CLS Bank sets a limit for debit positions. When this limit has been reached, the participating bank must replenish the account in the currency concerned before the CLS Bank will settle transactions charged to this account.

The settlement process takes place in three stages:

- stage 1 – delivery of settlement instructions;
- stage 2 – clearing;
- stage 3 – pay-out.

6.3.1 Stage 1: 11.00 CET - 7.00 CET

From 11:00 (CET) to 00:00 (CET) all banks send information about the foreign exchange transactions that are to be settled to the CLS Bank. At the beginning of this stage, each bank may also deposit initial funds into their accounts with the CLS Bank.

At the end of stage 1, the CLS Bank has an overview of all the transactions that are to be processed on that day. Based on this information, the CLS Bank draws up a 'pay-in' schedule specifying the net pay-ins required for the relevant payments, which all the banks are required to honour based on the assumption that all transactions will ultimately proceed. This schedule is sometimes referred to as a pay-in roster. The pay-in roster is an overview of the payment obligations of the settlement members. All initial pay-in amounts specified in the pay-in roster must be paid by 6:30 am (CET).

6.3.2 Stage 2: 7:00 CET – 9:00 CET

The settlement takes place with the CLS Bank on an order-to-order basis. This means that the CLS Bank processes each transaction separately. This is, therefore, referred to as a gross settlement system. In this case, an account of one of the participants at the CLS Bank is debited and, at the same time, the account of the counter party at the CLS Bank is credited. This simultaneous processing is the most important characteristic of the CLS system.

The CLS Bank processes the transactions in the sequence that they have been submitted. If the balance on the account concerned is insufficient, the collateral value has become too low, or the debit position in a certain currency has reached the limit, a transaction will not be processed and is directed towards the 'queue'. This implies that the CLS Bank will postpone the settlement until the paying bank has provided additional liquidity, either in the currency concerned or in a different currency. Providing additional liquidity is referred to as an interim pay-in.

During the settlement stage, the payment systems of all central banks involved must be open. After all, the participating banks must have the opportunity to still make additional pay-ins.

6.3.3 Stage 3: 9:00 CET – 12:00 CET

Once the settlement has been completed, the CLS Bank will update its entries to transfer the resulting balances of the settlements back to the accounts that the participating banks hold with their central banks. We refer to this as the payout.

The settlement of the foreign exchange transactions submitted takes place in stage 2 on an order-to-order basis, and this, therefore, concerns a gross settlement. However, the payouts in stage 3 take place on a net basis. After all, the amounts that the CLS Bank debits from the various accounts of the participants are the result of the debit and credit entries for all individually settled transactions.

For that matter, banks can also make interim pay-ins in stage 3 in order to eliminate authorised debit positions. Transactions that are in the queue will then be processed. At the end of stage 3 all accounts revert to zero.

Stage 3 ends for the Asia Pacific region at 10:00 (CET) and for Europe and North America at 12:00 (CET). All the central banks must also be open during this stage.

6.3.4 Example of the settlement of foreign exchange transactions

Following is an example of the way in which CLS Bank operates.

EXAMPLE

At the beginning of the day banks A, B and C, that are settlement members, have CLS Bank account balances amounting to EUR 150.00, USD 225.00 and JPY 10,000.00 respectively.

For the sake of convenience, this example is based on the following fictitious exchange rates: USD 1.00 = EUR 1.00 = JPY 100.00. The overall security is set at 90% (haircut of 10%).

The collateral value (countervalue in US) for each separate bank is:

A: USD 135

B: USD 202.5

C: USD 90

	CLS-accounts bank A			CLS -accounts bank B			CLS-accounts bankC		
	Euro	USD	Yen	Euro	USD	Yen	Euro	USD	Yen
In-payments	150	0	0	0	225	0	0	0	10000
	(135)				(202.5)				(90)

Note: all collateral values are given between brackets.

Phase 1

The banks deliver the following transactions to the CLS system:

1. Bank A buys USD 150 from bank B against EUR 150.
2. Bank A buys JPY 10,000 from bank B against EUR 100.
3. Bank B buys USD 100 from bank C against EUR 100.

Phase 2

The transactions (one to three) are placed in a queue before clearing occurs. The transactions are settled on a first-in-first-out basis.

1. Bank A buys USD 150 from Bank B against EUR 150.

This transaction can be settled. Bank A must pay EUR 150 mln and has this amount on its euro account with CLS. Bank B has EUR 225 mln on its USD account with CLS, which is more than enough to pay

USD 150 mln to Bank A. The following schedule depicts the transaction itself as well as the situation after the transaction.

	CLS-accounts bank A			CLS -accounts bank B			CLS-accounts bank C		
	Euro	USD	Yen	Euro	USD	Yen	Euro	USD	Yen
In-payments	150 (135)	0	0	0	225 (202.5)	0	0	0	10000 (90)
Transaction I	−150	+150		+150	−150				
Balance after transaction I	0	150 (135)		150 (135)	75 (67.5)		o	o	10000 (90)

2. Bank A buys JPY 10.000 from bank B for EUR 100.

CLS Bank settles the transaction.

After transaction 1, Bank A has no more euros in its EUR account. However, Bank A has sufficient collateral for transaction 2: 90% of USD 150 mln = USD 135 mln. On the basis of this collateral CLS Bank grants Bank A a temporary overdraft facility up to a maximum of EUR 135 mln (the EUR/USD exchange rate is 1,0000). As a consequence of transaction 2, Bank A would have an overdraft of EUR 100 mln, which is within the allowed overdraft level.

As Bank B also has sufficient collateral (USD 202.5 mln), it is granted an overdraft facility in JPY, up to a maximum value of USD 100 mln, by CLS Bank.

However, Bank A must repay its overdraft in EUR and Bank B must repay its overdraft in JPY before the end of phase 3.

	CLS-account Bank A			CLS Accounts Bank B			CLS Accounts Bank C		
	EUR	USD	Yen	EUR	USD	Yen	EUR	USD	Yen
Balance after transaction 1	0	150 (135)		150 (135)	75 (67.5)		o	o	10.000 (90)
Transaction 2	−100		+1000 0	+100		−10000			
Balance after transaction 2	−100 (−100)	150 (135)	10000 (90)	250 (225)	75 (67,5)	−10000 (−100)			10000 (90)

3. Bank B buys USD 100 from bank C against EUR 100

The third transaction may not proceed. Bank B has enough EUR on its account (also following the deduction of the requisite security for the JPY overdraft). Nevertheless, Bank C only has JPY 10,000 on its account (representing security with a value of USD 90).

This is not enough to serve as security for the payment of USD 100. If this transaction were to proceed, CLS Bank would be providing credit without any cover. The transaction is therefore placed in the queue until Bank C has increased the balance of its account with CLS Bank by an additional pay-in. Bank C executes an extra pay-in of USD 100.

CLS Bank then settles transaction 3.

	CLS account Bank A			CLS Accounts Bank B			CLS Accounts Bank C		
	EUR	USD	Yen	EUR	USD	Yen	EUR	USD	Yen
Balance after transaction 2	−100 (−100)	150 (135)	10000 (90)	250 (225)	75 (67.5)	−10000 (−100)			10000 (90)
Additional pay in								100	
Balance after additional pay in	−100 (−100)	150 (135)	10000 (90)	250 (225)	75 (67.5)	−10000 (−100)		100	10000 (90)
Transaction 3				−100	+100		+100	−100	
Balance after transaction 3	−100	150	10000	150	175	−10000	100	0	10.000

Phase 3

CLS Bank requires that all accounts are cleared by the end of phase 3. This means that Bank A must replenish its EUR account and Bank B must replenish its JPY account. As a result, Bank A transfers EUR 100 mln to the account of CLS Bank with the European Central Bank, and Bank B transfers JPY 10,000 mln to the account of CLS Bank with the Bank of Japan.

	CLS account Bank A			CLS Accounts Bank B			CLS Accounts Bank C		
	EUR	USD	Yen	EUR	USD	Yen	EUR	USD	Yen
Balance after transaction 3	−100	150	10000	250	75	−10000	100	0	5000
Extra pay ins	100					10000			
Balance after extra pay in	0	150	10000	250	75	0	100	0	5000

At the end of phase 3, CLS banks executes the pay outs.

	CLS account Bank A			CLS Accounts Bank B			CLS Accounts Bank C		
	EUR	USD	Yen	EUR	USD	Yen	EUR	USD	Yen
Balance after extra pay in	0	150	10000	250	75	0	100	0	5000
Pay-outs	0	−150	−10000	−250	−75	0	−100	0	−5000
Balance at the end of phase 3	0	0	0	0	0	0	0	0	0

Below, a diagram is included that shows the three stages of processing foreign exchange transactions by the CLS Bank. The diagram is based on the example cited above. We see the pay-ins by the three banks in stage 1. The central banks process the pay-ins. The CLS Bank enters the amounts on the sub-accounts of the banks.

The actual settlement with the CLS Bank takes place in stage 2. The processing of transaction 2, whereby Bank B buys EUR 100 from Bank A in exchange for JPY 10,000 is shown in the diagram. The internal CLS JPY account of Bank B is debited in favour of the internal JPY account of Bank A, and, at the same time, the internal EUR account of Bank A is debited in favour of the internal EUR account of Bank B. At the end of stage 3, the CLS Bank transfers the amounts from the sub-accounts, which both banks hold at the CLS Bank, to the accounts that the participating banks hold at the central banks in their home countries. The JPY payout to Bank A and the USD payout to Bank B are taken as an example. The payments are then processed by the central banks.

Figure 16   *The settlement of foreign exchange transactions through CLS*

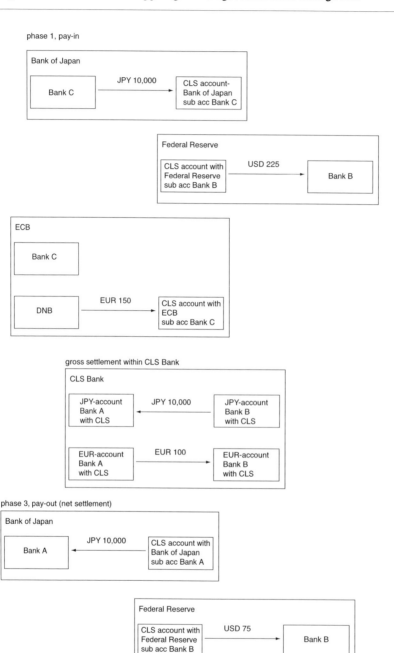

6.4 Risk management

CLS Bank requires that adequate security is available to cover a temporary overdraft in a currency. In addition, other security measures have been adopted in order to ensure that CLS Bank is also able to pay out any amounts that are credited.

Apart from the overdraft ceilings, the CLS Bank has established another security measure. Is has made arrangements with so-called liquidity providers. These are banks that have agreed to make a specified sum available in the event of a contingency, i.e. if a member bank exceeds its overdraft ceiling. The arrangements guarantee enough liquidity as may be required in the event that the participant with the largest overdraft ceiling defaults.

Chapter 17
Credit ratings

Introduction

399

A credit rating is a current opinion of an organisation's overall financial capacity to pay its financial obligations (issuer credit rating), or of the likelihood of repayment of a specific issue (issue credit rating).

An issuer rating focuses on the organisation's capacity and willingness to meet its financial commitments as they come due. Issuer credit ratings are based on current information supplied by the organisation, or obtained by a rating agency from other sources it considers reliable. Issuer credit ratings can be either long-term or short-term. Short-term issuer credit ratings reflect the organisation's creditworthiness over a short-term time horizon.

An issue credit rating reflects the current opinion of the creditworthiness of an organisation with respect to a specific financial obligation, a specific class of financial obligations, or a specific financial program (including ratings on commercial paper programs).

1
Credit ratings definitions

The most important rating agencies are Standard & Poor's, Moody's and Fitch IBCA. They reflect their current opinion in a character/figure combination. Standard & Poor's uses the character A to reflect that a company is reliable or 'investment grade'. Moody's uses the character P to indicate that an organisation is creditworthy. Fitch IBCA uses the character F for investment grade organisations. The following rates are commonly used:

A1 / P1 / F1

An organisation in this category has the strongest capacity to meet its financial commitments. Within this category, certain organisations are designated with a plus sign (+). This indicates that the organisation's capacity to meet its financial commitments is exceptionally strong.

A2 / P2 / F2

An organisation in this category has a satisfactory capacity to meet its financial commitments. However, it is somewhat more susceptible to the adverse effects of changes in circumstances and economic conditions than organisations in the highest rating category.

A3 / P3 / F3

An organisation rated 'A-3' has a fair capacity to meet its financial obligations. However, near-term adverse economic conditions or changing circumstances are more likely to weaken the capacity of the organisation to meet its financial commitments.

Moody's only distinguishes between a P1, P2 or P3-rating. All other organisations are rated 'Not Prime'. Standard & Poor's and Fitch IBCA, however, use special categories for less creditworthy organisations.

B

An organisation rated 'B' is regarded as vulnerable and has significant speculative characteristics. An investment in an organisation with a B rating is speculative. The organisation currently has the capacity to meet its financial commitments; but faces major ongoing uncertainties which could make it unable to meet its financial commitments.

Standard & Poor's uses three sub-categories: 'B-1', 'B-2' and 'B-3' to indicate finer distinctions within the 'B' category.

B1

Organisations with a 'B-1' short-term rating have a relatively stronger capacity to meet their financial commitments over the short-term compared to other speculative-grade organisations.

B2

Organisations with a 'B-2' short-term rating have an average speculative-grade capacity to meet their financial commitments over the short-term compared to other speculative-grade organisations.

B3

Organisations with a 'B-3' short-term rating have a relatively weaker capacity to meet their financial commitments over the short-term compared to other speculative-grade organisations.

C

An organisation with a 'C'-rating is currently vulnerable to non-payment and is dependent upon favourable business, financial and economic conditions to meet its financial commitments. An investment in such an organisation carries a high default risk.

D

An organisation rated 'D' has failed to pay one or more of its financial obligations (rated or unrated) when it came due. A 'D' rating is assigned when Standard & Poor's or Fitch IBCA believes that the organisation will fail to pay all, or substantially all, of its obligations as they come due.

Standard & Poor's uses an extra category in this segment: SD (selective default). A SD rating is assigned when Standard & Poor's believes that the organisation has selectively defaulted on a specific issue or class of obligations but will continue to meet its payment obligations on other issues or classes of obligations in a timely manner.

NR

An issuer designated NR is not rated.

2
Watchlist

A rating can be on watch. This means that there is a fair chance that the organisation's rating will change due to identifiable events and short-term trends. These may include mergers, recapitalisations, voter referendums, regulatory action or anticipated operating developments. Ratings appear on 'watch' when such an event or a deviation from an expected trend occurs, and additional information is necessary to evaluate the current rating.

3
Rating outlook

Rating agencies not only publish the current rating of a company, but also indicate their expectation of the development of the rating in the medium-term (six months to two years depending on the rating agency). This opinion regarding the likely direction of a rating over the medium-term is referred to as a rating outlook. A rating outlook may be positive, stable or negative.

Chapter 18
The European and the US money markets

Introduction

Each country that has its own national currency also has its own money market, where interest rate products (e.g. deposits) denominated in national currency are traded. Central banks use the money markets to achieve their monetary objectives, the most important of which is to keep inflation in check. As we will see, central banks seek to control inflation by setting money market interest rate levels in order to influence the money supply.

1
The money market

The money market is where interest rate-related financial transactions with terms of less than one year take place. Parties with short-term cash surpluses lend in the money market to parties with cash shortages. These loans receive interest, with supply and demand determining the level of interest. If the supply of cash is relatively large, interest rates will fall. A relative shortage of cash will result in rising rates. Central banks use this mechanism to influence the level of short-term interest rates by manipulating the liquidity positions of the banks.

1.1 The players in the money market

The parties who trade in the money market include:

- banks
- governments
- companies and institutional investors
- brokers
- central banks

1.1.1 Banks

Banks are some of the most important players in the money market. They continuously lend and borrow funds in the money market, sometimes dealing with each other directly but at other times operating through brokers. Banks use the money market to manage their cash (liquidity) positions. They trade in money market products with maturities varying from one day to one year, but are most active at the shorter dates. Bank proprietary trading desks also actively take short-term interest rate positions in order to generate trading profits.

Interbank interest rates set the benchmark or reference rate for all other money market rates, such as the rates for short-term bank loans to companies. EURIBOR (Euro Interbank Offered Rate) is the benchmark for the euro money market. Approximately 50 banks in Europe set EURIBOR daily for maturities ranging from one week to one year. There is also a reference rate for the overnight money rate: EONIA (Euro OverNight Index Average).

In the United States, the interest rate on treasury bills is used as the reference rate in the money market. Treasury bills are short-term financial instruments issued by the United States federal government.

Market participants can also make use of other benchmark interest rates, such as euro-LIBOR, USD-LIBOR and GBP-LIBOR. These are interbank rates set by the 16 London banks belonging to the British Banking Association. Additionally, LIBOR rates are often used for setting interest rates of financial derivatives such as interest rate swaps.

1.2 Companies and institutional investors

Multinational companies (MNCs) trade in the money markets either to earn interest on cash surpluses or to raise loans to cover short-term cash shortages. Apart from transactions with the bank, they also enter into transactions with other companies, with institutional investors and governments. Banks and brokers often play an intermediary role in such transactions. Smaller companies almost exclusively conclude transactions with the bank acting as counterparty.

Companies and institutional investors seeking to place a deposit usually ask several different banks to quote the rate they are prepared to offer. By 'shopping around' in this way, they force the banks to offer competitive rates.

1.3 Governments

Both central and local governments raise funds in the money market. They also regularly put surplus cash on deposit.

1.4 Brokers

When necessary, banks use the services of brokers. Brokers explore the market for their clients. They generally know which players are suited to a particular kind of transaction and which are not. Brokers receive commissions for the transactions they fulfil.

2
The role of the central banks in money markets

Central banks are responsible for the monetary policy of the country. Generally speaking, monetary policy is aimed at ensuring two goals:
- stable prices
- sustainable economic growth

Central banks tend to focus primarily on stable prices, or preventing inflation. They generally see this as a precursor to their second goal, achieving sustainable economic growth.

In order to attain these goals, central banks use monetary policy to control the money supply in the economy. By doing so, they can indirectly influence factors such as consumer spending, output, employment and prices. Monetary policy, then, is transferred to the 'real' economy through the money market. Although the impact of monetary policy in these factors may only be felt after a considerable time lag, the players in the financial markets react immediately.

Central banks use two kinds of instruments in monetary policy:

- instruments for influencing banks' cash positions
- interest rates

While an individual bank can manage its cash shortage, or surplus, by borrowing or lending from other banks, the banks collectively cannot expand (or decrease) aggregate liquidity in the market. They can merely pass around the existing funds. The total supply of cash is reflected by the commercial banks' current account balances with the central bank.

In most countries, central bank monetary policy operates as follows:

- – a policy is set targeting inflation and/or economic growth
- – a short-term interest rate is set that supports the set goal

The central bank trades securities with commercial banks in order to influence their overall cash positions and the level of money market rates. This procedure is referred to as open market operations.

Money market rates, or the rates that the money market players charge each other, do not diverge significantly from the rates set by central banks in its open market operations. The reason is simple. If market rates were to exceed central bank rates, the commercial banks would borrow from the central bank rather than other market players. Those with cash surpluses would, consequently, be unable to find counterparties willing to pay the higher market rates. By contrast, if market rates were lower than the central bank rates, all banks would try to borrow from the money market players other than the central bank, thus causing the market rates to increase. In both cases the process would continue until the market rates were virtually level with the central bank rate. Consequently, when setting their open market rates, central banks indirectly determine the exact level of money market interest rates.

Money market rate levels partly determine the pace of economic growth. Sometimes intense economic activity can lead to inflation. This occurs when the demand for goods in a country exceeds the production capacity. In this case, manufacturers are unable to produce more goods, even though the consumers want to buy more. The law of supply and demand then leads to higher prices.

In such cases, central banks will increase their interest rates. When interest rates are high, companies and individuals will be discouraged from borrowing. This, in turn, will lead to a slowdown in economic activity and can, ultimately, cause the prices of goods to fall. By influencing money supply growth, central banks can keep prices largely under control.

When there is no threat of inflation, central banks will prefer to keep interest rates as low as possible. Interest rates for credits will then also be low and companies and consumers will start to borrow more, thus giving economic growth a fresh impulse. Employment will also rise as a consequence.

2.1 The European Central Bank

Since 1 January 1999, all important decisions on monetary policy within the euro zone have been taken by the European Central Bank (ECB). The ECB, which is based in Frankfurt, is the hub of the European System of Central Banks (ESCB). The ESCB is made up of the national central banks of all EMU countries, plus the ECB. The most senior decision-making body is the Governing Council, which consists of the Executive Board of the ECB (a president, a vice-president and a maximum of four executive board members) and the governors of the participating central banks.

Individual central banks have the task of implementing the adopted policy in their country. Each national central bank, for instance, supervises the money supply in its own member state.

The ECB uses the following instruments to implement its monetary policy:

–   reserve requirements
–   open market policy (refinancing operations)
–   deposit facility and lending facility

2.1.1 Reserve requirements

The ECB reduces liquidity in the euro money market by imposing reserve requirements. The ECB requires commercial banks to maintain balances on their current account with the ECB equal to a specified fraction of their customers' deposits. These balances are known as reserve requirements. The fraction is set at such a level that the reserve requirement exceeds the total balances of the banks' current accounts with the ECB. The banks are, on balance, faced with a liquidity shortage. The banks in the euro zone are, therefore, forced to make use of the ECB's support operations. The ECB offers an interest rate on the required reserves which is equal to the refinancing rate.

2.1.2 Open market policy

Every week the ECB offers the banks in all participating countries the opportunity to subscribe at their central bank for a certain amount of liquidity under the refinancing facility. This involves repurchase agreements, where the banks temporarily sell financial paper to the ECB. The term of the majority of these transactions varies from one to two weeks. The refinancing facility of the ECB is exclusively used to expand the money market.

The interest that the banks are required to pay for this is the refinancing rate. The level of the refinancing rate is a key indicator for interest rates in the EMU money market, where the euro zone banks place deposits with each other. The refinancing rate is normally set somewhat above the minimum bid rate, which is the average of the official rates of the ECB.

Alongside short-term refinancing transactions, from time to time the ECB gives the banks the opportunity to conclude refinancing transactions with terms of one, two or three months.

2.1.3 The deposit facility

Sometimes a bank forecasts its liquidity position incorrectly. This may have led it to subscribe to the refinancing facility for either too little or too large an amount. During the term of the refinancing facility contract, the bank is then faced with either a cash surplus or a cash deficit.

A bank with a cash surplus or deficit, once all client demand and proprietary trading is concluded, will initially look for a bank with the opposite cash position to invest its surplus or to meet its funding requirements.

If there is a cash surplus on balance, the bank may not be able to find a counterparty that needs funds. The bank is then allowed to place its cash surplus on deposit with the ECB. This is known as the deposit facility. The interest earned on these deposits, the deposit rate, is typically 1% lower than the refinancing rate. Banks therefore will only make use of this facility as a last resort. The deposit rate places a floor beneath the money market rate.

2.1.4 The marginal lending facility

Banks with a cash deficit are able to borrow money at the ECB under a permanent lending facility known as the marginal lending facility. To qualify for this facility, they are required to place collateral. As the interest on this facility, the marginal lending rate, is normally about 1% higher than the refinancing rate, the banks will only make use of this as a last resort.

The interest on this facility places a ceiling on money market rates. Banks will naturally never pay a higher rate of interest on an interbank deposit than the marginal lending rate. Assuming they are able to provide the required collateral, they will always choose to use this facility if the market rates are higher.

The deposit rate and the marginal lending rate are the ECB's official interest rates. Normally, the mean of these two rates is presented in the media as being the official rate of the ECB. It is also referred to as the minimum bid rate.

Figure 1   *Instruments of monetary policy of the ECB*

Managing the liquidity positions of the banks	Interest Rates
Reserve requirements	Refinancing rate
Refinancing facility	Refinancing rate
Marginal lending facility	Marginal lending rate
Deposit facility	Deposit rate

2.2 The Federal Reserve System

As the central bank of the United Sates, the Federal Reserve System (FED) is responsible for the monetary policy of the United States. The organisation of the Fed is built on three layers:

- The Board of Governors;
- The Federal Open Market Committee (FOMC);
- The 12 district federal banks and their branches (Boston, New York, Philadelphia, Cleveland, Richmond, Atlanta, Chicago, St. Louis, Minneapolis, Kansas City, Dallas and San Francisco).

The FOMC implements monetary policy, principally by conducting open market operations in the federal funds market.

Large banks borrow and lend huge sums of money on a daily basis through the 'federal funds market'. This is a special part of the US money market. In the federal funds market short-term bank liquidity surpluses are traded mostly on an overnight basis. Banks with a shortage of federal funds borrow the required funds on an overnight basis from banks with a surplus. The rate the banks charge each other is called the federal funds rate (fed funds rate).

The federal funds rate is not set directly by the Federal Reserve. It is a free market rate, resembling EONIA in Europe, and is set by the laws of supply and demand of non-borrowed reserves on the federal funds market. The FOMC, however, manages the fed funds rate actively by participating in the market.

Like the Executive Board of the ECB in the euro zone, the FOMC decides on US monetary policy, so influencing the demand for, or supply of, the federal funds reserves of banks. The FOMC can determine the demand for, and supply of, reserves while simultaneously setting the fed funds rate by using the three following instruments:

- reserve requirements
- open market operations
  - outright operations
  - temporary operations
- the discount window

2.2.1 Reserve requirements

Under regulation D, all banks in the United States are subject to reserve requirements on their customers' deposits. The Federal Reserve requires commercial banks to maintain non interest-bearing deposits equal to a specified fraction of their customers' deposits with a Federal Reserve Bank. For large banks, this fraction is 10 percent. In recent years, the Federal Reserve has not changed this percentage. The reserve requirement is not used as an active monetary policy tool.

In managing their reserve positions, the banks attempt to balance two opposing considerations. As profit-seeking enterprises, they try to keep their reserves, which produce no income, close to the required minimum. On the other hand, they must avoid reserve deficiencies.

2.2.2 Open market operations

Reserve shortages, or surpluses, of the banks as a group are reflected in the overall supply and demand of the federal funds market. The FOMC influences the level of existing reserves through its open market operations. In doing so, the Fed influences the federal funds rate. In fact, the Fed even sets a target for the fed funds rate: the intended fed funds rate. The intended fed funds rate is the official interest rate of the Federal Reserve Bank.

The open market operations are executed by the open market desk (the Desk). Depending on the situation in the fed funds market, the Desk either buys or sells US treasury and federal agency securities on an outright basis, or on a temporarily basis.

If the Desk buys or sells securities on an outright basis, it increases or decreases the aggregate reserves in the banking system permanently. As a result of the public's continuously increasing demand for credit in the United States, the reserve requirement are growing constantly. As a result, the Fed usually conducts far more outright purchases than outright sales.

For short-lived needs to add or drain reserve balances, the Fed uses temporary operations. These are far more common than outright operations. If the Desk buys securities temporarily, the open market transactions are referred to as repurchase agreements. If the Desk sells securities temporarily, the open market transactions are referred to as matched-sale purchase transactions. With both types of transactions, the banks are asked to bid, or offer, interest rates they are willing to pay, or require to receive. The Fed accepts the most favourable offers until the volume of the offers equals the amount of reserve balances the Fed wants to add to, or drain from, the fed funds market. Most temporary open market operations are shorter than two weeks. Incidentally, the open market desk makes use of temporary open market transactions with a longer term.

Note that the ECB only uses open market operations to add liquidity to the money market. Another difference is that the ECB fixes a rate for the open market transactions, while the Fed only fixes the volume of those transactions.

2.2.3 The discount window lending facility

US banks that are faced with a cash deficit are also able to borrow money at the Fed under a permanent lending facility known as the Discount Window lending facility. The interest rate charged for these loans is the discount rate. The interest on this facility places a ceiling on money market rates. Since January 2003, the discount rate of well-capitalised banks has been 1% higher than the intended fed funds rates. Other banks have to pay an even higher interest rate if they use this facility. This is the reason why banks only use this facility if they are not able to access funds in any other way. Moreover, banks that frequently visit the Discount Window will be audited frequently by the Fed. Naturally, banks try to avoid this.

Unlike the ECB, the Fed doesn't have a deposit facility. The Fed never pays interest on the balances banks hold with it.

Following is an overview of the monetary instruments of the FED.

Figure 2   *Instruments of monetary policy of the FED*

Managing the liquidity positions of the banks	Interest Rates
Reserve requirements	No interest paid
Repurchase agreements and matched-sale purchase transactions	Fed funds rate
Discount facility	Discount rate

Chapter 19
ISO Currency Codes

Introduction

An ISO Currency Code is a three-lettter code to indicate a specific currency. ISO Currency Codes are commonly used in in financial messages and in financial contracts.

Figure 1   *List of most frequently used ISO Currency Codes*

Country	Currency	Code
Argentina	Argentine Peso	ARS
Australia	Australian Dollar	AUD
Brazil	Brazilian Real	BRL
Bulgaria	Bulgarian Lev	BGN
Canada	Canadian Dollar	CAD
China	Yuan Renminbi	CNY
Croatia	Croatian Kuna	HRK
Cyprus	Cyprus Pound	CYP
Czech Republic	Czech Koruna	CZK
Denmark	Danish Krone	DKK
Estonia	Kroon	EEK
Euro participants (see figure 2)	Euro	EUR
Hong Kong	Hong Kong Dollar	HKD
Hungary	Forint	HUF
Iceland	Iceland Krona	ISK
India	Indian Rupee	INR
Indonesia	Rupiah	IIDR
Japan	Yen	JPY
Korea	Won	KRW

Country	Currency	Code
Kuwait	Kuwaiti Dinar	KWD
Latvia	Latvian Lats	LVL
Lithuania	Lithuanian Litas	LTL
Macedonia, The Former Yugoslav Republic Of	Denar	MKD
Malaysia	Malaysian Ringgit	MYR
Malta	Maltese Lira	MTL
Mexico	Mexican Peso	MNXN
New Zealand	New Zealand Dollar	NZD
Norway	Norwegian Krone	NOK
Philippines	Philippine Peso	PHP
Poland	Zloty	PLN
Qatar	Qatari Rial	QAR
Romania	Old Leu / New Leu	ROL / RON
Russian Federation	Russian Ruble	RUB
Saudi Arabia	Saudi Riyal	SAR
Singapore	Singapore dollar	SGD
Slovakia	Slovak Koruna	SKK
Slovenia	Tolar	SIT
Sweden	Swedish Krona	SEK
Switzerland	Swiss Franc	CHF
United States	US Dollar	USD
Taiwan	Taiwan Dollar	TWD
Turkey	New Turkish Lira	TRY
United Arab Emirates	UAE Dirham	AED

Figure 2   *The participants of the Euro as of July 2006*

Austria

Belgium

Finland

France

Germany

Greece

Ireland

Italy

Luxemburg

Netherlands

Portugal

Spain

Index

418

decryption key 339
defensive hedge strategy 36
deposit 201
deposit account 56
deposit facility 408
deposit rate 408
DES 340
direct debits, DDs 87
direct link systems 102
direct participants 348
discount for cash payment 259
discount rate 411
documentary collection 88
downstream transaction 164
drawee bank 75
drawer 75
duration 49
duration of the cash conversion cycle
    278

E
EBA 369
EBIT 23
ECB 407
ECB payments mechanism 366
economic risk 283
ECP 364
EDIFACT 251
electronic cheque presentment 364
Electronic data interchange (EDI) 250
electronic signature 122
emergency pools 351
encryption key 339
enhanced correspondent banking 131
EONIA 60, 404
EONIA swap 329
EPM 366
e-procurement 252
ERP 370, 373
ESCB 407
EURIBOR 404
Euro Banking Association (EBA) 369

Euro Retail Payment (ERP) 370, 373
euro-LIBOR 404
European Central Bank 407
European Cross-border Credit Transfer
    Directive 372
European option 297
European Payment Council (EPC) 372
European System of Central Banks 407
exchange control regulations 139
exchange rate notation 287

F
face value of shares 19
factoring 263
FED 409
fed funds rate 409
Federal Agency short-term security
    203
federal funds market 409
Federal Open Market Committee 409
Federal Reserve System 409
file format 107
financial accounting 44
financial centre 43
financial management 11
financial ratios 352
financial risk management 33
Fitch I.B.C.A. 203
fixed assets 16
floor 334
FOMC 409
for collection 83
for regulation 83
foreign exchange forecast 287
foreign exchange risk 281
foreign exchange risk management 34
Foreign Exchange Yen Clearing System
    (FXYCS) 382
format con verter 103
format conversion 121
forward exchange contract 288, 290
forward exchange rate 290

maturity calendar (of accounts
     receivable) 266
Message Authentication Code (MAC)
     340
MICR 364
middleware 110
mid-office 45
minimum bid rate 408
mission of the treasury department 36
monetary policy 405
money market 403
money market fund 204
money market future 323
money market paper 203
Moody' s 203
multi-bank reporting 100
Municipal note 203

N
net debit caps 351
net profit 24
net profit margin 25
net settlement 124
net settlement system 122
Netting 224
netting 224
netting centre 224
network bank 134
New York Clearing House Association
     (NYCHA) 358
nominated bank 79
non-repudiation 118
non-resident account 137
nostro account 129
notional pooling 172

O
OECD 370
offensive hedge strategy 36
official interest rates of the ECB 408
off-shore account 137, 217
on-us cheques 361

open link systems 102
open market desk 410
open market operations 406
operating account 163
operating income 23
operational risk of settlement systems
     352
operational risks 45
order-to-cash cycle 245
order-to-order basis 391
OUR 74
out of the money 298
overdraft 55
overdraft facility 352
overnight index swap (OIS) 329

P
P.O. Box 107
Pan European Automated Clearing
     Houses (PEACH) 373
payer 72
paying in advance 74
payment conditions 248, 258
payment factory 230
payment term 258
payment-versus-payment 387, 389
PEDD 87
Personal Identification Number 122
PIN 91, 122
position control 47
position risk 45
presenting bank 88
presumed date of receipt 86
primary procurement 251
principal tasks of the treasury
     function 13
procurement process 249
production float 268
profit after tax 24
profit and loss account 23
profit before tax 24
profit centre 43

| 421

Treasurer 13
Treasury bills 203
treasury system 47
trigger balancing 166
Truncation 364
types of risk management strategy 36

U

under usual reserve 83
underlying period of a FRA 319
up-front 334
upstream transaction 164

V

Value at Risk 49
value balance 59
value dating 59
variation call 295

W

war chest 24
Watchlist 401
working capital 13, 239
working capital management 33
writer of an option 297

Z

Zengin Data Telecommunication
    System 384
zero balancing 165
zero-cost option 301

TREASURY AFFAIRS

JOURNAL ON TREASURY AND CORPORATE FINANCE

The role of the corporate treasury in non-financial companies is becoming more and more important. Recently, the role of the corporate treasurer has developed further and further – witness the development of active professional associations and the introduction of formal education schemes. *Treasury Affairs* (TA) is aimed at filling the gap between professional journals on treasury and academic journals on finance.

TA plans to cover all aspects of treasury management, broadly defined. This includes corporate finance. In other words, TA is interested in a broad spectrum of topics on cash management, all aspects of risk management, corporate finance, bank- and investor relations and liquidity management. Papers from practitioners as well as from academics are published. Ideally, TA aims to create a forum in which practitioners and academics can interact within the common treasury area. Therefore, TA welcomes papers with a practical orientation as well as deductive and empirical research studies, state-of-the art surveys and case studies of general treasury and corporate finance interest.

ISSN NR: 1570-0852

The journal is published by RISKMATRIX. All you need to do to get a complimentary copy of TA delivered at your desk, including subscription information and call for papers, is to submit your address information to Treasury.Affairs@riskmatrix.nl

RISKMATRIX

RISKMATRIX is an independent Dutch firm that offers support in treasury management and financial management to companies and non-profit organisations. The principal activities offered embrace publishing, training and consultancy. RISKMATRIX publishes books and other texts in the treasury and finance field. Publications may be ordered from specialised bookshops or directly from RISKMATRIX.

Address information
P.O. Box 176, 3970 AD DRIEBERGEN, The Netherlands, tel 31 343 556 801
www.riskmatrix.eu, www.riskmatrix.nl, info@riskmatrix.nl